Behind the Trail of Broken Treaties

Behind the Trail of Broken Treaties

AN INDIAN DECLARATION OF INDEPENDENCE

by Vine Deloria, Jr.

 University of Texas Press, Austin

International Standard Book Number 0-292-70754-1
Library of Congress Catalog Card Number 84-51686
Copyright © 1974 by Vine Deloria, Jr.
Copyright © 1985 by the University of Texas Press
All rights reserved
Printed in the United States of America

Fifth University of Texas Press Printing, 1994

Requests for permission to reproduce material from this work
should be sent to Permissions, University of Texas Press, Box
7819, Austin, Texas 78713-7819.

⊗The paper used in this publication meets the minimum
requirements of American National Standard for Information Sciences—Permanence of Paper for Printed Library
Materials, ANSI Z39.48-1984.

*All royalties from this book will go to the Institute for the
Development of Indian Law.*

Contents

Preface

The week of November 3–9, 1972, nearly a thousand American Indians in the caravan known as the Trail of Broken Treaties were in the nation's capital to present Twenty Points which they had designed as a partial solution to the pressing problems of the American Indian community. The events of that desperate week overshadowed the real issues of the caravan—which were highlighted in the Twenty Points and subsequent discussion—because attention was focused on the destruction of some government records and partial damage to the headquarters of the Bureau of Indian Affairs.

During the negotiations between the people of the Trail of Broken Treaties and the people representing the administration, the people representing the federal government promised to consider the Twenty Points and to report back their responses within sixty days. On January 9th, 1973, a response to the Twenty Points was released from the White House under the signatures of Leonard Garment and Frank Carlucci. The response was hardly adequate to the issues raised.

Among the Twenty Points were several (points one, two, four, five, six, seven, and eight) which involved restoration of the authority to make treaties with Indian communities, with the need to enforce treaty provisions for the protection of Indian individuals and with the need to place all Indian people under a new general category of status to be known as "treaty relations."

The treaty points were most strenuously rejected by members of the administration task force on the vague grounds that the Indian Citizenship Act of 1924 had precluded the United States from dealing with Indian tribes by treaty because the individual members thereof happened to be United States citizens.

The following is the administration's response to the first point of the Twenty Points, which involved a restoration of the constitutional authority to make treaties. This response generally characterizes the approach of the administration and seems to mean that the subject has been rejected without much consideration of the value of the proposal for contemporary times and in the context of the world situation today.

> Over one hundred years ago the Congress decided that it was no longer appropriate for the United States to make treaties with Indian tribes. By 1924, all Indians were citizens of the United States and of the states in which they resided. The citizenship relationship with one's government and the treaty relationship are mutually exclusive; a government makes treaties with foreign nations, not with its own citizens. If renunciation of citizenship is implied here, or secession, these are wholly backward steps, inappropriate for a nation which is a Union.
>
> Indians do need to "represent their own interests," and Indian tribes, groups, and com-

munities are finding increasingly effective ways of expressing these interests. There are several active and vocal nationwide Indian organizations; there are many tribal governments and these are being strengthened with full Administration support and endorsement. The President has even proposed that the administration and control of most BIA and HEW Indian programs be transferred to Indian tribal governments, at the latter's option, but the Congress has not yet approved this legislative proposal.

The President has proposed the creation of an Indian Trust Counsel Authority to represent Indian interests in the vital field of natural resources rights, but the Congress has not enacted this legislation.

The White House and every Department in this Administration meets frequently with Indian leaders and groups, listens to and pays attention to Indian recommendations and, as for example in the development of the Alaska Native Claims legislation, works with Indian representatives on matters vitally affecting Indian people. We will continue to go forward with these many, close relationships.

It is singularly unfortunate that the authors of the White House response to the Twenty Points had such a lack of understanding of the history of the relationship between the United States and the aboriginal Indian tribes of the North American continent. Setting aside the early period of exploration by the European powers, and taking only the recent years of American history as a guideline, the policy of the United States with respect to the Indian tribes has been one of expediency grounded only in the political considerations of the moment and without any lasting understanding of the nature of peoples, laws, governments, or responsibilities.

The result of this˙has been a tremendous rise in federal expenditures with few visible results, the creation of numerous liabilities by the United States toward the Indian tribes with whom they have a relationship, hundreds of cases of needless litigation, and not one solid or concrete path by which either the United States or the Indian tribes can understand the nature of their relationship or find a way to conclude their business with each other on mutually satisfactory grounds.

This book does not make any pretense of being a final statement on the legal and moral issues involved in the present situation. It is written to demonstrate that the proposal to reopen the treaty-making procedure is far from a stupid or ill-considered proposal. Rather it is one which would place the United States in the forefront of civilized nations in its treatment of the aboriginal peoples of the continent—a problem which even Japan and the Soviet Union have yet to solve. Moreover, by illuminating some of the twists and turns of the policies of the past, perhaps a better understanding of the status of the American Indian tribes can be seen in a world historical perspective— a perspective which the recent Vietnam war indicates is sadly lacking in contemporary American political understanding.

The responsibility of any nation, and the particular responsibility of elected officials of any nation, is not to justify what has passed for legality but to anticipate the conditions and problems of tomorrow and attempt to deal with them. The current confusion and violence in Indian country are a result of the failure to do so by generations of elected officials in this country. To continue to perpetuate myths about American Indians which have no basis in fact or in law is merely avoiding the larger issues confronting the nations of the world.

The concept of this book came into being in the context of the incident of Wounded Knee. Our plan was to present as fully as possible the background of ideas within which the declaration of independence of an Indian tribe would make sense. This has been a collective effort, for the most part, with many people thinking about the subject and several of us writing parts of the book. Chapters 5 and 10 were written and researched primarily by Kirke Kickingbird and Fred Ragsdale, and were then given critical and incisive review by William Veeder.

—VINE DELORIA, JR.

Behind the Trail of Broken Treaties

1. Preamble to the Present

In 1966 the National Congress of American Indians wanted to give an award to the then director of the Office of Economic Opportunity, R. Sargent Shriver. The N.C.A.I. had printed a special form which noted the achievements of the person receiving the award and stated that the award was for meritorious service to the Indian people. At the bottom of the form were several blanks under which the words "President," "Vice-president," and "Secretary" were printed. On the evening on which the award was to be made, the officers of the N.C.A.I. were gathered in the organization's offices, filling in the blanks with Shriver's name where it was appropriate. When they came to the blank for the President's name, one of the officers was stopped cold. "Is this our president who is to sign here," he inquired, "or theirs?"

The question was finally resolved after long and careful debate when the Indians decided that it was hardly likely that the President of the United States would be signing their form. The incident illustrates a fundamental fact of Indian existence: that the President of the United States may be a great White Father but he is not "our" president—he is "theirs."

Behind this attitude, which may appear curious to the non-Indian, is more than a racial distinction. For the most part, Indians have not accepted the mythology of the American past which interprets American history as a sanitized merging of diverse peoples to form a homogeneous union. The ties to tribal heritage are too strong, the abuses of the past and present too vivid, and the memory of freedom too lasting for many Indians. A substantial number of reservation Indians see the white man as little more than a passing episode in a tribal history which spans millennia. The white man may be the most destructive influence which the tribe has encountered, but he is still not regarded as a permanent fixture on the continent.

This attitude was noted by non-Indians in the decade just past. As the domestic social movement in America fractured on the Viet Nam war and the new ideology of the Third World began to emerge, Indians were regarded by left-wing ideologues as an integral part of the movement. The uncompromising ideology of Indian nationalism, which appeared to reject the values of Western society, seemed to many of the Third Worlders an indication that Indians were ready to join in a major movement to reform the American social and political order.

Imagining, therefore, that the coming Indian movement was an offshoot of the developments of the sixties, the New Left welcomed Indian activists at its rallies, included Indians in the roll call of the oppressed, and sought Indian endorsement for schemes of fundamental reform. The Indian activists learned the language of social protest, mastered the complicated handshakes used by the revolutionary elect, and began to raise funds for their activities. But the funding sources which were pouring money into the new fad of "self-determination" for minority groups were often astounded to learn that the Indians were not planning to share the continent with their oppressed brothers once the revolution was over. Hell, no. The Indians were planning on taking the continent back and kicking out all the black, Chicano, Anglo, and Asian brothers who had made the whole thing possible.

The idea was so preposterous to the good liberals and their guilt-laden supporters that it was considered a good movement joke. There was even hearty applause when an Indian mentioned the plan, and it invoked solemn confessions of sin from those revolutionaries who sought to acknowledge and heal the psychic scars carried by each of the oppressed groups. Few people were able to look backward to the four-hundred-year struggle for freedom that the Indians had waged and recognize that if the United States and its inhabitants had regarded the Indians as another domestic minority group, the Indians did not see themselves as such. They were inundated by foreigners, perhaps, but for the majority of Indians, their struggle was one of historical significance, not a temporary domestic discontent. Many Indians remained fully intent on raising their claims of national independence on the world scene.

Even the most sympathetic non-Indians had been schooled to deny this claim to international status made by the Indian tribes. Most of the literature on Indians has concentrated on the fierce and gallant fight of the Plains tribes against General Custer and the United States cavalry; the early part of American history, when Indians were the equals or superiors of the colonists, has rarely been written. Rather than a claim to international status, most non-Indian readers had been led to believe that, following the Plains Wars, the Indians meekly marched off to their reservations and lived in peace. The whole implication of the traditional Indian stereotype was that the Indians had become the best of American citizens within a decade of Wounded Knee.

For the American American the period of time from 1492 to 1860 was a hazy rendering of *The Deerslayer, Drums Along the Mohawk,* and *The Adventures of Pocahontas.* They knew little else except that Indians were poor (though a few had immense income from oil wells) and were trying to preserve their culture. As the contemporary Indian revival began to take shape and the news media, bored with the anti-war protests and civil-rights marches, became fascinated with Indians, the incidents marking the Indian protest trail were seen as another segment of the domestic social complex flexing its muscles. Rather than understanding the protests as a continuing struggle of Indians, the media characterized them as a new development, thereby missing the entire meaning of the protest issues.

In fact, the tragic climax of formal fighting between the United States and the Indians—the slaughter of Big Foot's band of Minneconjou Sioux at Wounded Knee, South Dakota—did not mark the end of the Indian struggle to preserve national identity. Although virtually unnoticed, the fighting continued through the twentieth century as surely as it had during the previous century of contact. The spectacular aspect of the conflict, which featured feathered war bonnets, slashing cavalry swords, and the flaming frontier, was simply missing, and without these dramatic and traditional symbols of Indian warfare, people thought that the Indians had been tamed.

Following the last series of treaties with the tribes in 1868, the federal government found itself with trusteeship over millions of acres of Indian lands and subject to increasing pressures by the Western settlers to open the Indian lands to homesteading. Such a course, if followed overtly, would merely have reopened the Indian wars, with an unhappy result for both the Indians and the settlers. The trick was to get at the Indian lands in such a manner as to make it appear as if the government was helping the Indians, not taking their lands once again.

An unusual coalition of forces began to line up around the question of the future of Indian lands. Cattlemen and railroads wanted the tribal reservations broken up and their lands opened to settlers. An increasingly active group of humanitarians wanted the individual Indians enticed away from tribal traditions and customs so that the great schemes for civilizing the Indians could prosper— for the humanitarians saw in themselves the progenitors of a new type of civilization that went far beyond settlement of the American West and had application in the Philippines, in Puerto Rico, and in the unclaimed islands of the world to which America was *destined* to lay claim.

Thus, as the 1880s arrived, there was sufficient pressure on the federal government to insure some kind of confiscation of Indian lands, and the idea of allotting the reservations—a happy ideology of the humanitarians that private ownership of lands would act in an instantaneous and magical way to civilize the Indian—became a demanded and popular political concept. Then Senator Henry Dawes of Massachusetts embraced the proposition that if every Indian family had its own piece of land, the natural greed in man would assume control of the individual Indian and create in him such dissatisfaction that he would become, as did the unhappy immigrants from Europe, a silent and peaceful farmer.

Battles raged in Congress over this concept, and

Senator Dawes fought Senator Henry Teller of Colorado, who knew too well that behind the naive ideas of the Eastern liberals lay the greed of the Western exploiters waiting to gain from the new policy before the liberals could understand what had happened. The humanitarians won the day by insisting that private enterprise had made America great and that since the natural course of evolution was from the hunting state to the farming state (ignoring the fact that the lands would be opened to the pastoral cattlemen—a step in the evolutionary process conveniently overlooked in the articulation of man's ascent from the savage state), the most humane policy conceivable would be the division of tribal lands among the members in tracts of 160 acres and the sale of the "surplus" to the federal government.

After several false starts, the Dawes Act, which incorporated the most prominent features of allotment that had been discussed, was passed, in 1887. Under the provisions of the act the President was authorized, whenever the tribes indicated that they were ready, to negotiate with the chiefs and headmen for a division of the tribal lands, and the "surplus," initially sold to the federal government, was to be used for new settlers under the homestead laws. Almost from its inception, the act was misinterpreted by the Bureau of Indian Affairs as a means of exploiting the Indians. Rather than waiting until the tribes petitioned for allotments, the Bureau began to threaten the tribes with dire consequences *unless* they agreed to immediate allotment.

Shortly after the passage of the act, the Bureau of Indian Affairs began to pressure the western tribes of Oklahoma territory to accept the act and cede their lands. A threat against the Kiowas, who owned vast areas in the southwestern part of the territory, frightened the western tribes, and they appealed to the Five Civilized Tribes for assistance in meeting the threat. In 1888 the tribes of the territory met at Fort Gibson, in the eastern part of the state, to discuss ways of forming an Indian state to foreclose any efforts by the United States to enclose them within the boundaries of a new state dominated by whites.

As the western tribes looked to the Five Civilized Tribes for guidance, they had every reason to be optimistic. The Cherokees, Creeks, Choctaws, Chickasaws, and Seminoles had come to the western lands some decades before and founded great republics, and so had experience in the ways of the white man. The Five Tribes delegates pointed out that, even with an Indian state, the old ways of governing the tribes, dependent in large measure on traditions related to the hunting and warfare culture of the past, would have to be altered. Recognition received by elder chiefs in battle would have to be surrendered, and new methods of electing chiefs would have to be instituted. The statesmen of the Creek and Cherokee Nations realized that any Indian state would be judged not on its accomplishments but on how closely it appeared to follow the practices and beliefs of the white man. The conference failed to take action, other than the appointment of a committee to draft a constitution and the promise of another conference the following June. In the meantime, the Bureau of Indian Affairs was working hard to put the allotment policy into effect.

The Five Civilized Tribes were exempted from the provisions of the General Allotment Act, but the other tribes which had been moved to Oklahoma were covered by the act. In the decade immediately after the enactment of the Allotment Act, most of the tribes in the Oklahoma area were made to accept allotment. As each reservation was allotted, the great

Oklahoma land rushes took place, and settlers poured into the former tribal lands to stake out their homesteads. The more land that was made available to the whites, the more they wanted the remaining land. By the early 1890s, the pressure to open the lands of the Five Tribes to settlement was at the bursting point.

The Five Civilized Tribes had faced opposition over lands before. In the 1830s gold was discovered on the Cherokee lands in Georgia, and the state passed laws which were intended to negate the laws of the Cherokee Nation. The Cherokees sued the state of Georgia in the Supreme Court and the court, torn between confirming the Cherokee treaty and upholding the sovereignty of Georgia, dodged the issue by ruling that the Cherokees could not sue in an original action in the Supreme Court because they were not a nation in the "foreign" sense demanded by the Constitution.

The following year, 1832, Samuel Worcester, a Christian missionary, allowed himself to be arrested while obeying both his conscience and the Cherokee laws. The case was appealed to the Supreme Court, with Georgia disdaining even to answer the complaint lodged against it by Worcester. In a historic decision, John Marshall ruled that the laws of Georgia were null and void over the Cherokee lands because of the treaties that the Cherokees had signed with the United States. Andrew Jackson, then President, is said to have remarked upon hearing the decision, "John Marshall has made his decision, now let him enforce it." Jackson refused to order federal troops to defend the Cherokee territory, and sent commissioners south to force treaties from the Cherokees and other tribes that removed them across the Mississippi into the then barren lands of Oklahoma.

In the next half decade following the *Worcester v. Georgia* decision, the Cherokees, Creeks, Choctaws, Chickasaws, and Seminoles were all forced to sign treaties and move west. But in the treaties they insured that removal would never happen again. The Choctaw treaty of Dancing Rabbit Creek, for example, promised that the tribe would never be allotted without its consent, nor would it ever be enclosed within the borders of a state of the Union. Each of the Five Tribes (who came to be called "civilized" because of their quick and skillful adaptation to the white man's ways) also secured a title to their lands in "fee simple." This title meant that the government had, or should have had, no authority over the lands of the tribe.

Since the 1830s the Five Civilized Tribes had become very strong, and had created small republics with schools, courts, businesses, and even plantations. They had offered their services to the Union during the Civil War, but had been rejected because the Northern generals felt that it would be improper to allow "savages" to fight against their white brothers of the South. So, abandoned by the federal government, some members of the Five Tribes signed treaties with the South, and regiments were organized by the Indians on behalf of both the North and the South.

Until the 1880s, the independence of the Five Tribes was nearly complete, but their ownership of extensive areas of land made them subject to political pressure from land speculators. Agitators in Kansas and Arkansas eyed the lands of the Five Tribes and conducted a continual campaign to discredit the governments of the tribes, thus hoping to create a situation where they could demand federal intervention and the eventual dissolution of the tribal governments. Congress disregarded the treaties in

the late 1880s, and in 1893 passed a law which provided for a commission to treat with the Five Tribes
for allotment of their lands and the opening of any
"surplus" lands to white settlement.

The Five Tribes refused to cede any land to the
United States, and the commission sent to deal with
them, headed by former Senator Henry Dawes, revealed its real nature when it became an apologist of
land confiscation instead of an impartial commission
to determine the legal basis for land purchase by the
United States. One of the chief arguments used by
members of the Dawes Commission against the Five
Civilized Tribes involved the presence of many non-
Indians within their boundaries. The tribes had allowed non-Indians to settle within their areas on the
condition that they respect the laws of the tribes.
But by 1893 the whites had become more numerous
than the Indians, and they continually agitated for
the dissolution of the governments of the tribes.
Needless to say, Congress was able to hear the complaints of the discontented whites where it could
not hear the legal arguments of the representatives
of the Five Tribes.

In direct opposition to the known desires of the
Five Tribes, Congress passed a law in 1895 authorizing a survey of their lands, and the following year it
directed the Dawes Commission to begin making a
roll of tribal citizenship. With the legal machinery
for dispossession grinding to its inevitable conclusion,
the Five Tribes were forced to come to terms with
the Dawes Commission. In 1897 Congress extended
federal law over the citizens of the Five Tribes and
required that the President approve all acts of their
elected councils. This action was tantamount to
nullifying their powers of self-government, and while
the tribes fought back with lawsuits to test the constitutionality of the federal laws, Congress kept push-

ing forward in its avowed intent to dissolve the governments and reservations of the Five Tribes.

In 1898 the final move was made when Congress passed the Curtis Act, which authorized the allotment of the tribal lands of the Five Tribes, divided their other property, and terminated their tribal governments. The excellent school system, which the respective tribes had devised, and which had produced more college graduates than the neighboring state of Texas, was dissolved and made part of the school system of the Bureau of Indian Affairs, which was probably the worst and least competent educational system in the world. The tribal governments became shadow governments, and the chief and other principal leaders were appointed by the President to oversee the conclusion of the distribution of tribal property.

Passing a law abolishing the tribal governments of the Five Tribes was one thing; accomplishing it in fact was another matter. The tribes fought back every way that they could. Indians had to be hunted down, captured and taken to the B.I.A. agency, and forced to accept allotments. Most of the traditional Cherokees and Creeks fled to the hills of the Ozarks rather than touch the pen to indicate that they would accept their allotted lands. A plan was devised whereby the fullbloods in the Cherokee tribe might take adjoining allotments and hold them in a unit under corporate title, but the Dawes Commission was committed to individualizing the Indian communal lands and refused to consider the plan.

The Choctaws went through incredible turmoil in their tribal affairs as progressives counseled the tribe to negotiate, hoping that some deal could be made with the United States, and traditionalists sought to develop a plan to move the tribe to Mexico or South America, where they could buy land and continue to govern themselves. This plan was discussed for nearly a decade, and when the Choctaws finally made a presentation to the Senate Indian Committee in 1906, they were ridiculed.

The Choctaws used the same reasoning the whites had used several centuries before to justify their flight from Europe:

> Surely a race of people, desiring to preserve the integrity of that race, who love it by reason of its traditions and their common ancestors and blood, who are proud of the fact that they belong to it, may be permitted to protect themselves, if in no other way, by emigration. Our educated people inform us that the white man came to this country to avoid conditions which to him were not as bad as the present conditions are to us. . . . All we ask is that we may be permitted to exercise the same privilege. . . .
>
> If the Choctaw and Chickasaw people as a whole were willing to lose their racial status, to become . . . white men in fact, we do not oppose the carrying out of their desires; but . . . we believe that the Great Father of all men created the Indian to fill a proper place in this world . . . a right to exist as a race, and that in the protection of that right . . . we are fulfilling the purpose of the Divine Creator of mankind.

Appeal to theology was no more effective than an appeal to the laws of the United States, and the Choctaws and Chickasaws were not only allotted, they were forbidden to expatriate themselves. (The Kickapoos did expatriate anyway, and moved to Mexico, where they were royally swindled. Some decades later, they moved back, although part of the tribe still remains in Mexico.)

As the final stages of allotment proceeded, the remaining fullbloods of the Five Tribes had to be arrested by armed posses in order to complete the allotment of the tribes. Several clashes between the Indians and the police ensued. Among the Creeks especially, feelings ran high. They were very bitter over the treatment they received from the United States. As late as 1912, nearly 10 per cent of the Cherokees had refused to take their allotments. The division of tribal assets, which was made by cash payments, resulted in the refusal by a substantial number of Indians to take any cash for the despoliation of their lives.

Resistance was not confined to the Five Civilized Tribes. The Navajos and Paiutes not only refused to follow government policy, they rejected all efforts to supervise their lives. As late as 1915, they were having sporadic clashes with government agents. In the remote areas of Arizona and Utah where they lived, it was impossible to exercise the tight controls which the government thought necessary, so occasional skirmishes broke out when agents attempted to enforce federal laws.

In the Pacific Northwest the tribes had a unique problem. They had been guaranteed the right to fish in their traditional grounds and stations by the treaties signed with the United States in 1854 and 1855. In these treaties the United States had sought to cement its claim to the lands of the Northwest following its settlement of the Oregon question with Great Britain in 1848. Although the United States viewed the treaties as confirmation of its title to the lands in question, the Indians who had lived along the rivers were not worried about the title to lands of the interior but sought only a permanent right to fish the rivers. After Washington and Oregon became states and the territory had been settled, the question of licensing sport and commercial fishing as a revenue source for the states eventually arose. The states maintained that they could control Indian fishing as part of their exercise of sovereign powers. The Indians claimed that their treaties forbade state control of their livelihood.

Almost every river and body of water was involved in the struggle over fishing rights. Along the Columbia, the Yakima and Nez Perce tribes attempted to exercise their fishing rights and were driven off by whites who had erected commercial fishing wheels at traditional spots claimed by the tribes. Finally a Supreme Court case had to settle the question, and the Indians were upheld in their claims.

On the western side of the Cascades, however, the smaller tribes waged a valiant but less successful fight against state regulation of their fishing. The Makah of Cape Flattery, for example, had always been sea-going whalers, and they were denied the right to hunt whales by a court decision made under a theory which was later reversed by the Supreme Court. The Lummi Indians of upper Puget Sound captured some Austrian fishermen who invaded their fishing grounds and held them until the Lummis were assured by the United States Attorney that they would be protected.

At every turn the tribes attempted to preserve something of the precious treaty rights which had been solemnly guaranteed to them only decades before. But on the whole, they were simply overwhelmed. For every victory that they achieved, a dozen defeats marked the train of events. Perhaps the best characterization of the period from 1890 to 1920 would be that of a time when the Indians sought to prevent further losses of their original status as independent nations. The struggle was tragic, since the Indians were fighting speculators who wanted their lands, bureaucrats who felt that they had no right to the lands, and philanthropic friends who felt that the best course for the Indian was to become a small farmer, and who therefore supported the whittling down of the tribal lands into small farming tracts.

The watershed of this process of disintegration of tribal land holdings was an insignificant lawsuit over the right to sell liquor to the Indians in New Mexico. In 1913 the case of *Sandoval v. United States* came before the Supreme Court. It involved a definition of the legal status of the Pueblo Indians, since, if they were legally under federal protection, it was illegal to sell them liquor. The Pueblos occupied a unique and nebulous legal position at best. They had received grants from the King of Spain in the 1500s which served to confirm the titles to their lands. These grants were continued under the various Mexican governments, and in 1848, at the Treaty of Guadalupe Hildalgo, which ended the Mexican War, the United States promised to secure the titles to them. They had thus been excluded from federal services and supervision since 1848, on the basis that, owning lands, they had citizenship rights and were unlike other Indians.

But citizenship under the United States was more onerous than it had been under Mexican rule. The courts of the territory were prejudiced against the Pueblos, and decisions regarding land title generally went against them. Whites simply moved in and claimed both the Pueblos' lands and their water rights on the Rio Grande. Forced tax sales had taken more Indian lands, and by 1913 the Pueblos had a mere fragment of their original holdings left. It was thus incongruous to maintain that they had been given either a just hearing by the people of New Mexico or protection by the federal government with respect to their rights.

Yet the United States wanted to control the sale

of liquor to Indians, since alcohol led to most expressions of discontent among all the tribes. Bootlegging spirits to the reservations was one of the remaining popular crimes in the frontier West, which was fading fast from its rough beginnings. In order to control the liquor trade, the United States had to maintain that the Pueblos were then and had theoretically always been under the control of Congress. The Supreme Court accepted the argument, and the result was to call into question the many land sales and homesteads which had been made on the Pueblo lands over a forty-year period.

The whites in New Mexico were livid over the decision, and, under Senator Hiram Bursum of New Mexico, promptly rallied to seek legislation which would nullify the effect of the Supreme Court decision. Various schemes were put forth to deprive the Pueblos of the right to their lands. Senator Bursum introduced a bill which would have forced the Pueblos to prove their rights to their remaining lands and any that they might have tried to reclaim under the Supreme Court decision. The bill passed the Senate and was in the House of Representatives before the Pueblos realized the danger it posed for them.

In a dramatic move toward unification, the Pueblo leaders sent out messengers to all of their villages, and gathered 123 of the headmen and governors of the Pueblos. The experience of facing a crisis was not new to these peaceful people. In 1680, while under cruel Spanish rule, the Pueblos had gathered under the great leader Popé. Planning carefully and executing the plan with surprising efficiency, the Pueblos had revolted against the Spanish and driven them south to El Paso del Norte, the present-day El Paso, Texas. They had managed to keep the Spanish out of New Mexico until 1692, when they were finally overwhelmed and reconquered.

The Pueblo elders planned a concentrated drive to

inform the American public of their situation, hoping that by massive publicity they could prevent the passage of the Bursum bill. They were not alone in their efforts. The General Federation of Women's Clubs, a national organization with a large and sympathetic membership, decided to assist them. The G.F.W.C. was able to interest a social worker named John Collier in the fight, and he took the lead in developing the strategy. With the newly organized New Mexico Association on Indian Affairs, a local group of whites who were sympathetic to the Pueblos' cause, Collier conducted a brilliant campaign, and the Bursum bill was defeated.

In 1924, as an alternative to the Bursum bill, the Pueblo Lands Act was passed, and its provisions reversed those that had been proposed by Senator Bursum some years before: They required that any white man claiming lands within the Pueblo boundaries prove *his* title. A special counsel was hired and assigned to the Pueblos to aid in the presentation of their case. By 1938 they had evicted nearly three thousand non-Indian squatters from their lands, and had taken both lands and water rights from non-Indian hands.

The Pueblos demonstrated to Indians everywhere that the erosion of Indian rights could be stopped by proper organization and a dramatic appeal to the conscience of the American public. Thereafter, Indian protests began to take up litigation as a serious tool in the battle to preserve their rights, and publicizing their problems became almost an automatic response when Indians found they were in trouble. If a tribe could find a sanctioned way to work out its problems, it did so. If not, then the people resisted as best they could, trying to publicize their misfortune wherever possible, and appealing to the moral sensibility of the American public whenever possible.

The Iroquois League of New York State worked

out an ingenious way to avoid a direct confrontation with the United States over the military draft during the First World War. The federal government was not certain it could draft Indians, since they were not citizens and many of the treaties had required the Indians to promise never again to bear arms. The government saw in the draft a means of both raising the treaty-rights issue and conscripting additional men into the Armed Forces for the war.

Realizing that the United States government had something more in mind than simple treaty interpretation, the Iroquois beat the government to the punch by a unique affirmation of their national status. In a special meeting, they declared war on Germany and authorized their young men to serve in the American Armed Forces as allies. The question of citizenship was avoided for the moment.

Following the war, there was great agitation by Indians for a general citizenship act. Men of numerous tribes had volunteered for combat and fought brilliantly for the country. Returning to find themselves in a second-class legal status, many Indians thought that they should be accorded voting rights in deference to their services rendered the government.

In 1924, after some years of discussion and the introduction of a number of citizenship bills which attempted to trade Indian lands for voting rights, Congress finally relented and passed a simple, one-paragraph statute that acknowledged that Indians would be considered citizens thenceforth without any detrimental effects on their tribal citizenship rights. The Iroquois politely sent a note to the United States informing the government that they were not then, had never been, and did not intend to become American citizens. They would not, they stated, consider that the 1924 statute had any effect with respect to them. They have never wavered from that official position in the years since.

The position taken by the Iroquois and demonstrated earlier in the appeal by the Choctaws for the right to expatriate has been a major attitude of Indians throughout the country for many years. American citizenship has been considered as incompatible with tribal membership during times of crisis among the people of many tribes. This attitude has varied only with the confrontation which the United States has forced upon the tribes. During the 1930s Congress passed the Indian Reorganization Act, which allowed the people on different reservations to organize tribal governments and exercise some measure of local government, subject to the approval of the Secretary of the Interior.

During the hearings on the proposed legislation, then Indian Commissioner John Collier called together "Indian congresses" in an effort to get the reservation people to support the Indian Reorganization Act. The traditionalist faction of some of the tribes made it evident that they did not want the new legislation. Many felt that it would supplant the treaty rights which they felt the government still owed their people. Others thought that the organization of a corporate form of government, which the legislation would have authorized, would negate their tribal citizenship and cause them to lose the rights of aboriginal nature which they still held.

The theory of the Indian Reorganization Act was that the tribe was to be legally created by the adoption of a constitution and by-laws which were accepted by majority vote and approved by the Secretary of the Interior. Some reservations had more than one tribe living on them, and if the reservations were each to be organized as one tribe with one legal status, what happened to the treaty rights which the tribes shared independently of each other? That was the argument used by traditionalists against the act.

The question was not a simple one. Throughout the intervening decades between 1890 and the present, tribes have had frequent recourse to the United States Court of Claims over various violations of their treaties. The burning question in Indian country whenever a settlement was pending was always whether the suit would serve to extinguish any tribal claim to national status. The question also arose during the 1950s, when the policy of Congress was to extinguish treaty rights and tribal political existence through termination legislation, which dissolved the constitution of a tribe and turned its assets over to a private trustee. Many traditionalists boycotted meetings called to explain the terminal legislation, on the grounds that the tribe was a sovereign nation and therefore could not be extinguished by an act of Congress.

The modern Indian movement for national recognition thus has its roots in the tireless resistance of generations of unknown Indians who have refused to melt into the homogeneity of American life and accept American citizenship. The idea that Indian problems are some exotic form of domestic disturbance will simply not hold water in view of the persistent attitude of Indians that they have superior rights to national existence which the United States must respect.

In the last two decades it was the Tuscarora people of the Iroquois Confederacy who began the type of protests which have now become so common. In the late 1950s the State of New York sought to expand its power-generating facilities at Niagara Falls, and it needed some of the lands of the Tuscaroras to use as a holding dam in order to complete its project. The state condemned the land, and the tribe sued. The case was appealed, and the federal court had to do mental gymnastics in order to find in favor of the state. Twisting language in an unprecedented manner, the federal courts characterized the New York Power Authority as a federal instrumentality with powers of condemnation, and denied the Tuscaroras the right to preserve their lands.

The response of the tribe was immediate. Gathering some supporters from the other Iroquois tribes, the Tuscaroras, led by Wallace "Mad Bear" Anderson, went to Washington to protest the taking of their lands. They demonstrated in front of the White House, with little noticeable effect. Then they invaded the Department of the Interior and attempted to make a citizen's arrest of the Secretary of the Interior. War whoops echoed down the staid halls of the government building, and startled bureaucrats watched as the Iroquois stalked the halls of Interior looking for the Secretary. He was spirited out a side door as the Indian contingent, blood in their eyes, came into his office.

Indians watched and laughed as the Interior Department tried to pass the incident off as the actions of a few communist-inspired radicals. But they never forgot that the Tuscaroras had stood up for Indian treaty rights and the international status of the tribes at a time when few men were willing to stand for any principles at all.

2. The Emergence of Indian Activism

The civil-rights movement of the sixties affected Indians in many profound ways. The obvious success of the marches and demonstrations in getting policies changed taught a very important lesson to many young Indians, who had seen their fathers and grandfathers thwarted by the immense bureaucracy of the federal government. The basic fact of American political life—that without money or force there is no change—impressed itself upon Indians as they watched the civil-rights movement, and the old fear of reprisal, which had plagued previous Indian efforts to change conditions, was partially dissipated.

The ideology of civil rights, however, was anathema to the majority of Indians. In the past they had experienced so many betrayals through policies which purported to give them legal and social "equality" that they suspected anyone who spoke of either equality or helping them to get into "the mainstream." The policy of terminating federal services to Indians, which had dominated the previous decade, was based upon giving Indians civil rights under the theory that, by abolishing treaty rights, Indians would receive full citizenship.

Tremendous pressures were generated to force Indians to conform to the civil-rights movement. Many liberals saw only the struggle for individual rights, and refused to consider the equally important fact of community existence and the corresponding legal right of a community to exist for its own sake. The radical individualism which civil rights encompassed frightened many Indians, since it was the same religious application of individualism which had been used to justify the allotment policy and had failed miserably.

Thus, when black leaders spoke of the Indian reservations as rural ghettos, a chill went up the spines of Indians, comparable to that in the old days when the bugle rang across the hills. While some of the tribes had been moved from their ancestral homes, the majority of the tribes still lived in the lands of their origin. Far from considering their reservations as ghettos, they were determined to save the remnants of their homelands and, if possible, prevent any further intrusion of whites into them. The Indian position was often seen by the supporters of civil rights as anti-American, and in many respects it was. The tribes were concerned about their separate existence as dependent nations for whom the United States had a responsibility. The Indian attitude might be called pre-American rather than anti-American, since it demanded that the original status of Indians be respected.

Yet, try as they might, Indians could not convince the non-Indians of the logic or historic validity of their ideas. The blacks and liberals who constituted the major following of the civil-rights movement could not believe that Indians had not been integrated into the bottom levels of American society, at least on an emotional basis. Whenever Indians tried to clarify their position, their arguments were interpreted as either the remnant beliefs of the missionary era or as unsophisticated and naive statements by those so isolated by time and distance that they were immune from the issues of the day. It was this unbelief of the early sixties that led directly to the misinterpretation of the later Indian movement as a Third World phenomenon.

A few Indians ventured into the civil-rights movement, however, and in 1963 several Indians attended the March on Washington. The sparsity of their numbers was a true measure of the importance which Indians placed on the civil-rights movement. The absence of any tribal delegations disappointed the liberals, but was an accurate gauge of Indian feelings. Sad to say, much of the early resistance of Indians to the civil-rights movement was simply inherited racial attitudes which Indians had learned from whites. The constant harping of conservatives in the Bureau of Indian Affairs and the Indian organizations that "Indians don't do those things" prevented some Indians from attending the march.

In 1964, however, things began to happen. The civil-rights movement dominated the headlines, and the Indian issues had rough competition even in Indian areas when the newspapers wrote of important social movements. The perennial question which newsmen posed for Indians regarded the absence of demonstrations and protests by Indians. If there were important issues, newsmen argued, why didn't the Indians make themselves heard? Thus it was that Indians were forced to adopt the vocabulary and techniques of the blacks in order to get their grievances serious consideration by the media.

The National Indian Youth Council, a small group of young Indians who were recent college graduates and sought change in the conditions of Indians, adopted some of the ideas of the civil-rights movement and held a "fish-in" in the Pacific Northwest. Washington State had become extremely rigid in its efforts to control Indian fishing. The state courts were convinced that no Indian rights existed, and they cooperated with the fish and game departments in convicting Indians who had been arrested while fishing. Some dramatic means were needed to publicize the treaty rights of the tribes, and so Marlon Brando and Dick Gregory went to the Northwest and helped organize the "fish-in."

There was a dramatic confrontation between the Indians and the state game wardens at Olympia, Washington, the state capital, and the Indian fishermen were arrested. Brando and Gregory were treated as naive outsiders who had been conned into helping the Indians; they were released with the admonition that the people of Washington State didn't like outsiders agitating "their" Indians. The reaction to the fish-in was generally bad for the Indians. The whites had convinced themselves that they had no racial problems because they were not gassing or hosing blacks, and they resented people "stirring up" the Indians.

Many tribal governments balked at the idea of demonstrations. In previous years they had fought the state over fishing rights and had reached tentative and informal agreements with the state agencies. The larger tribes had, in effect, sold out the rights of the smaller tribes by promising to police their own members. In return, the state mysteriously avoided confrontations with the larger tribes and concentrated its efforts on the smaller tribes, which were virtually helpless to defend themselves. Suddenly it seemed as if the whole balance of power and status quo would be upset and the fishing-rights issue on the basis of treaty promises would have to be litigated once again. This course of action had already been used by the larger tribes, and they didn't want to go through the whole thing again, so they opposed the fishing demonstrations.

Nevertheless, the fish-ins triggered a general Indian resistance in the Northwest against any further state intrusion on treaty fishing rights. The resistance spread from Washington State to Oregon and Idaho, and from fishing to hunting. Arrests of Indians followed, and soon there were a number of cases in the state courts involving the interpretation of Indian treaties. Perhaps the only facet of the problem which was not discussed was the number of Indians actually fishing. The population of the smaller tribes had not varied much during the preceding century. George Gibbs' census of Indians in the 1850s and the Bureau of Indian Affairs' figures for the 1960s showed populations of the fishing tribes as almost identical in numerical strength. But three million whites had entered the area in the intervening century, and they were determined not to allow the Indians to fish. That was the fishing "problem" in a nutshell.

The increased militancy of Indians began to spread across the country as people heard about the fishing-rights issue. Indians began to examine the conditions under which they lived, and they soon seethed with discontent and a new determination to correct the injustices. Local groups of Indians began to organize themselves and demand changes in their conditions. The new movement gave the tribal leaders some room to maneuver which they had never had before. The Indian field had always been very formally organized. Traditional Indians generally boycotted government meetings and held their own meetings. They provided a consistent but ineffective voice against government policy—consistent because they maintained the validity of the tribe's national status according to treaty, and ineffective because they forswore all recognized methods of raising the political issues necessary to resolve the dispute.

Tribal governments had to deal with the federal government on a one-to-one basis. Indians could not develop the necessary leverage on the government to make changes, since the tribal governments were the only formally organized groups in existence. With the development of protest groups, the tribal leaders had a chance to play off the government against the expanding activist organizations. The government officials knew that if they were unreasonable or did not make concessions to the tribal officials, they would be confronted by activists who sought even more radical change than did the tribal councils. Therefore, the United States, for the first time in its history, had to offer concessions to the tribes, in return for tribal support for some of its more exotic policies.

The demands of the younger Indians were not neglected in this new state of combat. The bureaucrats fully realized that while the young people were demanding far more than the federal government was willing to grant, these same people would one day take charge of tribal affairs or achieve other important positions within the Indian community. They could not, therefore, afford to alienate people who would be in the Indian business for many decades to come. There had to be a realistic compromise with the younger elements of Indian country if anything was to be accomplished. For the first time in history, then, Indians developed a strategy by which they could force the federal government to confront their problems and to live by its own avowed laws, through which it purported to have the power to govern them.

The first real test of this new situation came in Santa Fe, New Mexico, in 1966. Stewart Udall, then Secretary of the Interior, had just fired Philleo Nash, Commissioner of Indian Affairs, because of Nash's outspoken position against the termination of the Colville tribe in eastern Washington State. Udall had called a meeting of the highest officials in the Bureau of Indian Affairs to plan a new program for Indians. Part of the program, it was discovered a week before the meeting, was to disqualify the tribes as sponsoring agencies in the War on Poverty and turn the community-action funds over to the Bureau of Indian Affairs for programming.

The National Congress of American Indians discovered the plan and called for all tribes to come to Santa Fe and hold a meeting to oppose the projected goals of the Interior meeting. Representatives from sixty tribes arrived in Santa Fe to oppose Udall's program. In desperation Udall sent Robert Bennett, newly appointed Commissioner of Indian Affairs, over to the tribal meeting to play the piano for the assembled Indian delegates while he and his bureaucrats made their plans. At the N.C.A.I. meeting delegates drew up a plan for "self-determination" for Indian tribes, a phrase that was to echo through the minority groups three years later and catch the fancy of social-movement sloganeers.

On the second day the Indian elders planned to march to the Episcopal church, where the Bureau of Indian Affairs was meeting, and hold a silent vigil in protest against the Bureau's refusal to allow Indian observers to attend the meeting. Inside the church, attending the session, were representatives of the white-dominated Indian interest groups, such as the Association on American Indian Affairs, traditional supporters of the policies of the Interior Department. When plans for the march were relayed to Udall, he panicked and agreed to meet with the Indian officers of the National Congress of American Indians.

Udall's presentation was hardly of inspirational caliber. He related that certain Senators, notably Henry Jackson, Clinton Anderson, and Frank Church, were pressuring him to support a full termination program, and that he was at a loss to determine what he should do. His proposal was astounding. Udall said that if the N.C.A.I. would not object to the termination of the Agua Caliente tribe of California, he could buy five years of peace for the tribes, and during that time he would work to stop the termination policy altogether. The N.C.A.I. was furious, and vowed to fight everything Interior did until Udall dropped his plans for termination. Finding this unexpected resistance from the elderly tribal leaders, and recognizing the political hay which the National Indian Youth Council could make of this proposal, Udall humbly walked the dusty streets of Santa Fe back to his meeting and then sent word that the N.C.A.I. should appoint two men to observe the meeting. The termination of the Agua Caliente was a dead issue.

The Indian victory would have been complete except that Interior was not a group to surrender meekly to its Indians. To have done so would have been to forfeit the powers gathered over a century of increasingly dictatorial control over Indians, and an admission of incompetence and impotence by the Bureau of Indian Affairs. Thus, as the meeting in Santa Fe ended, Stewart Udall promised to create an "Omnibus Bill" which would incorporate all the problems of Indians into one major piece of legislation, and which he vowed to support personally. A tenuous promise was extracted by the N.C.A.I. that they would be consulted on the content of the legislation as it was being developed. Everyone left Santa Fe keeping a wary eye on everyone else. When people reflected on it, Santa Fe was a major victory for its time. Indians had forced the Interior Department to consult with them and allow them to attend a planning meeting for the first time in history.

As the summer of 1966 began, all was not well in Indian country. The Interior Department was unusually quiet, and rumors began to filter out that Udall had already commissioned people to draw up the legislation, without any prior consultation with the tribes. In this move Udall was probably betrayed by his career bureaucrats, since he never gave any indication during 1966 that he was repudiating the promises he made at Santa Fe, and he was not a deceitful man. At any rate, it was not long before the watchful eye of the N.C.A.I. had detected where the legislation was being prepared, and, by means as yet unrevealed, they obtained a copy of the legislation.

The N.C.A.I. analyzed the legislation during the summer and laid plans to ambush the Interior Department in the fall. A secret meeting was held in Denver with a dozen of the most influential tribal chairmen in the nation. After compiling their objections and reasons for objecting to the legislation, the N.C.A.I. set out to follow Commissioner Robert Bennett, who was given the thankless task of taking a trip around Indian country to solicit Indian opinions on what kind of legislation should be drawn up for the Omnibus Bill. Bennett gamely followed orders, and went to Minneapolis to hold his first consultation with the tribes. As he duly told the delegates that there was no legislation drawn up, the executive director of the N.C.A.I. was in the hall outside the meeting room, handing out mimeographed copies of the proposed bill.

Bennett bravely went on to Billings, Montana, to

talk with the tribes there, and when he arrived discovered that the tribes had already met and passed a resolution against the Omnibus Bill. Bennett tried to convince everyone that the bill they had was simply a proposal drafted in the form of legislation and not a serious piece of legislation, but it was no use. The tribal councils were wary, and many were totally convinced that they had been had. After the Billings meeting, the Bureau gave up all pretense of consulting with Indians and simply asked for suggestions to make the draft more accountable to the tribes' wishes. It was the second victory in a row for the N.C.A.I.

By early 1967 the Omnibus Bill was dead. It was introduced in Congress "by request," indicating that the Senators and Congressmen who put the bill in did so out of friendship for the administration and not because they intended to support it. The battle over the Omnibus Bill was the last unified resistance by the older tribal leaders. Thereafter, they carefully buttered their own bread with the Johnson administration, and later with the new Nixon administration, endorsing whatever policies they were asked to endorse. Perhaps the sign most indicative of things to come happened in Minneapolis in the fall of 1966, during Bennett's visit with the tribes of that area. A group of Indian protesters had picketed the area office of the Bureau of Indian Affairs the previous month, and they came to the regional meeting demanding to speak with the Commissioner about the problems of urban Indians. Among the group were a number who would be instrumental in the later activist movement, including some of the founders of the American Indian Movement.

By the late sixties the doctrine had been developed that "Indians don't protest," and such was the belief among a great many young Indians as well as tribal elders. People would point out the great benefits which had been received by tribes from the O.E.O. and remark that this had all been done without a single protest or demonstration. The fishing-rights activists continued their fight in the Pacific Northwest, but were still regarded by the major Indian leaders as a nuisance rather than a vanguard of things to come.

This calm was rudely shattered by the Poor People's March. In early spring of 1968, Dr. Martin Luther King, Jr., was contacting a number of groups about participation in the proposed march on the nation's capital later that year. A number of Indians accepted his invitation to come to a conference, and went to Atlanta to meet with the strategy group that was responsible for planning the march. When Dr. King was assassinated and the preparations for the march still went ahead, moneys soon became available for Indian participation. About a hundred Indians joined the Poor People's March and, as part of the protests conducted in Washington, held a rally at the Supreme Court to protest two decisions which the court had handed down concerning Indians. They also held a sit-in at Udall's office, demanding action on a number of points which they felt Udall, as Secretary, could solve.

By 1968 the increased spending on the Viet Nam war began to have its effect on Indians as well as other people. Job Corps camps which had been developed on some of the reservations were being closed for lack of funds, and there were continual cutbacks of the vital community-action funds, which provided the major source of funding for reservation programs operated by the tribes. Younger Indians had been the main beneficiaries of the War on Poverty, and their discontent grew with each cutback in program funds. The tribal leaders, on the other hand, had often used the programs for patronage appointments to strengthen their political hold over the reservations, and were not affected in the same way as were the young people. A conflict along generation lines became almost inevitable as the War on Poverty funds continued to dwindle.

The power movements which had sprung up after 1966 now began to affect Indians, and the center of action was the urban areas on the West Coast, where there was a large Indian population. "Red Power" naturally became a rallying cry, and the definition of Indian power began to take on a historic dimension, with appeals to the past glories of warriors such as Crazy Horse and Geronimo. While other groups might demand concessions from the government to change their present conditions, the Indian demands came to center on a restoration of tribal lands which had been taken illegally during the last century. Indians were keenly aware that they had been virtually independent nations only a century before, and many young Indians felt that the movement should concern itself with regaining their former status.

Yet, for the most part, the Indian movement was still in the rhetorical stage of slogans and speeches, reassurances of unity, and reawakenings of the resistance of the old days. Indians across the nation were speaking out against the treatment they were receiving from the federal government in the cities and on the reservations, but no overt actions were being taken. Perhaps if the government had made some effort to open the channels of communication at this point, the movement might have been thwarted. But the important legislation in Congress was stalled, and only trivial laws were passed. Both major political parties were concentrating on the Presidential campaign of 1968, and concerned themselves only with providing a few token red faces to demonstrate the universal scope of their political appeal.

On the border between Canada and the United States, events were unfolding that were to have a profound effect on Indians. Canada had been restricting the free movement of the Mohawks back and forth between the two countries, and many of the Iroquois felt that this was an infringement of their treaties with Great Britain, which Canada was pledged to uphold. The Mohawks blockaded the Cornwall Bridge, which links Canada and the United States in upstate New York. A number of Mohawks were arrested, but when they were tried in court for resisting arrest, it turned out that the treaty question was too hot for the Canadian government to handle, and the charges against them were dismissed.

The protest at Cornwall was covered by a number of papers, and the newspaper of the traditional Mohawks, *Akwesasne Notes,* gave full coverage to the incident. By 1968 *Akwesasne Notes* had developed into a national Indian newspaper with a circulation of nearly 50,000. It scoured both Canada and the United States for news about what was happening to Indians, and reprinted stories from both countries. News of the Cornwall Bridge became a prominent discussion topic of Indians across the continent, and the success of the Mohawks was noted carefully by the Indians who wanted action.

The American Indians were not waiting for Canadian leadership, however, as dissident Indians were beginning to organize in the Midwest. In the twin cities of St. Paul and Minneapolis, it was customary for the police to harass Indians on the weekends, and their arrest rate for drunkenness in these cities was far out of proportion to that of other groups in the metropolitan area. Clearly, something had to be done.

Some of the Indians in Minneapolis joined together

to form an Indian patrol to watch the actions of the police in the Indian section of town. They followed police cars around the area and acted as witnesses during arrests of Indians. If there was a question concerning the legality of the arrest, they defended the Indian and demanded his release. In thirty-nine weeks of careful patrolling of the Indian areas of the Twin Cities, the arrest rate was reduced nearly to zero, indicating that there had been extensive police discrimination prior to the organization of the patrol.

Out of this Indian patrol came the flashy and influential American Indian Movement. Some of its leaders were former inmates in the Minnesota prison system and knew well the dark side of the law. They were accustomed to police brutality and discrimination, and were determined to stop the harassment of Indians. As their fame spread, they began to travel to conferences to find out what other groups around the nation were doing. But their investigations revealed that, for the most part, tribal leaders were concerned with their own status in the eyes of federal officials and not with the welfare of their people. The more the A.I.M. leaders saw, the more they rebelled against the treatment of Indians across the nation.

The advent of the Nixon administration was greeted with some concern by Indians across the country. The last time the Republicans had been in office, they had developed and enforced the hated termination policy, and a number of tribes had lost their treaty rights through unilateral action by the Republican-dominated congress. Many Indians expected that once the Republicans were back in power, they would attempt something along the same ideological lines, and the Indians waited for the axe to fall. But they were pleasantly surprised. The administration appeared to be genuinely interested in correcting wrongs suffered by Indian people, and a general air of euphoria developed during the first year of the Nixon administration.

The pressures for protest began to grow too great to ignore, however, as the young Indians watched the anti-war activities continue to escalate and saw the other social movements gain general support and credibility with the public. By late 1969 the stage was set for action, but no one could predict when, where, and what the protest would be. In late October an Indian organization, the American Indians United, met in San Francisco for its convention. A day after the meeting ended, the San Francisco Indian Center burned down, and suddenly the Indians of the Bay area were left without a place to meet. The opportunity had suddenly presented itself.

A group of Indians had been planning to capture Alcatraz island, the abandoned former federal prison, since February of 1969, but had had no occasion to muster the forces necessary to do the job. Now, in late November, with the rainy season coming and the Indians concerned about the loss of the center, the time was ripe. Nineteen Indian students from San Francisco State and Berkeley landed on Alcatraz in early November and spent an anxious night hiding from the guards before being taken off the island. The incident caused a flurry in the local press, which did not serve to alarm the white population but which was a virtual call to action for the Indians of the area. On November 19th almost three hundred Indians landed on the island, and the next day the story mushroomed around the world. The Indians had captured the most famous island in America and were demanding that the government give them title to it.

Alcatraz became the focal point of Indian protest and the inspiration of Indians everywhere. Many

Indians regarded the capture of Alcatraz as the beginning of a new movement to recapture the continent and assert tribal independence from the United States, and it was finally this issue that Alcatraz came to symbolize. Tribal elders had sought for years to get the government to restore the lands of the tribes which had been taken for national parks and other uses at the beginning of the century. But they failed to realize that the struggle for Alcatraz could be used as a symbolic and political expression of the more general problem of instituting a program of land restoration by the federal government. Publicly they expressed abhorrence at the illegal invasion of government property, while privately they were delighted that some young Indians were tweaking the federal government's nose. Yet their failure to exploit the land issue when it was raised by the young activists was in a real sense the final emotional split between philosophies of change among Indians.

The government's immediate response to the invasion of Alcatraz was to channel more funds from the Office of Economic Opportunity to Indian groups in urban areas. Arrangements were made to fund an umbrella organization in the San Francisco Bay area as an alternative to funding the group on Alcatraz. In this way the administration hoped to defuse the impact which the occupation was having on Indians across the nation. Long after the activists left the island, the government embarked on a selective program of land restoration, returning Blue Lake to Taos Pueblo, Mount Adams to the Yakimas, and some 60,000 acres to the Warm Springs tribes of Oregon, but the restorations were more in the form of political payoffs for support than an acknowledgment of the justice of the case for land reform.

The inability of the Indian activists to discern their

impact or position with respect to the federal government began to emerge in the months following the landing at Alcatraz. The very success of the activists appeared to doom them to overestimate their impact and make mistakes. Richard Oakes, the charismatic Mohawk who had been instrumental in planning and leading the successful second landing on the island, saw his fame as a warrior spread. He attributed his fame to the invasion phase of the movement and failed to recognize the necessity of prolonged negotiations in completing the transfer of title to the lands which the activists wanted. Thus, Oakes made plans for additional invasions of federal property in northern California and at key places around the country. Other Indians followed Oakes' lead, and soon the only issue was landing on pieces of surplus federal property, not securing them in Indian hands through legislation or litigation.

The ideological basis for demanding a restoration of tribal lands was grounded in the treaty relationship of the tribes with the United States. This basis began to erode as activists viewed the treaties as an excuse for protests and not as the basis for establishing a clearer definition of the federal relationship. During the next two years the Indian activist movement degenerated into sporadic landings on federal property, accompanied by the demand that the property be turned over to them immediately under the provisions of the Sioux and Arapaho treaty of 1868. No one could ever find the provision which allowed this restoration, but restoration was demanded anyway. One of the major problems involved with this approach was that the government had no legal relationship with the activists by which it could have justified giving them the lands they demanded. Tribal governments grew wary of the staying power of the activists because they had dealt with the government long enough to understand that clearing title to lands was a complicated procedure, certainly nothing that could be achieved in a weekend of television appearances, and that permanent possession of restored lands required a legal entity such as a tribe to receive the title in trust.

The more the activists talked about the provisions of the 1868 treaty, the more the arena in which they worked changed. Tribal councils (with the exception of the small tribes in Washington State who were working on their treaty fishing rights) were generally unsympathetic concerning further action on treaties. They had all filed claims against the government with the Indian Claims Commission and were awaiting the settlement of their claims. While they realized that certain additional rights might accrue to them through the treaties, none could see any immediate and tangible benefits from demonstrations for land restorations based on treaties.

But a different force began to assert itself in Indian affairs as the discussions of treaties grew. Each reservation had a number of traditional Indians, largely fullbloods, who had preserved the tribal customs and had generally boycotted the tribal governments set up under the Indian Reorganization Act of 1934 on the basis of treaty rights. These people represented the Indian traditions in the best sense, were generally leaders in the tribal religious ceremonies, and were eager to see something done about the treaties. They took the activists seriously when they talked about treaties, and they began to give fairly substantial support to the idea of treaty reform.

The overtures made by the traditional Indians came at an opportune time for many of the new Indian leaders. Many had been taken from the reservations when they were children and had never lived in an Indian community. They had grown up in the slums of the cities of the West Coast and the Midwest and were toughened in the ruthlessness in which urban America schools her poor and disadvantaged. As more and more urban Indians joined the three major protest organizations—the American Indian Movement, the United Native Americans, and the Indians of All Tribes—they came into contact with young people who had grown up on the reservations and spoke the tribal language. This contact sparked a tremendous interest in the tribal language and traditions, and many of the urban Indians began to show up on the reservations, seeking the tribal heritage which they had been denied. They became the most militant of the advocates of cultural renewal.

The coalition had finally been forged which was to reshuffle Indian affairs beyond recognition. Urban Indian activists seeking an Indian identity and heritage and traditional Indians buttressed by the energies of the young combined forces and made ready to push the Indians who had accommodated the white man off the reservations. Caught between these forces were the tribal chairmen whom the government recognized and the large group of Indian professionals who were operating the programs of the tribes or working in government jobs. By mid-1972 the middle ground of progressive ideology in Indian affairs was fast eroding, and desperate confrontation was in the air over the issue of the nature of the modern Indian community.

3. The Occupation of the Bureau of Indian Affairs

1972 was the year for the Indian to gain the nation's spotlight. The ceremonials of the Plains tribes were filled to overflowing with Indians, many of them urban activists who had come to join in the revitalization of Indian cultures. The government, fearful of the quickened pace of Indian discontent, created its own organization, called the National Tribal Chairmen's Association. This group was used as a rubber stamp for the government's policies. Their public statements consisted mainly of paranoid reactions to the protests staged by the leading Indian organization of the nation, the American Indian Movement.

Throughout the year a sense of foreboding hung over Indian country. As the movement had developed from the days of the Alcatraz invasion in late 1969, the federal government had continued to co-opt the tribal governments, and while the activists gained national media reputations they watched promise after promise made by the federal government during demonstrations dissipate when their protests were concluded.

Early in January the Minnesota Chippewa tribe had won a major lawsuit over their rights to police fishing within the reservation boundaries, a decision that clearly grated on the nerves of the white resort owners who had used the lakes of the Chippewas for decades without paying the tribes any compensation. In the spring the American Indian Movement held a convention at Cass Lake, Minnesota, and there entered into a minor scrap over those fishing rights. The A.I.M. convention had been designed for unity, and the slogan of A.I.M. at that point was the support of tribal sovereignty. But tribal sovereignty began to take on many faces as the activists expounded on it. Tribal officials regarded tribal sovereignty as support for the decisions of tribal councils, especially in Minnesota, where the Chippewas had lost a great deal of their lands through allotments in the closing years of the last century. Tribal sovereignty over the remaining pieces of Indian land was a fragile right at best. Conversely, the activists interpreted this situation as an example of the failure of some of the tribal officials to take a stand on tribal rights which would be sufficiently militant to frighten the whites of the area. Their idea of tribal sovereignty seemed to date back to pre-discovery days, when each tribe was independent and able to confront its enemies in battle.

During the A.I.M. convention roads were blocked and guns drawn, but no violence ensued. The disputes seemed to be settled amicably, but the pattern of violent confrontation and the apparent willingness to use arms was established. On the deeper ideological front, it was also apparent that the years of activity had produced an increasing sense of disgust among the activists for the tribal governments, which were unwilling or unable to defend their own rights. The old yearning for a traditional form of government was no longer a rhetorical idea for many activists, and the mood began to reverberate through

Indian country for a return to a traditional form of government by casting aside the present governments as quickly as possible.

In June, as the summer round of pow-wows and ceremonials began, the concern of many Indians was to find a way to bring the Indian situation to the attention of the American public. Many of the tribal officials around the nation also felt a sense of betrayal at the continual shifting of federal policies and at the frequent cuts in their funds from the poverty programs. Indian country seemed ready to explode when, in state after state, there were incidents in which Indians were killed and no redress was made available to their relatives.

During the early spring there had been a major confrontation at Gordon, Nebraska, over the killing of Raymond Yellow Thunder, an elderly Sioux from the Pine Ridge reservation. Yellow Thunder had been beaten by five whites, stripped below the waist, and pushed into a dance hall, to the entertainment of the whites, who were having a celebration. He was found dead several days later, owing to the effects of the beating. Gordon officials had done nothing about the incident until the American Indian Movement called nearly a thousand Indians into the town as a protest. *Life* magazine covered the incident, and the situation was very tense for several days as nearly a thousand Indians invaded the town, demanding justice. The A.I.M. leaders had been prominent in the protest, and everyone figured that the Gordon incident would mark the end of senseless and brutal killings of Indians.

But the summer brought news of far-flung incidents involving Indian-killing. It appeared as if the whites of the West had decided to embark on an Indian war of their own, for no sooner had one incident cooled than another one arose. Indians marched for justice as a result of the killings of Indians in both California and Arizona, without receiving any relief in either state. The emotional commitment of the movement had now penetrated into every part of Indian country, and people were anxiously awaiting some word from the activist leaders as to what could be done to prevent more killings. Appeals to the Justice Department went unheeded.

During the Sun Dance at the Rosebud Sioux reservation in South Dakota, there was a discussion by a number of the activist leaders concerned with gathering all of the activists of the nation's tribes and preparing a march into Washington sometime in the fall. The idea was apparently patterned with some recollection of the impact which had been created by the March on Washington of 1963, when the civil-rights movement had demonstrated its remarkable national support. Plans were made to sound out the sentiment for such a march, and word began to spread around Indian country as to the possibility of such a protest.

There was a general sentiment in every section of the country for such a march, but the logistics appeared formidable, and as fall approached there was lacking an adequate sense of urgency to generate the energy for the march. As in other social movements, an unforeseen event provided the needed incident. In September Richard Oakes, leader of the Alcatraz invasion, was shot to death by a guard at a camp in California. Indian country was aflame with indignation, and the planners of the march decided to move.

A number of activist groups met in Denver, Colorado, to plan what would be called the "Trail of Broken Treaties" caravan. Plans called for the caravan to begin on the West Coast, pick up Indians as it traveled east, and arrive in Washington, D.C., during the final week of the 1972 Presidential campaign.

The idea was to build up both tension and publicity as the caravan proceeded across the nation, and to present a list of demands to both Presidential candidates in the week before the election. The Indians thought that if it were a close election, they could gain some important concessions from the candidates which might later be translated into reforms of some lasting significance.

The caravan began in October and wound its way eastward, stopping at every reservation within easy driving distance of the main route. For the first time, people began to realize the extent of discontent existing on the reservations. The Bureau of Indian Affairs had been instructed to refuse to assist any of the different groups that were proceeding east. The B.I.A. did its best to hamper the caravan. Nevertheless, as the caravan arrived at the reservations, it was generally greeted by large crowds and joined by many participants who also wished to present their grievances to the government.

The government would later interpret the Trail of Broken Treaties as primarily an urban movement, even though its members represented nearly every tribe, age group, political persuasion, and ideology in Indian country. Over 80 per cent of the group were residents of reservations, and old people were well-represented. Eastern Indians participated in substantial numbers. They had generally been denied any federal recognition, and the administration's tribal chairmen's organization adamantly and stupidly opposed extending federal services to them. Yet they were welcomed by their western cousins, making the caravan not only a national protest but one which, if successful, necessarily would involve a redefinition of federal responsibilities to Indians encompassing all segments of the aboriginal community of Indian people.

The caravan stopped in St. Paul, Minnesota, to plan the list of grievances and hold workshops on the various phases of the march. In several days of workshops the caravan members hammered out a list of twenty points which they felt fairly and adequately summarized a reform program for the government which would receive strong support from Indians. It was apparent by that time that Nixon would win the election, and much of the focus of the goal of the march shifted from presenting the Twenty Points to both candidates to simply presenting the Nixon administration with a program which it could easily put into effect.

The Twenty Points presented a new framework for considering the status of Indian tribes and the nature of their federal relationship. It harkened back to the days of freedom, when the United States courted the friendship of the tribes in its desperate battle to maintain its independence from Great Britain. The first point dealt with a restoration of constitutional treaty-making authority. It proposed the repeal of the 1871 appropriations statute which forbade further treaty-making with Indian tribes. The authors of the Twenty Points argued, and quite capably, that this prohibition had taken from the President and the Congress a constitutional power which they were bound to exercise as their official duty.

The second point proposed that a new treaty commission be established within the next year which could contract a new treaty relationship with the American Indian community on a tribal, regional, or multi-tribal basis. Any treaty proposed by the commission would be in effect for a period of twenty-five years and would include specific provisions for the protection of tribal members and tribal resources.

The fourth point (the third point had nothing to do with treaty rights) asked for a commission to review the treaty violations of the past and present and set up procedures for review of chronic treaty violations by both the states and the federal government. The explanation of this point noted that in the ten-year period from 1962 to 1972, Indian tribes had spent $40 million in litigation costs in an effort to force the government to fulfill its legal obligations under treaties. It noted that this money, if applied to developments on the reservations, would have been capable of generating substantial improvements in the conditions under which Indians lived.

The resubmission of unratified treaties to the Senate for approval was the fifth of the Twenty Points. The primary purpose, the Indians argued, was that it would restore the rule of law to the federal relationship. At issue were twelve treaties signed with California tribes but subsequently buried in the Congressional archives. It was obvious to everyone that the United States had indeed profited from the twelve treaties as if they had been ratified, since it had taken the lands of the California Indians and converted them to its own use. The California Indians had not received any benefits from their treaties, however, and in effect they were suffering from the unlawful actions of the United States. Ratification of the treaties would have clarified their legal status as tribes and assisted them in some of the lawsuits then pending in the Indian Claims Commission, since some of the suits involved the loss of lands described in the unratified treaties.

The sixth and perhaps the most fundamental point, and one that would be later prominent at Wounded Knee, was a demand that all Indians be governed by treaty relations. This point was partially an effort to respond to the questions raised by the non-federal status of the eastern Indians. They had been declared eligible for federal services during the 1930s, when the Indian Reorganization Act was instituted as federal policy. But the appropriations for travel to enable the federal government to organize them as federally recognized tribes had run out before the Bureau of Indian Affairs could finish its task. Since that time, they had been America's orphans, receiving no federal aid or recognition and little assistance from the states in which they lived.

The sixth point involved a similar consideration, and that was to define a specific contemporary legal status for Indian tribes. During the twentieth century there had been continual haggling by the Bureau of Indian Affairs over the status of tribes who had not signed a treaty but who had reservations set aside by the President under his powers to set up executive-order reservations. From time to time debate arose concerning either the title to the reservation lands, ownership of minerals and water of the reservation, or status of these reservations in regard to the civil and criminal jurisdictions of state and federal governments. The caravan participants were tired of hearing these arguments raised every time they wanted to do something. They wanted a clear definition of what it was they owned and what the nature of their relationship with the federal government was.

Even more, however, the participants wanted to define one basic status for all Indian people, which could be easily understood by Indians and which could not be whittled away by the actions of the different states. The Indians of Oklahoma, for example, had had their reservations abolished prior to the admission of the state to the Union, and their rights to federal services were blurred. Tribes in North and South Dakota, Montana, and Washington had received the benefit of a disclaimer clause inserted into their states' constitutions forbidding the state to lay any claim to individual or tribal property. The discrepancies in the status of the tribes could be demonstrated by other examples in other subject areas. The people felt that one basic definition would enable both Indians and state governments to better meet their basic responsibilities.

The seventh point asked for mandatory relief from treaty violations by state governments. Had the tribes been able to maintain a semblance of international status, a violation of their treaty would have been an act of war. But with the emphasis on their domestic status, tribes suffered greatly from the arbitrary actions of state governments, which continually violated their treaties with impunity. State courts would insist that they either found no violation of the treaty or that the treaty had become inoperative with the passage of time. As litigation over treaty rights proceeded, the tribes were often forced to climb the tedious ladder of appellate courts, seeking redress. The higher federal courts would generally uphold the arguments and status of the tribe, but such findings would rarely deter the state officials from immediately initiating another action against the tribe.

With the idea of mandatory relief, the Indians were asking that federal district courts be given the power to issue immediate injunctions against state agencies which would remain in effect until the court satisfied itself that an Indian treaty was not being violated. This proposal would have reversed the present situation, in which the courts make Indians prove a violation of their treaties before they will act. The seventh point, if accepted, would have allowed an immediate injunction to be issued against a state agency pending proof by the state that it was not violating an Indian treaty. By merely shifting the burden of proof upon complaint of treaty violation from themselves to the states, the Indians felt that their treaty rights could be made a serious part of the federal law. In the last analysis, such an amendment would have placed Indian treaties on the same basis as foreign treaties with regard to their enforcement.

The eighth and final point dealing with the treaty relationship asked for judicial recognition by the government of the Indians' right to interpret treaty provisions. During the 1920s a number of important lawsuits were taken against the United States. In those relatively early years of claims litigation, there were a number of old men in the respective tribes who had been present at treaty-signing ceremonies, and they were called as witnesses by the tribes during the course of the suits. But the Court of Claims immediately disqualified the Indian witnesses by ruling that their testimony would be biased because of their obvious interest in seeing the treaty provisions upheld.

There was also a great oral tradition among many tribes concerning the provisions of the treaties and their meaning. Fathers and grandfathers would pass along almost verbatim the words of the treaty commissioners which explained what the various articles and phrases of the treaties were supposed to mean. Courts had declared that this oral tradition could not be used by Indians in cases which involved treaties, and that only the writings and minutes taken by the government secretaries and officers would qualify, since they were considered "disinterested parties." That the oral traditions and proceedings of the treaties often coincided with records kept by the whites did not deter the courts from disqualifying the Indians and accepting the testimony of the whites.

Doubting the word of the tribal elders in a case involving a treaty was like proclaiming that the tribe was composed of pathological liars, and this matter of witnesses was understandably sensitive to Indians. The caravan participants did not know the rigid rules of evidence required by the federal courts, but they felt that they had been tricked, and the eighth point was designed to place the memory and credibility of the tribal elders on a par with the miscellaneous diaries of wandering preachers and traders who also happened to be present at some of the treaty negotiations.

In total, the points on the treaties had great importance. First, they were extremely accurate in their assessment of the feelings of Indians around the nation. Even months after the incident, whenever Indian people would learn of the points relating to treaties they would nod their heads in agreement and say, "It's about time someone said those things." Second, the points outlined a fairly sophisticated understanding of a type of relationship with the federal government that could best be defined as a quasi-protectorate status. It would have severely limited the arbitrary exercise of power by the federal government over the rights of the tribes. Most of all, the acceptance of the Twenty Points would have meant that the treaties which the United States had signed with the respective tribes a century earlier would have the rightful, legal status which they deserved, equal to the legal status accorded foreign treaties. As such, the treaties would have stood in a superior position to the laws of the several states, as promised by the United States.

The caravan participants, having composed the Twenty Points in Minnesota amidst the friendly confines of Chippewa country, wound their way eastward toward the nation's capital and arrived in Washington, D.C., on November 3rd, the Friday before the national elections. The bulk of the demonstrators went immediately to the Bureau of Indian Affairs, where they gathered in the auditorium to await word from their leaders as to the housing arrangements for their stay in the city. Some of the leaders, who had been in Washington for several weeks before the arrival of the caravan, had been delegated to arrange housing for the caravan people. But those responsible for housing had wasted their time enhancing their images as glamorous Indian leaders, and had done little to secure rooms for the people coming to town. Most of Friday afternoon was spent in trying to obtain from the Department of the Interior officials a suitable place to house the Indians who were pouring into the city. Several places were suggested, but these were turned down because of their inadequate facilities or their remote location from the main part of town. As the afternoon wore on, an arrangement was finally made to provide the Department of Interior auditorium for the protesters.

As the Indians started to leave the B.I.A. building, some of the guards began to push the younger Indians out the door. Instantly the situation changed. Fearful that they were being pushed out into the open to face the District of Columbia riot squad, the Indians seized the building.

From top to bottom, the building was blocked off. Desks and files were overturned, and passageways were blockaded to prevent any police force from easily taking the building. Legs were ripped off wooden desks and made into weapons for the confrontation that appeared to be imminent. The Commissioner of Indian Affairs, Louis Bruce, and a team of Indians went into the building to see if they couldn't bring the occupation to a close, but to little avail. They stayed the night, and then were ordered by their superiors to withdraw from the building.

The next several days were critical. The caravan leaders could barely keep their followers under control. Sporadic efforts by the police to harass the occupants of the building created a constant state of fear, and with each wave of harassment the building suffered additional damage as the Indians tried to plug the obvious weak points in their defenses. During the weekend the parade of celebrities began, and the Indians were visited by some of the famous personalities of the domestic social movement. Stokely Carmichael, the popularizer of Black Power from several years back, visited the building and pledged his all but invisible support. Carl McIntyre, the conservative evangelical minister, arrived and informed the Indians that they were being led by communists, a charge that carried little weight, appeared ludicrous in retrospect, and was greeted by gales of laughter from the Indians.

One of the humorous aspects of the occupation then ensued. The Rev. McIntyre told the Indians that they were not using the right tactics—that he was in full sympathy with their cause, but they should use the regular channels of dissent and not try to force a confrontation by occupying the building. Dennis Banks, one of the A.I.M. leaders, grew somewhat angry on hearing McIntyre's lecture, and challenged him to do something concrete. When McIntyre said he would give a demonstration of his support, Banks told him that Louis Bruce, the Commissioner of Indian Affairs, had been forbidden to stay with the Indians in the building. "He's a virtual prisoner," Banks stated, "and we want him let loose."

McIntyre got everything completely mixed up, and led his band of followers down the street to the Interior building. As they marched along they began chanting, "Free Morton, free Morton." Morton, of course, was Secretary of the Interior Rogers C. B. Morton, Bruce's boss, who had ordered the Commissioner out of the building. Interior officials, puzzled at this protest, began to barricade the doors of the Interior building, thinking that the Indians were trying to occupy that building also. McIntyre never did understand either who was Commissioner of Indian Affairs or who was being held captive. That's undoubtedly what happens when you are fighting communists.

A team of negotiators led by Hank Adams, Indian activist of the fishing-rights protest in the Pacific Northwest, worked out a partial solution to the occupation the following Monday morning, but by then the damage to the building had been compounded, almost to the point of total destruction. Sporadic deadlines given by the police had kept the Indians so watchful that they virtually tore the building apart trying to defend themselves from attacks which in fact never materialized. Finally, on Thursday, November 9th, the Indians left the building under a promise by the administration that no criminal charges would be filed for events which happened during the occupation. In addition, the caravan participants received some $66,000 in travel money to get them back to their reservations. The old people were flown home, and the younger people took buses and cars. Some Indians hung around Washington for several months, since they had no homes to return to and were satisfied to live off the brief glory of having been a member of the occupation, which was good for a meal and some drinks from newsmen for several weeks afterward.

Almost immediately, the accusations began to fly. Representatives of the conservative National Tribal Chairmen's Association, which was dependent upon the administration for its travel money and expenses, took a tour through the building and promptly expressed their outrage at its condition. They loudly protested the advance of the travel funds from the government, forgetting that the Bureau of Indian Affairs had, just a few months before, given them some $55,000 for their convention, held in Oregon.

The officials of the government just as promptly began spreading the story that the people who had occupied the building were primarily urban Indians without any real ties to the reservations. The fact that the Trail of Broken Treaties organization had a roster of its participants showing over 80 per cent of the addresses as reservation towns did not seem to register with the federal people.

As the weeks followed and the real stories of the occupation began to emerge, it became increasingly evident that the Indians had been had. Some of the Indians who had been in the building during the actual occupation went on the official tours of the occupation site. They were astounded to see extensive damage in rooms where they were certain there had been no damage. The walls were marked up with slogans and names and addresses where there had been no marks whatsoever at the time of departure. Some of the paint appeared fresh, an indication that it had been applied recently and not in connection with the Indians' takeover of the building.

Later events would indicate that the federal government had had a substantial number of agents among the protesters, and some were so militant and destructive as to be awarded special Indian names for their involvement in the protest. It became apparent why the government had been so willing to agree not to prosecute the Indians: The presence of agent-provocateurs and the intensity of their work would have made it extremely difficult for the government to have proven an intent by the real Indian activists to destroy the building.

Unnoticed in the general confusion of the occupation was the fact that, even in the midst of the turmoil, the Indians had been concentrating on the Twenty Points which they had come to Washington to discuss. During the early morning hours of Saturday, November 4th, they had sent off telegrams to the United Nations asking that a special investigating team be sent to Washington to observe the incident so that the whole matter of Indian rights could be considered by the United Nations when it next convened. A telegram was also sent to the Vatican, asking the Pope to revoke the Proclamation of 1493, which divided the New World between Spain and Portugal and which was later used to justify the legal doctrine under which the United States held its claim to the lands of North America. The only problem with this request was that the telegram was addressed to Pope John and not Pope Paul, who was then the reigning pontiff.

In early December the House Subcommittee on Indian Affairs held a hearing to determine the nature and cause of the protest. Unfortunately, it was restricted to government witnesses, and they made the most of their opportunity to paint the protest as the work of a few dedicated revolutionaries who had misled the Indian people. Damage estimates ranged from several hundred thousand to several million dollars. and some said that it was the most severe damage in Washington, D.C., since the British had burned the city in the War of 1812.

As the various groups of Indians had left the building and started their trek home, government agents had discovered that a substantial number of federal records were missing. During the weekend the A.I.M. leaders had loaded a number of boxes of files into trucks and cars and had taken them out of the city. They thought that they would uncover massive evidence of frauds perpetrated by the bureaucrats of the Interior Department against the tribes. But about all they found were chronological correspondence and some files on specific cases then pending in either the courts or Congress.

The Trail of Broken Treaties Papers got extensive

coverage from some of the newspaper columnists. Some of the A.I.M. leaders thought that they had scooped even Daniel Ellsberg's Pentagon Papers revelations, and went to New York City to ask incredible sums of money from unwary publishers for the rights to reproduce the papers. Spectacular announcements were made that at least a dozen Senators could be indicted from the evidence unveiled by the papers. When all the shouting died down, it appeared that the most important evidence of corruption and malfeasance present involved the ill-advised purchase of a paint factory by a Sioux tribe which was perfunctorily approved by the Bureau of Indian Affairs and a series of letters between officials of the State of Wisconsin and the Bureau of Indian Affairs concerning the investigation of two murders of Indian women in that state.

Hank Adams felt a deep responsibility to see that the papers were returned, and so he sent out word through Indian country that he would remain in Washington, D.C., and see that any papers shipped to him were returned to the proper authority. Adams had returned two batches of papers and office machines, and was about to return the first major shipment of papers, which had been sent to him from the Pine Ridge Indian Reservation in South Dakota, when he was foully betrayed by his federal contacts.

One Johnny Arellano, a Mexican-American undercover agent who had worked first for the District of Columbia police and then for the Federal Bureau of Investigation, hung around Hank's apartment and drove the remaining members of the Trail of Broken Treaties on their errands in the capital city. He went to the bus station to get the first large shipment of papers, and carried them up to Adams' apartment. The papers remained there overnight, and the next morning Arellano failed to show up to help Adams take the papers to the Bureau of Indian Affairs, where the return was to be witnessed by a member of the House of Representatives Ways and Means Committee staff.

Adams knew that he was running late in keeping his appointment and so, in desperation, he called Jack Anderson to see if Jack would send his assistant, Les Whitten, with a car to help Adams return the papers. Whitten, seeing a story in the dramatic return of the first major shipment of federal papers, hastened to Adams' apartment with his car. As they were loading the car, they were suddenly surrounded by F.B.I. agents, who arrested them and took them to the police station. They were kept there most of the day while the F.B.I. changed the affidavits that were used to justify their arrest—it seemed that the F.B.I. had planned on arresting Jack Anderson, not Les Whitten, and had sworn statements to support their arrest warrants stating that Jack Anderson was to pick up the papers and use them for his own purposes.

The case created a great controversy, since the Administration was already after Anderson because of his continual ability to ferret out information on its activities. He had revealed the nature of the United States' posture toward India during the Indian-Pakistani crisis a year earlier, and they were out to get him if possible. But they were able to arrest only Whitten, who was simply reporting his story. Nevertheless, the case was taken to the federal grand jury, and, after hearing the evidence, the grand jury refused to indict the two men, thus ending the F.B.I. involvement in the case with a slight embarrassment.

One of the terms for ending the occupation of the Bureau of Indian Affairs building had been that the administration would respond to the Twenty Points within sixty days. The caravan people felt that if the administration responded to their points, which were never presented formally because of the confrontation and occupation, they could then begin extensive efforts to get congressional hearings on the points. They planned a massive lobbying effort to get the needed reforms in the 92nd Congress, which began in January, 1973. The National Congress of American Indians, a large Indian-controlled private organization, was busy developing an "Impact Survey Report" to assess the effect of the occupation and thus clear the air for the hearings later in the spring. Indian country was poised to learn what posture the administration would assume toward the Twenty Points.

Finally, in January, the administration replied to the points. It was obvious that little attention had been paid to the document. The administration reply merely cited the positive accomplishments of the first Nixon term and promised more help during the coming term. But it rejected the whole idea of treaty reform, on the ground that individual Indians had been made citizens earlier in the century and no treaties could be made with individual citizens. The response was hardly accurate, since the Twenty Points asked not for individual treaties but for regional treaties with the then existing tribes and communities.

The previous record of the Nixon administration had been very good, and so the response given by the White House Task Force was a distinct disappointment to Indians everywhere. Until the occupation, the administration had been characterized as one of the most progressive in American history. It had seen that sacred lands were returned to the people of Taos Pueblo and Yakima, had restored other tribal lands, and had pushed through Congress a bill to resolve the land claims of the Alaska natives. Indians had come to expect a more enlightened and less emotional response by the administration.

Perhaps no group of Indians was more outraged at the response than the A.I.M. leaders, who felt that they had raised relevant issues concerning treaties only to discover that the treaty issue was regarded as unimportant by the administration. While they seethed with rage, the A.I.M. people vowed never again to surrender without receiving a definite commitment from the administration. This attitude of intractability would later be displayed at Wounded Knee, and the betrayal felt by Indians in January when they read the administration's response to the Twenty Points went a long way toward making the settlement of the Wounded Knee crisis more difficult.

4. The Confrontation at Wounded Knee

The desperation which had led to the Trail of Broken Treaties in 1972 now engulfed the Indian activists. It seemed as if there was no way to prevent the killing of Indians in the West. In January an Oglala Sioux named Bad Heart Bull was killed in Buffalo Gap, South Dakota. The circumstances of the killing were clouded, and when the man accused of killing the Indian was indicted on a mere manslaughter charge, the call went out from the A.I.M. leadership to gather in the Black Hills town of Custer and demand justice.

Indians from all over the nation came storming into the small Dakota town, and the local whites, fearful of what might happen, armed themselves and began blockading roads leading into the Black Hills. A protest march erupted into violence when the Chamber of Commerce building, a tiny boothlike structure, was set afire. Arrests were made, and general confusion reigned as the Indians' tempers hit the boiling point and local whites talked of killing Indians in terms reminiscent of big-game hunters looking for trophies.

The protest shifted to Rapid City, South Dakota, when the news came of the indictment of an Indian for murder somewhere in the northern part of the Black Hills. For several days tensions escalated and prolonged violence appeared imminent, but finally tempers cooled, and the Indians were assured some measure of justice. A.I.M. leader Dennis Banks grew so optimistic about the change of attitudes in Rapid City that he addressed the South Dakota legislature, promising a new era of race relations in the state. Things seemed to be under control, and so Dennis Banks and A.I.M. leader Russell Means went to the Pine Ridge reservation to rest and hold an eventful victory dance to celebrate their success in Rapid City, if it could be called success. All things considered, it was the last place on Earth they should have gone.

On the Pine Ridge reservation live the Oglala Sioux, one of the more memorable tribes of American Indians. They waged a successful war against the United States from 1864 to 1868 under the famous chief Red Cloud, a man who had no peer as a diplomat among Indians. In June of 1876, under the immortal Crazy Horse, the Oglalas swept the field against General Custer and his Seventh Cavalry, taking about half an hour to rout the finest unit of the day. By the time they finally retired to their reservation in the southwestern corner of South Dakota, the Oglala Sioux had been responsible for two of the three greatest defeats ever inflicted on the United States Army by Indians.

Their original reservation was over two million acres, and it was primarily grazing land, with some farmland in its southeastern corner. The Oglala Sioux adapted from hunting to ranching with comparative ease during the 1880s, and were one of the more successful tribes of the northern plains in making this transition. But ill fate seemed to be their lot. Red Cloud's prestige was international, and other tribes regarded him as the last and best hope when they were in trouble with the United States. Dull Knife and Little Wolf, the valiant Cheyennes, headed toward the Red Cloud Agency during their famous "Cheyenne Autumn" flight from Oklahoma. So great was Red Cloud's prestige that the other Sioux tribes refused to deal with the United States until they saw what Red Cloud was going to do. Generally, they decided to follow his lead.

In the late 1880s a new Indian religious movement began to sweep across the western states. Its prophet was Wovoka, a Paiute from the Walker River reservation in western Nevada. His doctrine was based upon visions which he had had while in a religious trance. He saw and talked with his relatives who had died, and they taught him a special dance of great significance. The world was shortly to come to an end, they related, and the dead Indians would return with the buffalo. The white man would be destroyed, and the earth which he had corrupted would be renewed. To a people recently forced to live in poverty on the high plains of the Dakotas, it was a welcome message, and many of the Sioux followed the teachings of the religion. The Army, fearful that it would lead to another war with the Sioux, pursued the new converts in an attempt to arrest them and end the movement.

Thus it was that the tiny band of Sioux people who followed the Ghost Dance religion fled from northern South Dakota in 1890 to seek the protection of Red Cloud. In early December of 1890 the government, fearful of the Ghost Dance—which was spreading throughout the West from its place of origin in Nevada—arranged to assassinate Sitting Bull, the Hunkpapa holy man of the Standing Rock Sioux reservation, when it was learned that he too had embraced the new religion. The government saw the assassination as a way to defuse the Ghost Dance situation and rid themselves of Sitting Bull, who had adamantly opposed allotment of the Sioux lands. So Indian police were sent to Sitting Bull's home to arrest him. An incident was arranged, and before the old holy man could even walk outside his house, he was shot. His followers, fearful of further retaliation by the government, fled south toward the Cheyenne River Agency.

The Cheyenne River Agency was divided into two basic areas. The Indians who had agreed to try the white man's road lived on the eastern side of the reservation, near the agency, on the Missouri River. The traditional Sioux who were still intent on keeping their old ways lived far to the west and stayed as far away from the influence of the white man as possible. The leading traditional chief was Big Foot, and it was to his camp that Sitting Bull's followers fled. The camp was predominantly women and children, because so many of the men had been killed in the wars of the previous decade. Big Foot, somewhat like Red Cloud, had used his personal prestige to protect the people of his camp, and so the frightened Hunkpapas of Sitting Bull sought his protection.

No sooner had they arrived when word went out from the agency that they must all report to the government agent. The government was more frightened than they were, and it had no intention of allowing any Indians to leave the reservations to which they had been assigned. The people in Big Foot's band were notified that unless they came immediately to the agency by the river, a two-day march in the cold winter weather, the soldiers would be sent after them. In panic the people took counsel, and decided to make the trek to Pine Ridge Agency, where they would be safe under the protection of Red Cloud. So, in the midst of the winter, with few weapons and little clothing or shelter, the people moved south into the Badlands of South Dakota, hoping to slip into the Red Cloud Agency undetected.

It was, at best, an impossible plan. The West had
not had a real Indian scare since the days of Chief
Joseph in 1877. Joseph had led his Nez Perces from
the Wallowa Valley of Oregon over a thousand miles
toward the Canadian border, throwing the states of
Idaho and Montana into a trauma and defeating several Army units sent to stop him. When he surrendered, only a few miles from the Canadian border,
the western settlers breathed easier. The following
year, Chief Dull Knife and his Cheyennes fled from
Oklahoma on a desperate march to Montana, evading
Army units, passing unnoticed through Kansas and
Nebraska, and finally being virtually annihilated by
the Army in a valiant and dramatic but hopeless fight.

The Army, the newspaper reporters, and the local
whites were all spoiling for a good old Indian war,
and they viewed Big Foot's band as real game.

The Oglala Sioux converts to the Ghost Dance had
gone to the Badlands to await the end of the world,
and the whites feared a general Indian uprising. The
agency itself was in a state of hysteria. The agent had
spent his time undermining Red Cloud's authority,
and he panicked every time a group of Indians gathered. With the news that Big Foot was coming south,
the agent lost his head and called for troops to repel
the invaders. As the units of cavalry marched into
Pine Ridge, the agency town, Big Foot's little band
trudged its way south, unaware of anything unusual.

The cavalry met the Indians south of what is now
known as Big Foot Pass, along Porcupine Creek in the
center of the reservation. The rest of the story is well-
known. Disarmed and surrounded at Wounded Knee
Creek, the little band of Sioux were ruthlessly slaugh-
tered by the Army, using Hotchkiss guns. The
wounded were left to die in a three-day blizzard, and
the United States handed out over twenty Congressional Medals of Honor to soldiers of the Seventh
Cavalry who had participated in the massacre. Red

Cloud was eventually able to calm the people after the massacre, but the Oglalas never forgot the sight of dying Sioux lying on straw in Pine Ridge during the Christmas season. Years later they would try without success to get the United States to pay some form of pension to the survivors, but the Army always insisted that the incident had been a great battle instead of a heartless massacre of women and children and a dying Chief Big Foot, and Congress refused to authorize compensation for them.

The United States broke the back of Oglala Sioux resistance during World War I. The people had developed large herds of cattle by 1916, and were fairly prosperous. They had extensive pony herds, and raised some of the finest horses in the Northern Plains. And they herded both cattle and horses in communal herds, refusing to take allotments and continuing to maintain their old band form of governmental structure. In 1917, under a new government policy, the agent for the Oglalas sold their cattle, allegedly for the war needs, and leased their lands out to white cattlemen who were bringing cattle up from the South to graze.

The cattle market broke following the war, making it impossible for the Oglalas to reenter the cattle business. Large corporate farm operations began to move into western South Dakota to practice the new techniques of dry-land farming which had recently been developed. The government forced allotment of the reservation lands, and then promptly sent out a "competency" commission, which was instructed to find as many "competent" Oglalas as possible in order that their lands could be taken out of the federal trust and sold. In short order, the white cattlemen and farmers had a stranglehold over the Oglalas through being able to both lease and purchase their lands. They never surrendered this advantage.

Over the years, as some of the Oglalas sold their lands and either spent their money or were cheated out of it, they came to live in the agency town of Pine Ridge. There were few jobs on the reservation; the ones that did exist were at Pine Ridge and were primarily patronage jobs, to be handed out at the discretion of the Indian agent. A large group of landless Indians, who were almost totally dependent upon the whims and generous natures of the different Indian agents, began to congregate at the agency town. In the back country the traditional Oglala people maintained their old ways and tried to hold on to their allotted lands. When the government finally devised the "leasing unit," by which it could lease a number of small Indian allotments as one unit to wealthy and powerful white ranchers—in effect taking the lands of the traditional Indians and giving them small rental payments—the destruction of these people was nearly complete.

The Indian Reorganization Act of 1934 gave the people of the reservation some measure of self-government. They organized a tribal council and made provisions for tribal control of the reservation. But the landless people at Pine Ridge provided a powerful voting block, which was carefully watched and eloquently wooed during elections, since they provided the margin of victory for the position of tribal chairman, the crucial and all-important post in tribal government. The tribal politics of the reservation developed very rapidly after the adoption of the tribal constitution in 1935. More than one election was decided by large and anonymous contributions by groups of ranchers. And more than one tribal administration was suspected of being obligated to the white ranchers, who sometimes controlled nearly 80 per cent of the reservation lands through the leasing-unit device.

During the 1960s the War on Poverty brought many new patronage jobs to the reservation, and the tribal chairman's position became even more critical in reservation politics. The tribal chairman could assign most of the important jobs in the tribe's poverty programs, and had at his disposal the selection of many of the committee posts which determined the policies of the programs. So the fight for tribal chairman became nearly an armed conflict between opposing groups of Sioux. Most of the tribal politicians tried to support the people of the back-country communities, the traditional Sioux, but almost always had to bow to the voting power of Pine Ridge village and promise extensive patronage jobs to important village people.

In 1972 two apparently unrelated events happened at Pine Ridge which were to have a profound effect on the life of the reservation. Russell Means, one of the American Indian Movement leaders and a tribal member who had lived most of his life in the cities of the West and the Midwest, decided to return to the reservation and study traditional religion with the tribal medicine men. He began a food-purchasing co-op for the people at Porcupine, a tiny village seven miles north of Wounded Knee, and let it be known that at some unstated but future date he would run for tribal chairman.

Richard "Dickie" Wilson, a plumber in the Pine Ridge village, ran for tribal chairman and won in a brutal election. He defeated Gerald One Feather, a fullblood from Oglala, one of the most remote and traditional communities on the reservation. One Feather lost the votes of the people at Pine Ridge village while he held most of the votes of the outlying districts, and it became apparent that the reservation was polarized between the country people and the people who were dependent upon the government and tribal jobs at Pine Ridge. When the American

Indian Movement swept into Gordon, Nebraska, to protest the death of Raymond Yellow Thunder during the winter of 1972, they repaired to the reservation for a victory dance and spent about ten days there, convening an informal Indian "grand jury" to discuss the abuses of the traders on the reservation.

The pride of A.I.M.'s accomplishments in Gordon was tarnished by their extensive protest and subsequent "grand jury." Richard Wilson was just being sworn in as tribal chairman as the A.I.M. members left the reservation, and he vowed that they would never conduct another extensive protest on the reservation, at least so long as he was chairman. When the Trail of Broken Treaties caravan occupied the Bureau of Indian Affairs building in Washington, Wilson went to his council almost immediately and received support for a resolution banning the activities of the American Indian Movement on the reservation. He made it clear that there would be no victory dances held by A.I.M. at Pine Ridge when they returned.

Relations between Russell Means and Richard Wilson were strained at best, because they were considered to be future political opponents. Their relationship deteriorated further during the protests at Custer and Rapid City, South Dakota, in February of 1973, when Wilson offered to send tribal police to help the white law officers put down the A.I.M. protest. By mid-February Wilson had developed a strong police force, which was theoretically designed to prevent A.I.M. protests but which had a tendency to lean very hard on all of Wilson's political opponents.

When Means and Banks returned to the reservation following the protests at Custer and Rapid City, the tribal police, who were now referred to as the "goon squad" by the frightened reservation residents, began to bear down, hoping to chase the two A.I.M. leaders away from the reservation. Incidents escalated the

tensions felt by both groups, and the Bureau of
Indian Affairs saw that federal marshals were dis-
patched to Pine Ridge. In short order the tribal headquarters were barricaded with sandbags, and groups
of roving tribal police stopped anybody who looked
suspicious. On February 27th some of Wilson's police
caught Russell Means and his lawyer in the local
shopping center and pushed them around. The next
morning A.I.M. occupied Wounded Knee and issued
its defiant cry of political independence to the world.

If Wilson had allies within the federal establishment that gave him support, Means had his allies
also, and Indians from all over the nation, not simply
A.I.M. members, began to rush to the reservation
in support of the protest. The popularity of Dee
Brown's book *Bury My Heart at Wounded Knee*, a
chronicle of the Indian wars from 1862 to the final
spasm of the Wounded Knee massacre itself, had
familiarized the American public with the story of
the last brutal encounter between red and white, and
so the little village was a familiar name to many
people. The overtones of potential violence, a possible
repeat of the original massacre, made the protest
appear to be a nightmare replayed on television
every evening before the eyes of a horrified world.

The people at Wounded Knee allegedly took a
number of hostages when they captured the little village, and the newspaper headlines about Indian
hostages facing almost certain death thrilled the general public but threw a scare into South Dakota's two
United States Senators, George McGovern and James
Abourezk, both of whom had been very favorably
inclined toward Indians during their political careers.
George McGovern had been the only Senator to fight
for Indians in the bitter struggle over the hated
Heirship Lands bill in the early sixties. He had prevented the enactment of a law that would have allowed sale of allotted Indian lands without providing

funds to enable the tribes to purchase them. If enacted, the bill would have spelled doom for the Sioux reservations, which needed to preserve their land base very badly. Abourezk had grown up on the neighboring Rosebud Sioux reservation, where his uncle was an Indian trader. He was familiar with Indian problems, and knew better than most people in Congress how to approach them.

The two Senators arrived on the reservation the second day of the occupation, willing to do whatever they could about settling the dispute. Witnesses stated that McGovern was able to calm the federal officials, who were almost past the point of hysteria and who considered a quick shooting war the best way to resolve the incident. Abourezk, who headed the Subcommittee on Indian Affairs of the Senate Interior Committee, took special pains to get the two opposing sides talking to each other, and generally brought things under control. He began to realize that the protest was not just another urban-reservation Indian confrontation, as the Bureau of Indian Affairs officials were already labeling it.

The American Indian Movement leadership at Wounded Knee was not the determining factor of the protest. A number of local groups had asked A.I.M. to investigate their rights under the Fort Laramie treaty of 1868; one group supporting the protest had been formed to defend the civil rights of individual Oglalas against the excesses of the tribal police, and another had determined to break the back of the hated "unit leasing" policy, which they felt prevented them from combining their individual allotments into a community grazing unit in the old traditional way. The A.I.M. leaders quickly discovered that they had become a focal point and tactical squad for the many discontented groups on the reservation, and not simply the leaders of the movement.

In determining the issues which had to be resolved

before they would leave Wounded Knee, the people decided to push the question of the rights guaranteed them by the Treaty of 1868. Many felt that the other wrongs—loss of lands, loss of traditional tribal government, and police brutality—could be resolved if the treaty question was handled satisfactorily. So, on the second day of the occupation, the call went out for Senator William Fulbright to hold hearings in his Senate Foreign Relations Committee on the Sioux treaties and their violation by the United States.

This demand was bold, dramatic, and probably legally sound. Indian treaties had been ratified and proclaimed in the same manner as had foreign treaties. The federal courts had frequently concluded that Indian treaties had the same legal status as foreign treaties, and that the same doctrines of interpretation should be used to interpret the provisions of both kinds of treaties. In addition, the Library of Congress and the Senate Parliamentarian, when queried on the question of Indian treaties, both issued informal and not-for-quotation opinions regarding the probable jurisdiction of Fulbright's committee to hold hearings on Indian treaties. In spite of the Congressional Reorganization Act of 1946, when the old Indian Committees of the two houses of Congress were abolished and jurisdiction was conferred upon the two Interior Committees, both the Senate Parliamentarian and the Library of Congress felt that with respect to the treaty documents themselves the Foreign Relations Committee had full powers to hold hearings on all treaties of the United States. Only Senate protocol stood in the way of the Foreign Relations Committee's acting on the request of the Wounded Knee occupants.

Demanding hearings in the Foreign Relations Committee had been an old saw in Indian country, but no one had taken the idea seriously enough to actually contact the Committee to see what its reaction would be. Rather, the demand for hearings was an emotional appeal used by Indian politicians to give their audiences a boost in morale. Indians across the nation paused and looked at the Wounded Knee occupation in a different vein when the demand for hearing went out. It was one thing to issue rhetorical demands but quite another to gather the support of the Indian people themselves for such a demand, and people were very interested to see what would happen.

The nature of the Indian force occupying Wounded Knee astounded Indians and whites alike. This was no ordinary protest of young Indians intent on making headlines (although plenty of headlines were made and eventually accusations were leveled against Banks and Means for manipulating the media). Rather, a strong contingent of Sioux traditional peoples were at Wounded Knee. Revered medicine men and several well-known holy men were taking part in the occupation. Representatives of the Iroquois League were at Wounded Knee, and the Iroquois had always received the utmost respect for their precise knowledge concerning treaties and the sovereignty of Indian nations. The more Indian people saw of the Wounded Knee protest, the more seriously they began to take it.

As the occupation went into its second week, the government began to toughen its stand. Ultimatums were issued almost daily by the federal officials against the people occupying the tiny village, and deadlines were drawn beyond which it appeared the government was not prepared to continue. On the second Friday of March the tensions seemed to peak. The government issued an order that everyone leave the village by six o'clock or it would come in shoot-

ing. The National Council of Churches sent representatives to the reservation, who pledged to stand between the besieged Indians and the federal marshals
when the shooting began. This vow gave the federal
marshals food for thought. It would be bad enough to
kill Indians on the site of the bloodiest massacre in
American history, let alone a group of preachers.
Tensions began to ease. Word seeped out that the
deadline was not really a deadline after all.

It had not been only the valiant action of the people from the National Council of Churches that had
caused the cancellation of the deadline, however, as
telegrams and letters of support for Wounded Knee
had been pouring into the White House all through
the preceding week. With the attention of the world
concentrated on Wounded Knee, the Nixon administration could ill afford to allow its jet planes to sweep
the village and release their bombs, as rumors were
predicting.

Then there was the little matter of the reservation
people. As the deadline for withdrawal neared, the
reservation communities grew tense. Many of the
Oglalas had relatives at Wounded Knee. While many
of the people were adamant Wilson supporters, they
could not stand idly by and watch the federal marshals kill their sons, uncles, cousins, and fathers. So,
on the morning of Friday, March 9th, the word
spread throughout the reservation that a crisis was
at hand. By afternoon the roads to Wounded Knee
were jammed by cars filled with Indians trying to get
to the little village. They were determined to stop the
federal marshals from killing their relatives. Some of
the people were so angry at the occupation that they
probably would have killed their relatives themselves,
given a chance. But they were determined not to
allow anyone else to harm a hair on the heads of the
people at Wounded Knee. So, instead of confronting

a mere three hundred Indians armed with mail-order rifles, the federal marshals faced over a thousand Indians, the majority of them converging on Wounded Knee from behind the federal forces. The deadline was extended very quickly. It is said that the line of cars from Porcupine heading for Wounded Knee was nearly seven miles long. That's a lot of Indians, no matter how you figure.

As the weekend arrived, plans were made to leave the village. The federal government had offered some fairly generous terms to the occupants of the village, and many people felt that the point had been proven and it was time to leave. But the question of tackling the severe and persistent reservation problems began to loom larger and larger. No satisfactory answers had been found, the administration had promised little, and the reservation residents were genuinely fearful of reprisals by Wilson's men following the departure of A.I.M. Thus, local rather than national issues began to weigh more heavily in the discussions by the Indians on the subject of ending the occupation.

At this point the government's perfidy in the November takeover of the Bureau of Indian Affairs paid its tragic dividend. As the discussions continued, it was agreed by all concerned that they had been betrayed by the government in their last confrontation. While the White House Task Force had promised to review all of the Twenty Points and make its response, little had been done of any depth or significance by that task force. Rather, it had made perfunctory answers to questions which the Indians had considered of overwhelming importance. Were they, then, to lay down their arms, walk out of the village, and live on the vague promises made by the same government negotiators?

On Sunday, March 11th, Russell Means announced

on national television that the Oglala Sioux Nation had been formed and that it had declared its independence from the United States, that it was to determine its own borders, as defined by the treaty of 1868 with the United States, and that it would shoot anyone who violated those borders. The trauma gauge in the White House ruptured. It was apparent that the negotiations of the previous ten days had not begun to cover the issues which the Oglalas felt important, and that the government would have to do better immediately, for the situation was now out of control.

The declaration of independence also proved traumatic to Indians. Many had accepted the violations by the United States of their treaties as the inevitable course of events, and had filed claims in the Indian Claims Commission to get some compensation for the loss of their lands. Challenging the fundamental illegality of the actions of the United States was another matter. Everyone knew that the United States had acted illegally but realized that often "might makes right," and always seems to when Indians are concerned. People had accepted their lot as unpleasant but final. Now the fundamental nature of the federal relationship had been raised once again.

The people at Wounded Knee lost no time in pushing their advantage. They sent emissaries to New York, and Indians began to show up at the United Nations seeking the assistance of friendly nations which might raise the question of the Sioux treaty before that body. While few tribal governments openly supported the Wounded Knee people, Indian country secretly glowed with the knowledge that the mouse had finally roared. And not a few tribal officials began to examine their own treaties with the United States to determine how they could respond to the general cry for reform of the treaty relationship.

The occupation lasted seventy-two days and was finally brought to an end by the successful negotiations of a number of people on both sides. Hank Adams, who had negotiated the settlement of the occupation of the Bureau of Indian Affairs building in November 1972, played an important role in bringing the Wounded Knee protest to a successful conclusion. He was able to sidestep the multitude of low-level flunkies at the White House and deal directly with Leonard Garment, who later assumed control over a large part of the administration's policy for domestic affairs following the Watergating of John Ehrlichman and H. R. Haldeman.

Perhaps the major point of contention in the settlement was the promise of the White House to send out a team of negotiators to meet with the traditional chiefs and medicine men of the Oglala Sioux on the treaty of 1868. In mid-May a negotiating team did arrive, and spent several days at Fools Crow's camp, at Kyle, South Dakota, discussing the problems of the Oglala people and the remedies which the government could offer to solve the problems created by the violation of the 1868 treaty. But, as one of the government people was quick to point out, it was Congress, not the executive branch, which had the final authority to reform the treaty rights of the Indian tribes. Another meeting was promised, and a series of letters containing points for discussion were exchanged.

During the historic occupation of Wounded Knee, two Indian men were killed by gunfire and a federal marshal was partially paralyzed. Thousands of rounds of gunfire were exchanged nightly, and millions of dollars of damage was done to the village. The only structure of the village which did not re-

ceive some damage was the mass grave in which Big
Foot and his people were buried. The federal government spent millions of dollars on law enforcement,
with little visible effect. When the Indians' weapons
were finally turned in, only a few broken rifles were
discovered. The protesters had spirited away the
other weapons they had brought to Wounded Knee.

Both sides counted a moral victory. The federal
government had been able to contain the protest,
and had eventually outlasted the Indians, a feat not
unfamiliar to a bureaucracy. The Indians had developed a new pride in themselves which transcended
tribal loyalties and instilled in Indian children everywhere the image of the brave Indian warrior, which
had been missing in Indian society for two generations. Even the old non-Indian social activists of the
sixties had been given a chance to stand in the sun-
light of publicity once again as they individually
made their pilgrimage to Wounded Knee to pledge
their support, a gesture as futile as it was symbolic.

On a deeper, more intellectual level, and of world
significance, Wounded Knee marked a historic
watershed in the relations of American Indians and
the Western European peoples. The theory of treaties as articulated by the Oglalas called for a re-
examination of the four centuries of contact between
Indians and whites on the continent. In demanding
independence for the Oglala Nation, the people at
Wounded Knee sought a return to the days of pre-
discovery, when the tribes of this land had political
independence and sovereignty. They sought the recognition by the nations of the world of their rightful
status as nations in the community of nations.

Wounded Knee marked the first sustained modern
protest by aboriginal peoples against the Western
European interpretation of history, for the Oglala
Sioux refused to accept the definitions which the

American legal system had used to cover up the status of Indian tribes and make them appear to be merely a minor domestic problem of the United States. In their declaration of independence, the Oglala Sioux spoke to the world about freedom for all aboriginal peoples from the tyranny of Western European thought, values, and interpretations of man's experiences.

The world press was attracted to the Wounded Knee protest for a number of reasons. Europeans had always been curious about Indians. In recent years they had formed a "noble savage" cult, in which the Indians received more than their share of favorable commentary. But, more important, Europeans had become aware, partially because of the collapse of their colonies in other parts of the world, of the deep desire of smaller nations to gain a place in the family of nations. Since World War Two many small nations had received political independence and become members of the United Nations. For the most part, these new nations were carved out of the former colonies in Africa and Asia. But new nations had arisen from the Western Hemisphere.

The trauma of the French in Indo-China and Algeria had made a deep impression on the people of Europe. They had recognized, where the United States had not, that the world had indeed shrunk and our planet could not afford to place its destiny in the hands of any one nation or group of nations. Rather, the community of nations had to become a community in which even the smallest nation had rights which could not be violated. To see a tiny Indian tribe attempt to cast off the bonds of colonialism and become a free nation fascinated the European journalists who visited the United States and made the journey to Wounded Knee.

The Third World ideology which proved so useful to Europeans in interpreting the events of the world in the last two decades seemed to be fulfilling itself in North America as well as Africa and Asia. Wounded Knee meant that American Indians were determined to seek their rightful place in the world, that they had declared their independence, if not physically then spiritually, from the past, and that they were entering a new phase of world existence which had previously been denied to them. And it was heady material for any journalist.

In the chapters that follow, we will review the basis for the claim to world recognition made by the people at Wounded Knee. No one can be certain that they would make their claim in such a manner, or that they would endorse the theories which we will expound. What is certain, however, is that a great many bodies lie buried in America's past and that at Wounded Knee the first spade of dirt was turned in an effort to revive these buried secrets and force their reconsideration.

The frightening aspect of the declaration of Indian independence has many facets. It seems incredible to many Americans that Indians have feelings distinct from those of other Americans. This attitude had been developed by the sanitized version of world history which is taught in the American educational system. Children are taught that it was inevitable that Indians would be subjugated and become American citizens. Indian political allegiance is therefore assumed to be American. To understand why it is not, take the hypothesis that a plague suddenly reduces the white population to a very small figure, while the Indian population remains high. Do the Navajos, who then become relatively abundant and powerful people, have an allegiance to the remnants of the United States government? Or are they free to assert their political independence?

What the occupation of Wounded Knee has done has been to remove the cloak of isolation behind which Americans hide from the rest of the world, and confront them with the question of what constitutes a nation. Does a nation cease to exist when it is conquered or overrun by a larger nation? Or does it remain a nation so long as its people give it allegiance? Can the Oglala Sioux nation be consumed by the United States through the confiscation of its lands? Or does it exist so long as the people consider themselves Oglala Sioux?

Once the Indian nations were the equal of any power on earth. The European nations scraped and bowed before the Indian chiefs, hoping for allies to insure the existence of their colonies. Without the Hurons, the French would have been unable to exist in North America, and the Iroquois enabled the English colonies to withstand the might of the French and their Indian allies. It was a frightened George Washington who wrote to the Passamaquoddies:

> When I first heard that you Refused to send any of your Warriors to my Assistance when called upon by our Brother of St. Johns I did not know what to think. I was afraid some enemy had turned your hearts against me.

While the Indian misfortunes are presently hampering tribal survival, who is to say that Indians cannot regain their independence some time in the future? Can one view the re-creation of the state of Israel after two thousand years of exile and seriously maintain that the Oglala Sioux will never again ride their beloved plains as rulers of everything they see? Or that the might of the Iroquois will not once again dominate the eastern forests?

Consider. Consider what follows.

5. The Doctrine of Discovery

Few Americans have ever taken the time to learn precisely how the settlement of the continent was justified by the Europeans. Mythological stories of the first Thanksgiving have often merged with the equally vague idea that the lands were empty and waiting for the civilizing hand of European man. Did the Europeans, badly needing a place to pray, simply walk ashore and begin allotting lands, laying off plots, and planning for future suburbs? No, the Europeans were forced to deal with questions concerning the ownership of lands, and the morality and, indeed, the legality of taking lands claimed by the original inhabitants. Exploration and settlement required a good deal of intellectual effort, which resulted in concepts by which European men could relate to North American men. The Europeans were equal to the occasion, and developed a theory which, naturally, gave them all of the advantages.

The new theory had theological overtones of great importance which would be reflected in the great Spanish debates of 1550 at Valladolid about Indians, as well as in the writings of English, French, and Swiss intellectuals. The new agreement was called the "doctrine of discovery," and was an integral part of international law, as defined by the European nations, for several centuries. In practice the theory meant that the discoverer of unoccupied lands in the rest of the world gained a right to the land titles as against the claims of other European nations. It accorded the Indians only aboriginal title.

"Aboriginal title" is a legal concept, ultimately endorsed by the Supreme Court of the United States, which describes the nature of ownership of land held by the Indians within the legal framework of the Anglo-American judicial system. It is a concept which has its origins outside of the courts of the Anglo-Saxon heritage. Since it is a pragmatic, politically created concept of the European powers, in discussing it we are forced to use the Western perceptions of what the Indian use of land and ownership meant. This requires that we reject our knowledge of the Indian civilizations and consider Indian rights in light of what Europeans imagined them to be in the European system.

The attempted integration of Indians into the existing structure by Europeans was on both a conscious and an unconscious level. It was done not for the benefit of Indians but for the preservation of the existing European civilization. Fifteenth-century Europe was a marvelously structured and self-assured universe. Europeans were a pugnacious and hardy people, tempered by the constant warfare that had raged for hundreds of years across their continent, and were immune to the diseases that would devastate the rest of the world. One might call them the weeds of mankind. They were refining a vast and efficient military (especially naval) technology. Strains of nationalism were increasing. The Spanish had begun to test their strength by defeating the Moors at Granada, ending a thousand years of

Moorish influence on the continent and driving the Jews from the country. The financing of an expedition by Columbus to discover a new spice route to the Indies was further manifestation of this rising nationalism. The Spanish were confident of their place in the hierarchy of the world, assured by the exactness of their knowledge and controlled by the tenets of their church. The return of Columbus and his Indian slaves marked the end of the grand illusion that the known world was finite and rational, and the beginning of modern Europe.

Upon Columbus' return from his voyage of discovery, the Spanish monarchs soon became aware of Portuguese intent to challenge Spanish right and interest in these new lands. It was convenient for Spain that Pope Alexander VI was Spanish and considerate enough to issue a series of papal bulls which benefited the Spanish rulers. Ferdinand and Isabella were granted an exclusive interest in the lands and islands to the west of the Azores and Cape Verde Islands in May of 1493. While Ferdinand and Isabella were pleased, João II of Portugal was not. The ensuing Portuguese and Spanish communication resulted in the Treaty of Tordesillas, in 1494. It established a Portuguese-Spanish division of the world. By defining geographic boundaries, the Treaty of Tordesillas prevented a potential clash of interests and a potential clash of armies.

Henry VII of England had turned down the Columbus brothers and their wild ideas about reaching the Indies by sailing west. When John Cabot, another Genoese, appeared in England in the years immediately following Columbus' voyage with a scheme which would make England's merchants the financial equals or superiors of the Venetian spice traders, Henry decided to accept a proposition in which Cabot paid for the cost of the voyage. Cabot's successful voyage to Newfoundland would form the foundation for the English claim to North America. Following the Cabot voyage, the other European powers would send expeditions to North America, clearly indicating their intention not to be bound to the Spanish-Portuguese division of the world according to the papal bulls, which, Sir Walter Raleigh pointed out, "could not gore so well as they could bellow." At this point, the Europeans had to work out a method of establishing and preserving their land claims. Spain and Portugal had set examples in their voyages of exploration, and they had set an example in their land division, not by papal bull but by the Treaty of Tordesillas. This was the genesis of the doctrine of discovery. It can be ascribed to a desire for accommodation among the international powers. It was developed in total disregard of the fact that these new lands were occupied by the Indian nations. However, it was a proposition to which the Europeans readily adhered, because there appeared to be enough land to propitiate the various powers. Most important, they did not want to have to go to war: Any profit that they might find would be exceeded by military costs if they had to fight to protect their interests.

Once it was apparent that great wealth could be generated from colonial possessions, the leaders of Europe became concerned that unless conflicting claims to land in the New World were resolved peacefully, a new round of warfare in Europe might be touched off. To prevent this from occurring, the European nations came to a gentleman's agreement with respect to claims in the New World. Thus, a corollary of the doctrine of discovery was created, to the effect that disputes in the New World between colonists would not carry over into Europe. Therefore, if a French trader was murdered by Spanish adventurers on the Mississippi River, the incident was of political importance only to the Spanish Viceroy and the French Governor. They were expected to work out any reparations which might be necessary. The converse was not true, however, and the seventeenth and eighteenth centuries saw the frequent transfer of European conflicts to the North American colonists by the mother countries.

As exploration developed, so did the rationales behind the doctrine of discovery. The discussions in ensuing centuries would include Vattel, Victoria, Las Casas, Sepulveda, Locke, Montesquieu, More, Blackstone, and many others. The white Europeans were to have the Indian lands because the Indians were infidels rather than Christians, hunters rather than farmers, monsters rather than men, or by reason of the generous gifts of European civilization and technology, or by reason of conquest, or by reason of the fact that the king owned everything. We are now aware of the logical or factual error of these writers, and of their resort of pure fabrication in concepts such as conquest.

The Spanish Charles V's resort to scholarship must have been less than satisfactory. The great debate in 1550 between Las Casas, arguing for Indian rights, and Sepulveda, arguing against Indian rights, was inconclusive. The great theologian and jurist Franciscus de Victoria was providing his Spanish monarch with such unsettling answers about his overseas empire as the following:

> . . . the aborigines in question were true owners, before the Spaniards came among them, both from the public and private point of view.

Felix Cohen in his *Handbook of Federal Indian Law* summarized Victoria's argument this way:

Since the Indians were true owners Victoria held
discovery can be justified only where property is
ownerless. Nor could Spanish title to Indian
lands be validly based upon the divine rights of
the Emperor or the Pope, or upon the unbelief or
sinfulness of the aborigines. Thus, Victoria concluded, even the Pope has no right to partition
the property of the Indians, and in the absence
of a just war, only the voluntary consent of the
aborigines could justify the annexation of their
territory. No less than their property the government of the aborigines was entitled to respect by
the Spaniards, according to the view of Victoria.
[p. 46.]

The Swiss jurist Vattel had first attempted to explain the doctrine of discovery, and had developed a
theory which could best be described as benign and
universal communism. According to the Vattel theory, each nation took that portion of lands which its
way of life required, and the inevitable development
of sedentary civilization's complex economic system
meant that lands which had been devoted to hunting and grazing had to be turned to agricultural use.

By 1650 the great oceanic explorations had given
way to civilization, although much of the Pacific remained to be explored. Instead, the nations of Europe
turned on the Americas like the Visigoths on Rome.
The riches in furs in North America and gold in
South America brought thousands of plunderers
whose sole concern was making a quick fortune with
which they could return to the old country. They
were unconcerned over the legal standing of Indians,
and since they had no intent of staying and coloniz-
ing, the question of land title never arose.

The lethargy of the English in exploiting the New
World was a combination of several factors: 1) the

lack of immediate riches in the lands they discovered; 2) a constant outlet for aggression in the politics at home; and 3) basic misjudgment of the land's potential. With the restoration of the Stuarts in 1660, a measure of civil order returned to England. With the conclusion of the Thirty Years' War and the Peace of the Pyrenees, Europe's interest turned to a less savage occupation: the more intense struggle for power and money. Europe's interest in the New World during the next hundred and fifty years can be classified in three categories: 1) areas where the local products were easily extractable and had an immediate market in Europe; 2) forced labor where the local economics could be reorganized, usually through the institution of slavery, to procure the product for the world market; and 3) the transplantation of Europe into America, a phenomenon that existed in two forms in conjunction with the exploitative concept and as new frontiers were transformed into European-style homes. It is with the emerging frontier philosophy that the real question of Indian title arose.

The English who arrived at Jamestown in 1607 were concerned over the title of lands, since property was the basis for Anglo-Saxon law. The colonists and the mother countries were faced with the problems of defining the rights of Europeans against Europeans in conflicting claims in the New World. But what was the extent of Indian property rights as against Europeans', and how were these rights, if existent, to be treated?

The second question facing the colonists was much more difficult to answer. The problem of assuming the Indian title to lands had both legal and moral implications. No settler wanted to settle or purchase lands which might have some aspect of Indian title remaining with them. Nor did the colonists want to suffer the accusation by the European nations that they had swindled the inhabitants of the New World. The Puritans particularly felt that confiscation of property was wrong regardless of who practiced it or against whom it was directed.

The eventual solution to the problem was the creation of a complex theory that encompassed tradition, morality, and the old Anglo-Saxon property concepts. Again, the crucial distinction between methods of land use and the creation of wealth which characterized the European and the Indian became important. While both groups "occupied" the lands to which they claimed title, various reasons were advanced to justify the "higher" use of the colonists as opposed to the "lesser" use of the Indians. It was this basic theory that found its strongest articulation in *Johnson v. McIntosh.*

Counterbalancing the Puritan guilt of the wrongness of taking another's property was the realization that they were up against the wall. Obviously, to recognize the Indian title as sacred as the title of an English landowner would have left them in an untenable position: They would have been unable to purchase any land at all. To ignore the Indian would spell disaster. To escape the dilemma, they espoused different theories to justify the taking. The justifications were not presented in any sort of chronological order, nor was any one colony necessarily committed to supporting any particular theory. It is easy to argue inconsistent theories when the only judge is one's conscience.

The most obvious justification for reducing the status of Indian occupancy rights was Sepulveda's argument, which was resurrected to remove Indians from the class of people that laws apply to. This justification depended primarily on a recognition of military superiority and a proper psychological attitude. As soon as the colonists had built up the military strength to ignore the previous generosity of Indians, this became a popular notion.

The Puritans needed not only justification, but approval from God; not surprisingly, they looked to the Scriptures for guidance. After careful examination, they found that not one right existed to the land but two, civil and theological, and both were ordained by God. The Bible provides that man must go forth and multiply; since man cannot multiply where there is no room, the discovery of a new continent was by divine revelation. America was obviously meant to be occupied by Christians fulfilling their deity's command. While the right to ownership was not fully covered by this argument, legal title was of little concern; the issue was whether the Scriptures could provide guidance. While many leading colonists pointed out the absurdity of the argument, reason vanished before practical political realities of the day.

The second rationale embodied the classic Puritan work ethic. The famous English jurist Blackstone wrote of the evolution of private property, and, as seen by him, property was fundamental to the civilization of man. Europeans failed to see that their classification of states of man's civilization was a justification of conditions after the fact, and depended upon a willingness to accept complex technology as the sole criterion for determining the value of societies.

The role of the farmer, his natural right of ascendancy over the hunter and grazer, his paramount right to possess the land, the necessity to create courts to enforce the rights of the farmer—all these were a continuing theme in the exploitation of the American continent. These themes appeared to the average colonist to be simply a common-sense explanation of the universal laws of nature. The transmutation of land use from a natural right shared by all men to a private-person right protected by governments was not questioned. The ascendance of the agriculturalist, with the prototype of Adam in the Garden of Eden, was a multi-purpose theme which justified Western conceptions of property and was sanctified by both God and the laws of men.

One of the final and more sophisticated arguments for taking the lands of the aboriginal peoples involved the transmission of the benefits of civilization to the uncivilized. Taking the lands by whatever means possible was justifiable because, in return, the Indians were receiving the great benefits of Western civilization, which had allowed the European peoples to create such military and economic power as to make it possible for them to dispossess other peoples. The argument was most familiar when posed in Rudyard Kipling's famous admonition to "take up the white man's burden."

While England, France, Spain, Holland, and Sweden were laying claim to the North American continent on the basis of the doctrine of discovery, and European theologians, philosophers, and jurists were justifying this doctrine, some colonists were coming to different conclusions about rights to the land, despite the pan-European intellectual, religious, and social matrix. One of these men was Roger Williams:

> As early as 1633 Roger Williams believed that the king had no moral right to claim by right of discovery the land occupied by the Indians. To Williams the patents of Massachusetts Bay, Plymouth, and the other colonies were of no value, for the king had granted something that he did not possess. As a true Christian, Williams felt he could not recognize these illegally granted rights. He proposed to purchase for a reasonable

price the land of the Indians, deeming it the only proper means of acquiring the right to occupy the lands.

This struck at the heart of the early colonial governmental plan, which was based upon the same patents and rights as the rights to land. This was possibly as much the cause of Roger Williams' banishment from Plymouth as were his purely religious views. Carrying his conviction into practice when he started to settle at Rhode Island, Williams immediately purchased land from the Indians. On March 24, 1637, Cononicus and Miantonomo, the two chief sachems of the Narragansett, confirmed the grant made two years earlier to Williams. (Marshall Harris, *Origin of the Land Tenure System in the United States*, pp. 163–4.)

Although it met with initial success, it was ultimately a vain attempt, for "Williams, despite his brave stand against the royal patent, was eventually forced to request a charter from the English parliamentary government in order to prevent the Rhode Island Colony from being devoured by her neighboring English colonies." (Wilcomb Washburn, *Red Man's Land, White Man's Law*, p. 41.)

Following the American Revolution, it became necessary for the United States to find some relationship between its patricidal act of rebellion and the philosophical principles which appeared to govern mankind. Part of the justification of the American Revolution had already been expounded in the Declaration of Independence, and during the war itself Thomas Paine had articulated a "Common Sense" justification of the acts of colonial rebellion in terms that made the revolution appear as an evolutionary and progressive step by the Americans.

The new government attempted to follow the lead of Great Britain in developing its Indian policy. In 1763 the King of England had set aside the lands of the western slope of the Appalachian Mountains through Royal Proclamation for the Indian tribes of the continent, and banned further exploration and settlement west of this line until there had been adequate negotiations with the tribes who would be affected. The United States Congress, in its famous Ordinance of 1787, followed this precedent and defined the pattern of settlement for the old Northwest (which covered the area of Ohio, Michigan, Wisconsin, and the states of the Great Lakes/Ohio Valley region). Article 3 of the Ordinance stated that the "utmost good faith" would be shown to the Indian tribes and that their lands would never be taken without their permission, except in "just wars" authorized by the Congress.

Yet settlement proceeded rapidly, and no sooner was one section of the country explored than the inevitable parade of pioneers and fugitives from justice would move into the area, establish settlements, begin trade and commerce, and petition Congress for statehood. If the settlement of the western country was predictable, it was not according to the principles set down in the 1787 Ordinance. More often than not, Congress was forced by political pressure to pass what became known as "Pre-emption Acts," which validated land titles of those people who had violated federal laws and settled in the West while it still belonged to the Indian tribes.

In all of this confusion, the articulation of the status of the Indian tribes and the nature of their land titles lagged behind the development of the national political identity. During colonial times, the eastern lands were quite often acquired from the Indians by purchase, despite any grants from the

King that the colonists possessed. When the settlers began to encounter the larger and more powerful tribes in the Mississippi Valley and Illinois country, they discovered that all lands had to be purchased. As the controversies swirled around the development of the policy of removing the Indians from the lands east of the Mississippi—which came to fruition in the 1830s—the nation was forced to examine its treaties with the Cherokees, Creeks, and Choctaws of the south and the powerful Miami confederacy of the Indians' Illinois country, and the question of the full nature of Indian title arose.

The early 1800s brought new pressures on the leaders of the federal government and the federal courts to determine the precise nature of Indian right and title. The issue was of great importance for several reasons. The United States was purchasing great areas of land from Spain and France. While it was understood in international law that these acquisitions were primarily the purchase of the right to extinguish existent Indian title, what constituted sufficient extinguishment of title (e.g., treaty, force, sale, trespass) had to be judicially determined. Rather than resolve Indian problems, the courts had to determine titles to lands between two competing non-Indian claimants, usually settlers and land speculators.

Second, the federal government had reached a crisis with the states concerning where the ultimate political power with respect to federal lands was to be vested. A pact was concluded between Georgia and the United States in which Georgia agreed to cede her claims to land west of the mountains in return for the United States' extinguishing Indian title within her borders. A conflict arose over the agreement, and eventually boiled over in the famous Cherokee cases.

The Cherokees sued in the Supreme Court to prevent the State of Georgia from forcing the issue of their removal without the permission of the federal government. The Cherokees lost their case on a jurisdictional question, but the following year the Supreme Court held that the federal government's power over Indians was plenary and the State of Georgia had no right to exercise jurisdiction over Indian lands. Implicit in this holding was that they could ignore Indian title. Chief Justice Marshall pointed out that the doctrine of discovery did not invalidate Indian rights, since it only went to the power to extinguish and that power rested solely with the hand of the federal government.

The federal courts were confronted with the task of defining the status of the Indian land title. The Constitution remained purposely vague with respect to Indians, and in the then-developing state of federal law, and particularly federal constitutional law, no one wanted to take a step which might prove injurious in the future. Thus it was that the precise nature of Indian land title was defined by the courts. The judges referred to the ancient authorities of the European nations to justify and bolster their decisions, which were generally a reflection of the political realities of the day. The problem was not so much the development of law as it was the postponement of the task of defining the nature of the relationship between the expanding United States of America and the Indian tribes occupying the interior of the continent. From this period of legal confusion and constitutional development and geographical expansion came the U.S. theory of aboriginal title.

The articulation of this right claimed by the Europeans and assumed by Americans was explained by Chief Justice John Marshall in the landmark case *Johnson v. McIntosh*, 8 Wheat. 543 (1823). In defining the doctrine of aboriginal possession which was to characterize American domestic law, Marshall reviewed the origins of the doctrine of discovery and the acceptance by the United States of its rights under this concept.

On the discovery of this immense continent, the great nations of Europe were eager to appropriate to themselves so much of it as they could respectively acquire. Its vast extent offered an ample field to the ambition and enterprise of all; and the character and religion of its inhabitants afforded an apology for considering them as a people over whom the superior genius of Europe might claim an ascendancy. The potentates of the old world found no difficulty in convincing themselves that they made ample compensation to the inhabitants of the new, by bestowing on them civilization and Christianity, in exchange for unlimited independence. But, as they were all in pursuit of nearly the same object, it was necessary, in order to avoid conflicting settlements, and consequent war with each other, to establish a principle which all should acknowledge as the law by which the right of acquisition which they all asserted should be regulated as between themselves. This principle was that discovery gave title to the government by whose subjects, or by whose authority, it was made, against all other European governments, which title might be consummated by possession.

The exclusion of all other Europeans necessarily gave to the nation making the discovery the sole right of acquiring the soil from the natives, and establishing settlements upon it. It was a right with which no Europeans could interfere. It was a right which all asserted for themselves, and to the assertion of which, by others, all asserted.

Those relations which were to exist between the discoverer and the natives were to be regulated by themselves. The rights thus acquired being exclusive, no other power could interpose between them.

In the establishment of these relations, the rights of the original inhabitants were, in no instance, entirely disregarded; but were necessarily, to a considerable extent, impaired. They were admitted to be the rightful occupants of the soil, with a legal as well as just claim to retain possession of it, and to use it according to their own discretion; but their rights to complete sovereignty, as independent nations, were necessarily diminished, and their power to dispose of the soil at their own will to whomsoever they pleased was denied by the original fundamental principle, that discovery gave exclusive title to those who made it.

While the different nations of Europe respected the rights of the natives, as occupants, they asserted the ultimate dominion to be in themselves; and claimed and exercised, as a consequence of this ultimate dominion, a power to grant the soil, while yet in possession of the natives. These grants have been understood by all to convey a title to the grantees, subject only to the Indian right of occupancy.

The history of America, from its discovery to the present day, proves, we think, the universal recognition of these principles. . . .

The United States, then, have unequivocally acceded to that great and broad rule by which its civilized inhabitants now hold this country. They hold, and assert in themselves, the title by which it was acquired. They maintain, as all others have maintained, that discovery gave an exclusive right to extinguish the Indian title of occupancy, either by purchase or by conquest; and gave also a right to such a degree of sovereignty as the circumstances of the people would allow them to exercise.

The power now possessed by the government of the United States to grant lands resided, while we were colonies, in the crown, or its grantees. The validity of the titles given by either has never been questioned in our courts. It has been exercised uniformly over territory in possession of the Indians. The existence of this power must negate the existence of any right which may conflict with, and control it. An absolute title to lands cannot exist, at the same time, in different persons, or in different governments. An absolute must be an exclusive title, or at least a title which excludes all others not compatible with it. All our institutions recognize the absolute title of the crown, subject only to the Indian right of occupancy, and recognized the absolute title of the crown to extinguish that right. This is incompatible with an absolute and complete title in the Indians.

We will not enter into the controversy, whether agriculturists, merchants, and manufacturers have a right, on abstract principles, to expel hunters from the territory they possess, or to contract their limits. Conquest gives a title which the courts of the conqueror cannot deny, whatever the private and speculative opinions of individuals may be, respecting the original justice of the claim which has been successfully asserted. The British government, which was then our government, and whose rights have passed to the United States, asserted a title to all the lands occupied by Indians within the chartered limits of the British colonies. It asserted also a limited sovereignty over them, and the exclusive right of extinguishing the title which occupancy gave to them. These claims have been maintained and established as far west as the river Mississippi by the sword. The title to a vast portion of the lands we now hold originates in them. It is not for the courts of this country to question the validity of this title, or to sustain one which is incompatible with it. . . .

However extravagant the pretension of converting the discovery of an inhabited country into conquest may appear, if the principle has been asserted in the first instance, and afterwards sustained; if a country has been acquired and held under it; if the property of the great mass of the community originates in it, it becomes the law of the land, and cannot be questioned. So, too, with respect to the concomitant principle, that the Indian inhabitants are to be considered merely as occupants, to be protected, indeed, while in peace, in the possession of their lands, but to be deemed incapable of transferring the absolute title to others. However this restriction may be opposed to natural right, and to the usages of civilized nations, yet, if it be indispensable to that system under which the country has been settled, and be adapted to the actual condition of the two people, it may, perhaps, be supported by reason and certainly cannot be rejected by courts of justice. . . .

Nine years later, in another landmark case, Chief Justice Marshall would add further commentary on discovery in *Worcester v. Georgia*.

America, separated from Europe by a wide ocean, was inhabited by a distinct people, divided into separate nations, independent of each other, and of the rest of the world, having institutions of their own, and governing themselves by their own laws. It is difficult to comprehend the proposition, that the inhabitants of either quarter of the globe could have rightful original claims of dominion over the inhabitants of the other, or over the lands they occupied; or that the discovery of either, by the other, should give the discoverer rights in the country discovered, which annulled the pre-existing right of its ancient possessors. . . . But power, war, conquest, give rights, which, after possession, are conceded by the world; and which can never be controverted by those on whom they descend. We proceed, then, to the actual state of things, having glanced at their origin; because holding it in our recollection might shed some light on existing pretensions.

The great maritime powers of Europe discovered and visited different parts of this continent, at nearly the same time. The object was too immense for any one of them to grasp the whole; and the claimants were too powerful to submit to the exclusive or unreasonable pretensions of any single potentate. To avoid bloody conflicts, which might terminate disastrously to all, it was necessary for the nations of Europe to establish some principle which all would acknowledge, and which should decide their respective rights as between themselves. This principle, suggested by the actual state of things, was, "that discovery gave title to the government by whose subjects, or by whose authority, it was made, against all other European governments, which title might be consummated by possession." 8 Wheat. 573. This principle, acknowledged by all Europeans, because it was the interest of all to acknowledge it, gave to the nation making the discovery, as its inevitable consequence, the sole right of acquiring the soil and of making settlements on it. *It was an exclusive principle, which shut out the right of competition among those who had agreed to it; not one which could annul the previous rights of those who had not agreed to it. It regulated the right given by discovery among the European discoveries; but could not affect the rights of those already in possession, either as aboriginal occupants, or as occupants by virtue of a discovery made before the memory of man.* It gave the exclusive right to purchase, but did not found that right on a denial of the right of the possessor to sell. The relation between the Europeans and the natives was determined in each case, by the particular government which asserted and could maintain this pre-emptive privilege in the particular place. The United States succeeded to all the claims of Great Britain, both territorial and political; but no attempt, so far as is known, has been made to enlarge them. So far as they existed merely in theory, or were in their nature only exclusive of the claims of other European nations, they still retain their original character, and remain dormant. So far as they have been practically exerted, they exist in fact, are understood by both parties, are asserted by the one, and admitted by the other.

Soon after Great Britain determined on planting colonies in America, the king granted charters to companies of his subjects, who associated for the purpose of carrying the views of the crown into effect, and of enriching themselves. The first of these charters was made before possession was taken of any part of the country. They purport, generally, to convey the soil, from the Atlantic to the South Sea. This soil was occupied by numerous and warlike nations, equally willing and able to defend their possessions. *The extravagant and absurd idea, that the feeble settlements made on the seacoast, or the companies under whom they were made, acquired legitimate power by them to govern the people, or occupy the lands from sea to sea, did not enter the mind of any man.* They were well understood to convey the title which, according to the common law of European sovereigns respecting America, they might rightfully convey, and no more.

This was the exclusive right of purchasing such lands as the natives were willing to sell. *The crown could not be understood to grant what the crown did not affect to claim; nor was it so understood.* . . .

The actual state of things, and the practice of European nations, on so much of the American continent as lies between the Mississippi and the Atlantic, explain their claims, and the charters they granted. Their pretensions unavoidably interfered with each other; though the discovery of one was admitted by all to exclude the claim of any other, the extent of that discovery was the subject of unceasing contest. . . . [Emphasis added.]

In these two famous Indian cases Marshall articulated the doctrine of discovery very well, but there seems to be some question as to whether he adhered to the doctrine. The doctrine was to apply to uninhabited countries only. While the United States purported to succeed to the interests of Britain, whose claims ran from ocean to ocean, the fact that there were Indian inhabitants on the continent gave England nothing. It would be pure folly to assert that in 1832 (and even more in 1788) the United States had conquered the Indian nations.

Perhaps the consistency of the United States in maintaining its doctrines of land tenure should account for part of their legal reality. Not all of the land of the continental United States was purchased or taken directly from the Indians. Several large sections of the country, such as Florida, Louisiana, Oregon, Alaska, and parts of Arizona, were purchased from the European monarchs. While the United States purchased only the right to extinguish the Indian titles in the first four instances, it is noteworthy that land titles already recognized by the previous monarch were considered valid even after the United States assumed control of the lands.

In Louisiana the Spanish and French settlements around St. Louis and New Orleans had already established plats and tracts of lands to which titles had been given. When the United States purchased the Louisiana lands, it recognized the existing titles even though, in many cases, the lands described did not fit into the land patterns described in the United States Land Office regulations.

The lands in Florida, which had been settled since the early 1500s, were the subject of several lawsuits, and from these suits came the doctrines which recognized the titles given by the previous sovereign. In *Mitchel v. United States*, 9 Pet. 711 (1835), a case which involved the validity of a title given by the Indians with the consent of the King of Spain, a circumstance which occurred under John Marshall's doctrine of government primacy in the right of purchase, the court ruled that all prior transactions in the territory were superior in title to subsequent title derived from the United States. In a later case, *Choteau v. Molony*, 16 How. 203 (1853), the American doctrine of discovery merged with the European when the court decided that unless the Spanish crown recognized the principle of Indian consent, the title was not valid. Since the Americans were then the only people concerned with the operation of the doctrine of discovery, this fundamental concept remained unchallenged.

The latter part of the nineteenth century was marked by a massive move west in America, by the Homestead Act, and by the railroad grants, which were gifts by the United States of large pieces of land that was usually occupied by Indians. According to the principles of *Johnson v. McIntosh*, the grants required that title be extinguished. While the principle of law would appear to be dispositive of the situation, the importance of the railroads and the pressure of homesteaders required that the courts restate the principle and define the nature of title Congress could grant if Indian title was not extinguished.

Holden v. Joy 17 Wall 84 US 211 (1872) is the leading case on homesteads. There the plaintiff attempted to avoid the issue of Indian title by arguing that, in opening land for settlement, Congress had preempted Indian title. Treaties entered into by Indians were contra the interest of the Homestead Act because they were made by the President and the Senate, which was unconstitutional since Congress alone had the power to dispose of public lands. The court rejected this argument by pointing out that aboriginal title existed prior to the creation of the United States, and that land did not become public until title was extinguished.

The scope of Indian title was held in *United States*

v. Shoshone Tribe 304 US 111 (1938) to extend to every element of value that would accrue to a non-Indian landowner; it was further held that a treaty did not lessen the title of the "undisturbed possessions of the soil from time immemorial."

Out of this case derived several principles:

1) Indians had title to all of the land.

2) Only the United States had the right to extinguish that title.

3) That title existed independent of its recognition by the United States.

4) The extinguishment could not be made by subsequent grants.

5) Indians had an interest in all land in which title had not been extinguished.

The treaty process is a shorthand way of viewing the history of America's expansion. The evolution of the treaty—from a mutual agreement between sovereigns, each ostensibly giving and receiving, to the rubber-stamp land conveyances that opened the West —reflects a concept that sovereignty is not static nor absolute. It is nothing more than a construct to describe the relationship of political entities. It varies according to time and place. Sovereignty as expressed by the Jamestown colony to the Indians on the James River bears little resemblance to the ideas of sovereignty of the Indian tribes of California in relation to the State of California. But this does not mean that sovereignty is a meaningless concept. Implicit in the relationship is recognition of a degree of independence by the stronger to the weaker. This recognition of the residuals of complete freedom and control is the sovereignty which courts seem to discuss in the Indian cases that reach them. Treaties in the formative years of the existence of the United States were a type of sovereign manifestation because they were exercised under the independent wills of the respective contracting parties.

In 1871 the House of Representatives engaged in a bitter but victorious conflict with the Senate. Under the Constitution the Senate was given the power to ratify treaties made by the executive branch of government. Treaties with both foreign nations and Indian tribes came under this constitutional power of the Senate. But the power of appropriating money to pay the treaty annuities resided in the House of Representatives, and every year the House was required to pass an extensive and exhausting appropriations bill to pay for the itemized treaty annuities to the respective Indian tribes. Feeling that Indians were now a domestic affair and not a subject of international concern, the House forced the Senate to agree that thereafter no Indian nation would be recognized as having the legal capacity to contract treaties with the United States.

The remedy which the House proposed, joint legislative consideration of Indian matters, was hardly a progressive step. For a period of thirty-eight years Congress passed legislation, aptly called "agreements" with the Indians, which was merely congressional endorsement of agreements made in the field by employees of the Interior Department or by specially appointed Presidential commissioners. The fact that several agreements made with tribes were rejected by the Congress, and many agreements proposed by the government were rejected by the tribes, would indicate that because of this recognition of the independence and control by the tribes over geographical territory, the international theory of treaties still remained a viable operating principle.

When the treaty concept is used in its international sense (and quite a few American Indian leaders still cling to this conception of the nature of their treaties), the documents themselves become less personal and more generally subject to the policy considerations which have been used to underline their legal effect. The sense of morality and fair dealing which characterizes a treaty on the international scene is moved from the specific terms of agreement between nations to the general sympathy invoked from the American public whenever the broken Indian treaties are discussed. It is the difference between a legal right and a moral obligation, and the courts have never been moved to enforce morality without tremendous public pressure.

The validity of Indian title in its international sense does not depend upon government recognition but on the transfer mechanisms by which the lands are converted from Indian title to government title and into private ownership titles. As the treaty process was allowed to deteriorate from a sacred pledge of faith between nations to a series of quasi-fraudulent real-estate transactions, the United States evidenced by its conduct that it did not view the treaties as binding upon it. The great and sweeping land-cession treaties, such as those signed by I. I. Stevens, the government negotiator at that time, in the Pacific Northwest, were for the purpose of acquiring legal title to the lands in a formal sense that would satisfy the minimum requirements of the American system of law. They could not conceivably be considered as taking away from the tribes their national recognition or their residual rights as nations.

Treaties are made to be broken; this is the accepted practice of the nations of the world. But property conveyances are holy writs, at least among the nations subscribing to the Western European concepts of property rights. That a nation would be asked to sell its lands, thus extinguishing its political life, would be absurd in European terms, and it is this residual right of political existence which underlies the present Indian demand that the treaties be honored. While the lands are mostly gone, the national character of Indian existence remains, and continues to exert itself in incidents such as Wounded Knee.

The traditional argument of the United States government is that Indian tribes, because of the doctrine of discovery, became domestic subjects of the new United States government upon its assumption of discovery rights from Great Britain. But the whole idea of aboriginal title, from Victoria to the present, dealt with transactions between Europeans and non-Europeans in the field of real estate, with Europeans given a decided edge in purchase rights. Aboriginal title did not extinguish the political rights of the Indian tribes, and they still have the right to be recognized among the nations of the earth, even with the domestic legal doctrines of the United States guaranteeing the validity of their titles as held in a protected status by the United States against the European nations.

6. Dependent Domestic Nations

The doctrine of discovery described the nature of legal title owned by the aboriginal peoples of the North American continent as that title would be recognized by the invading European nations. While the initial theory held that only vacant lands could be claimed by the Europeans, the United States swiftly shifted the emphasis from vacant lands to all the lands, giving the inhabitants an occupancy title and thus precluding Indian tribes from ever asserting a final or valid title to their lands. Even today the assertion of the ultimate power of the United States over Indian lands means that, should Indians ever want to sever their relationship with the federal government completely, they would still be within the reach of the government's power to confiscate their lands.

The major issue of recent Indian activism began with a demand for land restoration, and in this sense it was a countermovement by Indians against the interpretation of their treaties as real-estate contracts. Claims of the universal validity of the Fort Laramie treaty of 1868 and its mysterious clause which empowered Indian activists to claim abandoned lighthouses, prisons, and surplus federal property was only the initial phase of a more fundamental movement to reclaim national status for tribes and to force a reconsideration of the treaties in light of the political implications which they might have today.

Thus it was that the Wounded Knee siege dwelt on the provisions of self-government and undisturbed use of the Sioux lands and not specifically the restoration of lands already taken. While the people at Wounded Knee wanted a total restoration of lands in western South Dakota, they based their contentions on the political recognition of the Sioux Nation as contained in the treaty and not upon any clause of the treaty which gave them the power to reclaim lands. It is therefore the history and meaning of treaties that has become important to Indians today, the manner in which the treaties limited exercise of self-government or eroded the power of the tribe to deal with other nations, and not particularly the redefinition of tribal land titles.

The history of the Indian treaties is extensive, and we cannot examine all of the provisions of every treaty to determine whether the tribe limited its commerce with foreign nations to the extent that the tribes could no longer be said to have any semblance of residual national character. Perhaps the clearest description of the nature of Indian political existence was articulated by Justice Johnson in the landmark case of *Cherokee Nation v. Georgia*, the case which has dominated all legal theory concerning American Indians for nearly a century and a half.

Justice Johnson was one of the two justices agreeing with Chief Justice John Marshall that the Cherokee Nation was not a foreign state in the sense that the Cherokees could initiate an original action against the State of Georgia in the Supreme Court. While John Marshall classified the Cherokees as a "dependent domestic nation," a definition that has plagued everyone ever since, Johnson took as his cue the lessons of history, and said of the Indian tribe's legal existence:

> Their condition is something like that of the Israelites, when inhabiting the deserts. Though without land that they can call theirs in the sense of property, their right of personal self-government has never been taken from them; and such a form of government may exist though the land occupied be in fact that of another. The right to expel them may exist in that other, but the alternative of departing and retaining the right of self-government may exist in them. And such they certainly do possess; it has never been questioned, nor any attempt made at subjugating them as a people, or restraining their personal liberty except as to their land and trade.

The other two justices in the case, Thompson and Story, were of the opinion that the Cherokees were indeed a foreign nation within the terms laid down by the jurisdiction requirements of the Constitution for the Supreme Court. Justice Thompson wrote a particularly strong dissenting opinion in an effort to buttress the national and foreign status of the Cherokees:

> The terms state and nation are used in the law of nations, as well as in common parlance, as importing the same thing; and imply a body of men, united together, to procure their mutual safety and advantage by means of their union. Such a society has its affairs and interests to

manage; it deliberates, and takes resolutions in common, and thus becomes a moral person, having an understanding and a will peculiar to itself, and is susceptible of obligations and laws. National being composed of men naturally free and independent, and who, before the establishment of civil societies, live together in the state of nature, nations or sovereign states, are to be considered as so many free persons, living together in a state of nature. Every nation that governs itself, under what form soever, without any dependence on a foreign power, is a sovereign state. Its rights are naturally the same as those of any other state. Such are moral persons who live together in a natural society, under the law of nations. It is sufficient if it be really sovereign and independent; that is, it must govern itself by its own authority and laws. We ought, therefore, to reckon in the number of sovereigns those states that have bound themselves to another more powerful, although by unequal alliance. The conditions of these unequal alliances may be infinitely varied; but whatever they are, provided the inferior ally reserves to itself the sovereignty or the right to govern its own body, it ought to be considered an independent state. Consequently, a weak state, that, in order to provide for its safety, places itself under the protection of a more powerful one, without stripping itself of the right of government and sovereignty does not cease on this account to be placed among the sovereigns who acknowledge no other power. Tributary and feudatory states do not thereby cease to be sovereign and independent states, so long as self-government, and sovereign and independent authority, is left in the administration of the state.

Testing the character and condition of the Cherokee Indians by these rules, it is not perceived how it is possible to escape the conclusion, that they form a sovereign state. They have always been dealt with as such by the government of the United States; both before and since the adoption of the present constitution. They have been admitted and treated as a people governed solely and exclusively by their own laws, usages, and customs within their own territory, claiming and exercising exclusive dominion over the same; yielding up by treaty, from time to time, portions of their land, but still claiming absolute sovereignty and self-government over what remained unsold.

John Marshall's description of Indian tribes as "dependent domestic nations" has become the dominant phrase used in describing the Indian tribal legal status. It was actually a concept used to effect a compromise between the political realities of the day and the ideas of Marshall's fellow judges, who viewed the status of the Cherokee Nation as much closer to an independent nation than Marshall would allow the court to maintain publicly. Comparing the various theories of the legal status of Indian nations articulated in the *Cherokee Nation* case, we find three divergent descriptions of the nature of Indian political existence. Justice Thompson conceived the Indian nations as independent and probably "foreign" nations. Justice Johnson described the Indian nations as existing in a state of expectant national status comparable to the Israelites waiting in the desert. Chief Justice Marshall saw Indians as dependent domestic nations with rights of self-government and a clear legal right to occupy their traditional lands.

None of these theories, incidentally, in any way supports the extravagant claims now made by the United States and the Department of the Interior concerning their absolute power over the lives and lands of American Indians. If anything, at least two of the theories lend strong support to the contentions of the Indian activists at Wounded Knee that the Indian nations have residual right to national existence and self-government which has been violated by the United States. And the theories of Justice Thompson and Johnson would be valid today in describing many of the present quasi-independent states who have sought the protection of larger nations.

That these three basic theories of Indian political status have existed side by side for nearly two centuries would seem to indicate that the question of Indian political independence has yet to be resolved. The Indian treaties would seem to support at least parts of each theory. The argument of the federal government that the treaties were documents recording political surrender by the tribes in return for annuities from the government and reservations on their traditional homelands is a strong one, but the facts do not bear out this conclusion.

The first treaty signed between an American Indian tribe and the United States took place only three years after the beginning of the Revolutionary War, at a time when no one knew for sure whether the colonists would gain their freedom or the King of England would soon have a gigantic hanging party of rebellious subjects. In September 1778, a delegation of Americans visited the chiefs of the Delaware Nation at Fort Pitt, in western Pennsylvania. They sought permission from the Delaware Nation to travel over its lands in order to attack the British posts in southern Canada.

The third article of the treaty stated that

. . . whereas the United States are engaged in a just and necessary war, in defense and support of life, liberty and independence . . . and as the most practicable way for the troops of the United States to some of the posts and forts is by passing through the country of the Delaware nation, the aforesaid deputies, on behalf of themselves and their nation, do hereby stipulate and agree to give a free passage through their country to the troops aforesaid. . . . And the said deputies on behalf of their nation, engage to join the troops of the United States aforesaid, with such a number of their best and most expert warriors as they can spare, consistent with their own safety.

Plainly, the colonists were on the ropes in the West, and had the Delawares refused to allow passage, the United States might have been faced with a violent Indian war in addition to its scrimmage with the British. To have pretended decades later that the American Congress had always asserted its claim to Indian lands under the doctrine of discovery, or that it had always regulated the internal affairs of the Indian tribes in its guardianship capacity, is sheer self-serving rhetoric when the nature of this first treaty is understood. If the Delaware treaty exemplified the way that the United States asserted its plenary power over the Indian tribes, it was certainly a humble way of doing so.

The desperation of the colonists is apparent when one examines the sixth article of the treaty:

. . . And it is further agreed on between the contracting parties should it for future be found conducive for the mutual interest of both parties to invite any other tribes who have been friends to the interest of the United States, to join the present confederation, and to form a state whereof the Delaware nation shall be the head, and have a representation in Congress: Provided, nothing contained in this article to be considered as conclusive until it meets with the approbation of Congress. And it is also the intent and meaning of this article, that no protection or countenance shall be afforded to any who are at present our enemies, by which they might escape the punishment they deserve.

Far from considering the Indian tribes as domestic wards, the early colonists saw as the major possibility of annexing more territory the option of extending the tribes statehood in the new confederation. In 1785 this offer was also tendered to the Cherokees of the deep South:

That the Indians may have full confidence in the justice of the United States, respecting their interests, they shall have the right to send a deputy of their choice, whenever they think fit, to Congress.

The federal policy was to contain their western frontier by getting the tribes to view the United States as a benevolent union which they might someday join. In neither the Delaware nor the Cherokee treaty is any claim made regarding the primacy of the United States over the self-governing functions of the tribe.

The treaty of peace ending the Revolutionary War, signed in 1783 between Great Britain and the United States, recognized the United States as a nation with international status and fixed the extent of the boundaries of the new nation with respect to the possessions then claimed by the King. The Indian tribes within the old Northwest Territory, roughly bounded by Ohio, Indiana, Illinois, Michigan, and Wisconsin, were faced with the necessity of recognizing that Great Britain's right to extinguish their land titles had passed to the United States when the peace treaty created a boundary between the United States and Canada.

The Indian treaties signed immediately after the signing of the peace treaty reflect this change in claims from Great Britain to the United States. The Wyandotte treaty of 1785, for example, contained the provision that

> The said Indian nations do acknowledge themselves and all their tribes to be under the protection of the United States and *of no other sovereign whatsoever.* [Emphasis added.]

In a formal sense, the United States was demanding exclusive recognition by the Indian tribes against the European nations. But Great Britain did not reduce its efforts to win the allegiance of the tribes away from the Americans. Rather, the covert competition for Indian favors between England and the United States escalated.

By the end of the Revolution the British traders had penetrated the old northwest territories to an amazing degree. Their operations were so complex and far-flung as to give them a virtual monopoly. Thus, while the United States had formal sovereignty over the tribes of the region, the British had practical control of the area, and the tensions between the avowed American policy of claiming political sovereignty and the liberal and realistic British attitude toward the tribes made the new American policies appear ludicrous. The American forts were few in number compared to the string of outposts manned by the British along the international border. And the strongest allies of the British, the Iroquois League, refused to respect the international border at all, regarding their traditional lands as exempt from the lines drawn on a map in a foreign city across the ocean.

Canada appeared to be vulnerable to attack from the United States because it had extensive borders with few natural boundaries to offer protection. Continual agitation by people in the United States concerning the conquest and annexation of Canada made it imperative that the English Crown be ready to defend its last North American possession. Between Canada and the Ohio River the lands were controlled by an informal confederacy of the Wyandottes, Miamis, Delawares, Shawnees, Ottawas, Chippewas, Kickapoos, and Potawatomi, and these tribes were very favorable to the British interests because of the liberal trading policies of the Crown.

As early as November 1783, Governor Haldimand of Canada wrote to the British government and suggested that the area be made a buffer state between Canada and the United States, and that the recognition of American interests in the area be limited by the British recognition of the formal international status of the tribes. Tensions escalated, and an undeclared war broke out between the tribes of the old Northwest and the Americans. The conflict lasted, intermittently, until 1795. The Mohawk Chief, Joseph Brant, who had gone to Canada after the Revolution, made himself a chief agitator for tribal independence in the region, and for over a decade the United States was generally unsuccessful in subjugating the tribes to its sovereignty because of the strong stance taken by Brant against alliances with the Americans.

Finally, in 1795, General Anthony Wayne defeated

the assembled Indian tribes and forced them to sign the treaty of Greenville in August of that year. The treaty was the first real assertion of American strength in the old Northwest since the founding of the nation. At best, it caused the tribes to seek further assurances from the British concerning the support they could expect from the Crown should the tribes wish to engage in further warfare with the Americans. The ill feelings between the Indians and the Americans continued to grow, and found their expression in the plans of Tecumseh, the great Shawnee warrior, who dreamed of uniting all of the tribes of the region into one anti-American confederacy. Tecumseh strongly objected to the frequent sale of lands to the United States by individual tribes. To counteract this trend, he taught that the Great Spirit had only lent the lands to the tribes to be used. Like water and air, land could not be divided and sold, Tecumseh advised.

Tecumseh worked hard to bring the tribes together, traveling great distances to spread his message. He even visited the distant lands of the Choctaws and Chickasaws, hoping to induce them to join his Indian military alliance and secure the whole western boundary of the United States against further expansion. But the southern Indians, to their eventual regret, refused to align themselves with the northern confederacy, and when his brother, Tenskwatawa the Prophet, attacked the Americans prematurely and lost the Battle of Fallen Timbers, Tecumseh's fragile coalition of tribes was thrown into a premature war with the Americans.

The northwest Indians fought the United States sporadically from 1808 until 1811, when General Harrison defeated them in the famous battle of Tippecanoe. Tecumseh fled to Canada and sought British help against the Americans. War between the Americans and the British appeared inevitable at that point because of the continued British depredations against American shipping and the demands by the war hawks in the United States Congress to have at it. When war was declared in June, 1812, Tecumseh immediately proceeded into the Ohio valley area and rallied the tribes against the Americans. The Shawnees, Miamis, Wyandottes, and Potawatomi began an offensive against the frontier settlements, and as the war progressed the Chippewas and some Sioux entered the fight on the British side.

Far from having secured the passive acceptance by the tribes of American sovereignty during the first three decades of its existence, the United States had succeeded in provoking the hostility of the tribes from the Ohio River to the Missouri River and as far south as the Floridas. As American history is now interpreted, the War of 1812 was basically a quarrel over the rights to international commerce between the United States and Great Britain, and the illegal impressment of American seamen into the British navy is seen as the chief emotional cause of the war. But if the war is understood in its frontier aspect, the continuing hostilities between the United States and the tribes of the old Northwest from 1783 to the War of 1812, the war itself must be understood as the final spasm of Indian efforts to play Great Britain off against the United States in order to preserve their own political independence.

As discussions over the peace terms began between the United States and Great Britain in 1814, Lord Castlereagh, the British secretary of state for foreign affairs, instructed the British peace commissioners:

> Upon the subject of the Indians, you will represent that an adequate arrangement of their in-

terests is considered by your Government as a
sine qua non of peace; and that a full and express recognition of their limits shall take place;
you will also throw out the importance of the
two States entering into arrangements, which
may hereafter place their mutual relations with
each other, as well as with the several Indian
nations, upon a footing of less jealousy and
irritation. This may be best effected by a mutual
guarantee of the Indian possessions, as they
shall be established upon the peace against en-
croachment on the part of either state. . . . The
best prospect of future peace appears to be that
the two Governments should regard the Indian
territory as a useful barrier between both States,
to prevent collision; and that, having agreed
mutually to respect the integrity of their territory, they have a common interest to render
these people as far as possible, peaceful neighbors to both States. (*American and British Claims
Arbitration*, Cayuga Indians, "Answer of the
United States," National Archives, 1934.)

The British government intended to gain a concession which they had failed to get at the peace table
following the American Revolution—the creation of
an internationally recognized Indian state which
would act as a buffer between the ambitious Americans and their Canadian neighbors.

The negotiations broke down on this specific point.
The Americans felt that the new provision would be
a step backward in their status as defined by the
Paris peace treaty of 1783. The British realized that
without a strong Indian state interposed between the
advancing American frontier and the Canadian border, the activities of their traders would be severely
if not permanently compromised. At least part of the

problem in resolving the debate was the fact that nearly a hundred thousand American citizens were already living in the northwest territories on Indian lands, and removing them would be politically impossible for any American president.

The American peace commissioners pointed out

> . . . [that] the territory of which Great Britain wishes now to dispose is within the dominions of the United States was solemnly acknowledged by herself in the treaty of peace of 1783, which established their boundaries, and by which she relinquished all claims to the government, propriety [property] and territorial rights within those boundaries. No condition respecting the Indians residing there was inserted in that treaty. No stipulation, similar to that now proposed, is to be found in any treaty made by Great Britain, or, within the knowledge of the undersigned, by any other nation.

The Americans would not allow the British to improve upon their position of 1783, even to end what everyone agreed was a senseless and unnecessary war.

As the controversy continued, the Americans began to back away from their previous rigid position. In order to reassure the British of the humanity of their Indian policy, the United States alleged that

> . . . the Indians residing within the United States are so far independent that they live under their own customs, and not under the laws of the United States; that their rights upon the lands where they inhabit or hunt are secured to them by boundaries defined in amicable treaties

between the United States and themselves; and that whenever those boundaries are varied, it is also by amicable and voluntary treaties by which they receive from the United States ample compensation for every right they have to the lands ceded by them. They are so far dependent as not to have the right to dispose of their lands to any private persons, nor to any Power other than the United States, and to be under their protection alone, and not under that of any other Power. Whether called subjects, or by whatever name designated, such is the relation between them and the United States. That relation is neither asserted now for the first time, nor did it originate with the Treaty of Greenville.

The Treaty of Greenville neither took from the Indians the right, which they had not, of selling lands within the jurisdiction of the United States to foreign Governments or subjects, nor ceded to them the right of exercising exclusive jurisdiction within the boundary line assigned. It was merely declaratory of the public law, in relation to the parties, founded on principles previously and universally recognized.

The final solution to the controversy was the insertion into the peace treaty of a special article covering the political status of the Indian tribes of the interior of the continent. Being a compromise, it was more confusing than either the British demand for Indian independence or the American demand for total subjection of the tribes to the United States had been.

Article IX. The United States of America engage to put an end, immediately after the ratification of the present treaty, to hostilities with all tribes or nations of Indians with whom they may be at

war at the time of such ratification; and forthwith to restore to such tribes or nations, respectively, all the possessions, rights and privileges
which they may have enjoyed or been entitled to
in one thousand eight hundred and eleven, previous to such hostilities: Provided always that
such tribes or nations shall agree to desist from
all hostilities against the United States of America, their citizens and subjects, upon the ratification of the present treaty being notified to such
tribes or nations, and shall so desist accordingly.
And His Britannic Majesty engages, on his part,
to put an end immediately after the ratification
of the present treaty, to hostilities with all the
tribes or nations of Indians with whom he may
be at war at the time of such ratification, and
forthwith to restore to such tribes or nations
respectively all the possessions, rights and privileges which they may have enjoyed or been entitled to in one thousand eight hundred and
eleven, previous to such hostilities: Provided
always that such tribes or nations shall agree to
desist from all hostilities against His Britannic
Majesty, and his subjects, upon the ratification
of the present treaty being notified of such tribes
or nations, and shall so desist accordingly.

The solution was in fact no solution. The agreement was that both the United States and Great Britain would restore the tribes with whom they had
been at war to the political status which those tribes
had enjoyed prior to the commencement of the war.
The United States, if you will recall, was concerned
primarily with protecting its international status in
the eyes of the European nations and maintaining
their recognition of its right to extinguish Indian
titles within its boundaries. The political status of the

tribes, therefore, remained pretty much as Victoria would have defined it: as nations with a right to political existence and valid land titles.

Following the signing of the peace, the United States began an extensive campaign to sign peace treaties with the tribes of the West in order to prevent further expansion of British influence in the Plains and Far West. The tribes of the Ohio region had already signed a peace treaty with the United States in 1814. The treaty required the tribes not to make peace with Great Britain without the permission of the United States, thus in effect undermining the American arguments concerning the relative independence of the tribes of that region. The British did not understand the nature of the treaty during the negotiations, however, and so the nature of the political status of the tribes was never questioned.

In 1815 the United States signed treaties with the Potawatomi, the Piankashaws, the Sioux of the Lakes, the other western Sioux, the Omaha, the Kickapoo, the Wyandotte, the Osage, the Sac and Fox, the Iowa, and the Kansas, and the following year contacted several other western tribes which had engaged in war on behalf of the British. In each treaty text was the admission, by the tribe concerned, that the United States would be acknowledged as exercising political sovereignty over the tribe and would conduct the tribe's foreign relations. In later years the United States would attempt to interpret these treaties as having extinguished the political independence of the western tribes. Such was not the case. The treaties were simply the United States' method of fulfilling its treaty promise to Great Britain.

Of the area now composing the continental United States, Great Britain was thenceforth a political power only in Oregon territory. The United States

was free to deal with the tribes of the interior un-
hindered by the opinions or policies of the European
nations. Shortly after the end of the War of 1812,
the policy for Indians began to change, and the pious
assurances it once had given to Great Britain concerning the Indian tribes vanished. Political demands
to clear the Indians from the Mississippi valley by
advocates of western settlement resulted in the infamous removal policy, which was finally, brutally
perfected by Andrew Jackson in the 1830s.

For nearly a decade, from 1823 to 1832, the eastern tribes were forced from their ancestral homes in
the Ohio and Mississippi valleys and moved to the
barren plains of Oklahoma and Kansas. Even the
Seminoles in Florida were removed to the West, as
the intense drive to develop the agricultural wealth
of the deep South meant clearing the land of trees,
animals, and Indians, not necessarily in that order.
But even in the removal treaties the political independence of the tribes was recognized. In the famous
treaty of Dancing Rabbit Creek, which resulted in the
removal of the Choctaws from Mississippi to Oklahoma, Article IV promised:

> Article IV. The Government and people of the
> United States are hereby obliged to secure to the
> said Choctaw Nation of Red People the jurisdic-
> tion and government of all persons and property
> that may be within their limits west, so that no
> Territory or State shall ever have a right to pass
> laws for the government of the Choctaw Nation
> of Red People and their descendants; and that
> no part of the land granted to them shall ever be
> embraced in any Territory or State but the
> United States shall forever secure said Choctaw
> Nation from, and against, all laws except such as
> from time to time may be enacted in their own

National Councils, not inconsistent with the Constitution, Treaties, and Laws of the United States; and except such as may, and which have been enacted by Congress, to the extent that Congress under the Constitution are required to exercise a legislation over Indian Affairs. But the Choctaws, should this treaty be ratified, express a wish that Congress may grant to the Choctaws the right of punishing by their own laws, any white man who shall come into their nation, and infringe any of their national regulations.

This promise was a serious proposal. The very next article of the treaty promised that the United States would protect the Choctaws against "domestic strife and foreign enemies."

The political implications of the treaty of Dancing Rabbit Creek were clear. John Marshall's theory of dependent domestic nations was not articulated in the provisions of this treaty, but rather that of dissenting Justice Thompson, who had decided that Cherokees were a foreign nation in the constitutional sense of the term. The United States promised never to enclose the Choctaw tribe within the boundaries of any state or territory which it created. If the Choctaws did not have a foreign status, they were at least a protectorate with some international status.

During the Civil War the Five Civilized Tribes offered to join the Union side, recognizing that their treaties bound them to the United States as military allies. But the Union forces rejected the overtures of the tribes, stating that the use of Indians against the Southern whites would be barbaric. Since the Confederates were much closer to Indian country than were the federal forces, the Five Civilized Tribes had little choice but to sign treaties with them. Again, as in the American Revolution, the whites promised political equality to the Indians. (A historical note: The Confederate treaty is the only treaty in which the text actually reads "as long as the rivers flow and the grass grows." The phrase is frequently found in the proceedings of other treaties but never in the actual text.)

The Indians, unfortunately, had sided with a loser again, and the Confederacy collapsed after a bitter struggle of four years. The Five Civilized Tribes were in a most difficult position, and in order to get back the political status which they had had prior to the beginning of the war, they had to agree to enroll their freed slaves into citizenship in their tribes. The Confederate treaty was regarded more as an embarrassment by the United States than as an unfaithful act, and lawsuits decided in later years would simply mention that the treaty relationship with the United States had existed throughout the Civil War, as if the whole venture into political independence symbolized by the Confederate treaty had never existed.

Treaties with other tribes sometimes supported the theory of protectorate and sometimes supported the idea that Indian tribes were a domestic creature of the United States. The treaty of Medicine Creek, signed in 1854 in the Pacific Northwest, for example, forbade the Indians to trade at Vancouver's Island, a British trading post in Canada and the most important British settlement on the West Coast. Such a provision recognized, at least in a backhanded manner, the freedom of the Pacific Northwest tribes to deal with both the United States and Great Britain.

The first treaty signed with the Comanches, in 1835 at Camp Holmes, in the Creek Nation, illustrates how far the United States was from subduing the Plains tribes. The Cherokee, Creek, Choctaw, Seneca, Osage, and Quapaw tribes, fearful of the depredations of the Comanches and desirous of participating in the Santa Fe trade, asked the United States to intercede with the Comanches and seek the right of free passage from the Comanches through their country.

No effort was made by the United States to secure a pledge of allegiance from the Comanches, and there was no acknowledgment by the Comanches that they recognized the United States as their sovereign. The United States offered to pay full indemnity to the Comanches for any ponies stolen by the whites who might pass through their country. Article IX of the treaty attempted to distinguish between the relationship which the Comanches had toward the United States and that which they had with Mexico, in whose territory they lived:

> The Comanche and Witchetaw nations and their associated bands or tribes, of Indians, agree, that their entering into this treaty shall in no respect interrupt their friendly relations with the Republic of Mexico, where they all frequently hunt and the Comanche nation principally inhabit; and it is distinctly understood that the Government of the United States desire that perfect peace shall exist between the nations or tribes named in this article and the said republic.

Far from being subservient to either the United States or Mexico, the Comanches and Wichitas held control over a vast area into which neither Americans nor Mexicans strayed without permission. If the doctrine of discovery had theoretical validity in Europe or the universities and law schools of the United States, it had little relevance on the staked plains of the Southwest, where the Comanches and their allies held sovereignty by force of arms.

As the continent came under the plow and the

military strength of the tribes dwindled through the attrition of a hundred nameless skirmishes, the treaties and agreements began to reflect one-sided real-estate transactions rather than further clarification of the political status of the tribes. John Marshall's offhand remark that the relationship between the Indians and the United States resembled "that of a guardian to its ward" was transformed by the federal courts and Congress into a full-blown theory of wardship under which Congress had unlimited and plenary power to dispose of the lives and property of Indians without any more justification than that it had the power and, by definition, the wisdom to do so.

Symptomatic of this expanding assertion of unlimited powers was the sequence of events by which the federal government abolished the Five Civilized Tribes of Oklahoma. They had escaped the provisions of the General Allotment Act in 1887, led the futile conference to establish an Indian state in 1888, and were regarded as the major stumbling block to total domination of the tribes by the employees of the Bureau of Indian Affairs. So long as efficient democratic Indian governments existed and the less organized tribes could seek their advice and counsel, the massive schemes of social engineering envisioned by the Bureau, the church groups, and the philanthropists would fail.

In 1893 Congress passed a law setting up a commission headed by former Senator Henry Dawes. The commission was directed to negotiate with the governments of the Five Tribes to secure land cessions from them and secure their agreement to allotments of tribal lands. The tribes resisted so violently that Congress thought it necessary to use additional pressure, and two years later, in 1895, another law was passed, authorizing a survey of their lands and the drawing up of a roll of their citizens. It was apparent that the United States was going ahead with tribal dissolution regardless of the treaty rights. Under this unrelenting pressure, the Choctaws agreed to negotiate, in 1896, and the following year Congress followed this concession with a law requiring the President to approve every act of the tribal councils.

Congress then moved in for the kill when, in 1898, it passed the Curtis Act, sponsored, ironically, by Charles Curtis, a one-eighth-blood Kaw and Osage Indian from Kansas. Under the provisions of this law, the allotment of the lands of the Five Civilized Tribes was authorized, along with the division of their other property. Their governments were terminated, and the business of the former governments was placed in the hands of Presidential appointees. The excellent school systems of the tribes—which among the Cherokees had produced more college graduates than were then living in either Texas or Oklahoma—were merged into the public school system. The territory of Oklahoma was now ready for admission into the Union.

The naked exercise of legislative power in defiance of the long-standing treaties was simply a *fait accompli*. Even the fee simple titles which the tribes held were considered void, a strange development in Anglo-Saxon law. The later articulation of this Congressional power came in 1906, in the case *Lone Wolf v. Hitchcock*, when Congress did essentially the same thing with the Kiowas and Comanches. In that case the Supreme Court, rewriting history with a flourish, ruled that Congress had always had absolute powers over Indians and their property, an assertion fraudulent on its face considering the long history of treaties with the tribes.

Even in the darkest days of Indian political existence, the United States made sure that it had at least a symbolic agreement by the tribal members to the actions which the United States proposed. Although the government had successfully smothered the political life of the Indian tribes, it did not wish to appear blatant before the world in its acts of aggression. So the requirements of the Ordinance of 1787, the first major policy statement of the new nation regarding Indians, that the United States would never take the lands of the Indians without their consent except in just wars, remained a haunting reminder of the days when the United States was forced to deal with the Indians on a just and moral basis.

The contemporary demand of American Indians for a restoration of the treaty relationship must be seen in this historical setting. Few tribes would have signed treaties with the United States had they felt that the United States would violate them. The promises of self-government found in a multitude of treaties, the promises of protection by the United States from wrongs committed by its citizens, the promises that the tribes would be respected as nations on whose behalf the United States acted as a trustee before the eyes of the world, were all vital parts of the treaty rights which Indians believe they have received from the United States.

John Marshall characterized the Cherokees, and by extension the other Indian tribes, as in a state of tutelage. The implied meaning of this phrase was that at some future time the tribes would assume full status as nations in the world community. There was never an indication that the tribes were to be destroyed and their individual members merged into the great American mass as citizens. Rather, many treaties specifically reserve the right of tribal membership and allow the process of expatriation to the tribal member through the taking of allotments.

The recent series of incidents in Indian country is

based upon a political reading of the treaties and not a reading of the treaties as symbolic real-estate documents. The history of the treaty relationship between the United States and the Indian tribes contains a strong tradition denying that tribes are wards of the government and describing them as expectant nations with eventual status as nations in the family of nations of the world.

In 1934 the Kansas (or Kaw) tribe filed a suit against the United States for lands taken from the tribe during the previous century. The basis which the tribe used to establish liability of the United States was a wardship theory. The tribe maintained that the treaty of October 15, 1815, which it had signed with the United States and in which it acknowledged the sovereignty and accepted the protection of the United States, was sufficient to establish the wardship status of the tribe. Therefore, the tribe argued, the United States had a responsibility to deal fairly with its ward.

After having heard this doctrine expounded by the Bureau of Indian Affairs and acclaimed in the halls of Congress for nearly a century, the Kansas tribe thought they had finally hit upon the proper theory to describe their relationship with the United States. Not so. The United States Court of Claims, in a startling reversal of popular doctrine, stated:

> Pursuant to the provisions of the Treaty of Ghent between the United States and Great Britain, ratified February 17, 1815 (8 Stat. 218), the United States entered into a treaty of peace and friendship with the plaintiff tribe on October 28, 1815. The purpose of the treaty as proclaimed in the preamble was the re-establishment of peace and friendship between the United States and the plaintiff tribe of Indians and placing them

in every respect upon the same footing upon
which they stood before the late war [the War
of 1812] between the United States and Great
Britain. . . .

The stipulation that the plaintiff tribe acknowledged itself to be under the United States
and no other nation in no way divested the plaintiff tribe of its sovereign power to enter into
treaties with the United States on equal terms or
lessened its obligations under such treaties when
made. The purpose and effect of the treaty were
to place the contracting parties upon the same
footing in every respect upon which they stood
before the war with Great Britain. No contention
is made that the relationship of guardian and
ward existed between them before the war. Certainly this relationship could not be created by a
treaty that merely re-established their pre-existing political relations. The contention that this
was the effect of article III of the treaty is without merit. (*Kansas or Kaw Tribe of Indians v.
United States*, 80 C. Cls. 264–325, 1934.)

The Indian treaty, therefore, according to the
courts of the United States, did not establish the
wardship relationship with it. The only valid interpretation of tribal political status which this decision
leaves is that of dissenting Justice Thompson, that
the Cherokees, and by extension the other Indian
tribes, remain in a very real sense foreign nations
with respect to the United States. It is this tradition
that the current Indian movement seeks to support.
And if the wardship status was not established in the
treaties, the only documents in which the Indian
tribes contracted with the United States government
on a legal basis, then the international basis of Indian existence must still be good legal doctrine.

It should be no mystery and no sedition, therefore, to recall the proclamation of Wounded Knee: that the Oglala Sioux have announced to the world their political independence from the United States.

7. The Plenary Power Doctrine

The relationship between American Indian tribes and the United States government is not built exclusively upon either the doctrine of discovery or the multitude of treaties and agreements signed over a hundred-year period. Rather, from the very beginning of the republic there was an acknowledgment by the framers of the Constitution that the new nation would have to deal with the Indian tribes. Discussions initially involved the respective powers of the states and the new federal government to deal with the Indian tribes within the old colonial borders. Massachusetts, for example, claimed lands known as the western reserve (in what is now Ohio), and the difficulty of treating with the Indian tribes of that region from Boston was apparent.

New York had always dealt with the Iroquois League on an equal basis, and had concluded several land-cession treaties. The state government insisted that several more treaties, actually fraudulent land cessions, had been made by the Iroquois. It was loath to surrender its treaty-making powers to the federal government when the Iroquois still owned a large portion of the western part of the state. North

Carolina and Georgia were also reluctant to give the federal government power to control Indian affairs, since they had the large and powerful Cherokee nation within their boundaries. But the folly of allowing every state to deal with Indians as it wished, and the possibility of continual Indian wars which this option forecast, made it imperative that the federal government create some central power to deal with the Indians. Extensive sales of the unsettled Indian lands of the West were also seen as a means of paying off the massive federal debt incurred during the Revolution. When the debate reached the pocketbook issue, the federalists won, and Congress was given power to deal with the Indians.

The Constitution of the United States mentions Indians in Article I, section 1, clause 3. The clause regards the apportionment of direct taxes and representatives among the several states, and simply mentions how the population of each state will be determined, "excluding Indians not taxed." The phrase has not been understood as a justification of Indian tax exemption, although some Indians have been prepared to argue as much. Rather, it has remained as enigmatic as on the day it was written. The only conclusion that can be drawn regarding the interpretation of the phrase is simply that Indians would not be counted when compiling statistics on either direct taxation or population for determination of representatives to Congress.

The most important mention of Indians in the Constitution is in Article I, section 8, clause 3, in which the powers of the Congress are enumerated. The clause reads:

> To regulate Commerce with foreign Nations, and among the several States, and with the Indian tribes.

If it were not for the fact that the interstate-commerce clause has been used to justify so many things of which the original framers of the Constitution could not have conceived, one would feel that the use of this phrase to justify the actions of the United States toward Indians was highly suspect. From this simple wording has come the justification for confiscation of Indian lands, kidnapping of Indian children for government boarding schools, and the myriad other things which the United States has perpetrated on Indians.

Perhaps the most consistent use of the phrase has been in the area of separation of powers. It has been interpreted to mean that both the courts and the executive branch have secondary powers with respect to Indians, while Congress has the primary power over Indians and Indian property. Many cases have been taken by the tribes in an effort to secure some exposition by the Supreme Court of their rights against the exercise of these unlimited powers by Congress. In almost every instance, the court has declared that the Constitution commits Indian Affairs to Congress and that matters dealing with Indians are essentially political matters, to be settled only by Congress.

Thus it was that during the conflict between the Five Civilized Tribes and the United States regarding the disposition of tribal assets, the Cherokee Nation sued Secretary of the Interior Ethan Allen Hitchcock to prevent him from leasing their lands for mineral exploration. If the Supreme Court wanted a chance to uphold the inherent right of sovereignty of an Indian tribe, the case was a classic. Yet the Supreme Court maintained:

> The power existing in Congress to administer upon and guard the tribal property, and the

power being political and administrative in its nature, the manner of its exercise is a question within the province of the legislative branch to determine, and is not one for the courts. (*Cherokee Nation v. Hitchcock*, 187 U.S. 294, 1902)

Since Congress was given the power to regulate commerce with the Indian tribes, the court felt that there were no limits set on that power. All Indian efforts to limit the scope of the congressional power by constitutional principles came to naught.

The most extensive articulation of this power, as we have briefly discussed previously, was in *Lone Wolf v. Hitchcock*, the Kiowa case on allotments. The President, under a directive from Congress, had appointed the Jerome Commission, to go to Oklahoma and there enter into an agreement with the Kiowas and Comanches for the allotment of their lands. The commission reported that it had gotten the necessary number of signatures of the adult males of the two tribes required by the Medicine Lodge Treaty of 1867, and that the tribes had agreed to cede most of their reservation to the United States.

But the signatures on the agreement were fraudulent (the Secretary of the Interior admitted as much later), and the leading chief of the Kiowas, Lone Wolf, filed suit against the Secretary of the Interior, asking that he be prohibited from carrying out the terms of the agreement, specifically allotment of the reservation. The case was appealed to the United States Supreme Court, and the court reached its decision quickly, declaring that Congress could change the specific terms of the Kiowa and Comanche treaty.

"Plenary authority over the tribal relations of the Indians," the court stated, "has been exercised by

Congress from the beginning, and the power has always been deemed a political one, not subject to be controlled by the judicial department of the Government." The historical accuracy of the court was not in question. Had it been, the Kiowas would surely have won since, as we have seen, the facts of history did not support this conclusion. Of more importance was the willingness of the court to rule that an Indian question involving the nature of Congressional power was a political question and not open to judicial inquiry. There was, therefore, no effective way in which tribes could appeal the actions of the U.S. government other than by political action.

With the basic protections of the Constitution closed to the Indian tribes by the doctrine of plenary powers, the only recourse would seem to have been provoking an incident to which the United States would have to respond politically, for even the vote was denied to the Indians. There was no practical way in which political dissent or reform could be expressed. The development in 1906 of the doctrine of the political nature of Indian questions by the Supreme Court of the United States led directly to the Wounded Knee situation of 1973. Indians had come to realize, by 1973, that political activism was their only hope. Even assuming the best of intentions by Congress, they could not achieve a modicum of justice.

Not only were the courts closed to the tribes for redress in cases where their property and political rights had been violated, but the courts also excluded individual Indians from the other protections of the Constitution. The great civil-rights amendments to the Constitution, the Thirteenth, Fourteenth, and Fifteenth, were interpreted by the federal courts as excluding American Indians in their operation when the courts found that the

Fifteenth Amendment did not grant suffrage but only prohibited discrimination where suffrage already existed.

The clearest case of the exclusion of Indians from voting citizenship was that of *Elk v. Wilkins.* In that case an Indian had voluntarily left his tribe and taken up the pursuits of civilized life. He had moved to Omaha, Nebraska, and established residence, getting a job and earning his own way in the world. Then he decided to vote.

Elk claimed that he had been born in the United States and had severed his relations with his tribe, as required by his treaty. Under the theory of aboriginal title and the doctrine of discovery, the lands of the tribe upon which Elk had been born were within the limits of the United States; if we accept the theory which the American commissioners argued with the British negotiators following the War of 1812, there were no "foreign" places on the continent to which the United States did not lay claim. And if we accept John Marshall's theory of Indian land tenure and political status, it should be clear that Elk was well within the sovereignty and supervision of the United States.

Yet the court made a distinction between citizenship by birth and citizenship by naturalization in order to deny Elk his rights to vote under the Thirteenth and Fourteenth Amendments to the Constitution. The court declared:

> The persons declared to be citizens are "all persons born or naturalized in the United States, and subject to the jurisdiction thereof." The evident meaning of these last words is, not merely subject in some respect or degree to the jurisdiction of the United States, but completely subject to their political jurisdiction, and owing them direct and immediate allegiance. . . .

Indians born within the territorial limits of the United States, members of, and owing immediate allegiance to, one of the Indian tribes (an alien, though dependent power), although in a geographical sense born in the United States, are no more "born in the United States and subject to the jurisdiction thereof," within the meaning of the first section of the Fourteenth Amendment, than the children of subjects of any foreign government born within the domain of that government, or the children born within the United States of ambassadors or other public ministers of foreign nations.

Thus, while federal courts were busy maintaining the plenary power of Congress over Indians, and classifying Indian tribes as wards of the federal government, and denying an international dimension to Indian political existence, the individual Indians seeking to exercise their constitutional rights were being told that they were, in effect, "no more than the children of [foreign] subjects."

Unwittingly, the United States was preserving for the Indians of the future a peculiar dimension—a foreignness, if you will—to their political existence which could not be denied. To find, then, at Wounded Knee and other places, the assumption by American Indians that their tribes had international status and that they owed no allegiance to the United States, should not be strange in light of *Elk v. Wilkins*.

The federal court concluded that while Elk had done everything that it was possible to do to achieve the status of citizenship, including fulfilling the treaty requirement that he sever his relations with his tribe and take up the white man's way of life, Elk could not receive citizenship without the United States performing a positive act indicating its acceptance of him as a citizen. Although originally a member of a "dependent domestic nation," Elk was required to perform all of the naturalization functions of a native-born European, Asian, or African in order to exercise his voting franchise.

The denial by the federal government of citizenship and the protections of the Thirteenth, Fourteenth, and Fifteenth Amendments of the Constitution served to place individual Indians outside of the constitutional framework. Their only citizenship was in nations having a "foreign" relationship to the Constitution. The status defined was exactly that maintained by the Cherokees in their original action in the Supreme Court against the State of Georgia, which had been denied by that court for political reasons.

In 1924 the United States passed a general act, known as the Indian Citizenship Act, which unilaterally made all Indians residing in or born in the limits of the United States American citizens. The question raised by Indians upon learning of the act concerned whether the United States could extend citizenship on a unilateral basis. If it previously had required Elk to wait for a positive act on the part of the United States before he could become a citizen, would it not require a positive act on the part of the Indians in 1924 to become United States citizens?

The Iroquois served notice on the United States that they did not want American citizenship.

The Constitution purported, as we have seen, to relate the Indian tribes to the emerging American political system. But, as we have also seen, the only significant mention of Indians was in the interstate-commerce clause. One of the important aspects of American citizenship is the right to the protections offered by the Bill of Rights. If the Indian tribes truly were dependent domestic nations which had surrendered their governmental functions to the United States, or which had never had self-government because of the exercise of the plenary powers of Congress over them, it would be correct to assume that the United States has enforced the protections given to individuals in the Bill of Rights. Such has not been the case.

Indian tribes have always governed their own tribal domestic affairs. Until recently, the Bill of Rights did not extend from the Constitution into tribal governments, as one would have expected it to do if Indians were indeed in the state of tutelage described by John Marshall. Until 1968, when Congress extended the Bill of Rights to cover the relationships between tribal governments and tribal members, Indian tribes were not affected by the constitutional protections when dealing with their own affairs. Even today, the 1968 Civil Rights Act is under constant challenge by tribes attempting to define how the Bill of Rights affects tribal sovereignty.

The first major litigation which attempted to define the individual Indian's constitutional rights against his tribal government involved the selection of a jury in the Cherokee Nation. Talton, a Cherokee, was convicted of murder by a Cherokee grand jury which consisted of five citizens of the Cherokee Nation. Talton filed a writ of habeas corpus against Mayes, the high sheriff of the Cherokee Nation, asking that he be released because the Cherokee grand jury was in violation of the Constitution of the United States, to which the Cherokee tribe was subject.

The case went to the United States Supreme Court in 1896; there was full expectation that the writ would be upheld, since Congress was at that very moment considering legislation to dismantle the Cherokee government. But the court astounded everyone when it turned down the writ and upheld the action of the Cherokee Supreme Court. In determining whether the Cherokee Nation was bound by the Constitution of the United States, the court reviewed some of the major decisions involving the rights to self-government of Indian tribes, and in particular the two famous Cherokee cases of three-quarters of a century earlier, *Cherokee Nation v. Georgia* and *Worcester v. Georgia*, which had destroyed the Cherokee treaty rights and made their removal from Georgia inevitable.

After commenting on the Cherokee rights to self-government as contained in treaties and statutes, the court continued:

> True it is that in many adjudications of this court the fact had been fully recognized, that although possessed of these attributes of local self-government, when exercising their tribal functions, all such rights are subject to the supreme legislative authority of the United States. . . .
>
> *Cherokee Nation v. Kansas Railway Co.* 135 U.S. 641, where the cases are fully reviewed. But the existence of the right in Congress to regulate the manner in which the local powers of the Cherokee nation shall be exercised does not render such local powers Federal powers arising from and created by the Constitution of the United States. It follows that as the powers of local self-government enjoyed by the Cherokee nation existed prior to the Constitution, they are not operated upon by the Fifth Amendment, which, as we have said, had for its sole object to control the powers conferred by the Constitution on the National government.

As the court described it, the relationship of the Cherokee Nation to the United States was hardly that of tutelage but rather a protectorate relationship in which the United States had a minimum power to interfere with the self-government of the Cherokee people. Since the Cherokees had existed as a political entity before the establishment of the United States, they did not become subject to the provisions of the American Constitution when they became a protectorate state of the American government. Where the federal and state governments were required by the Constitution to remain within certain limits in their exercise of power, the Cherokees were subject to no such limitations. They did not even have to adhere to the Bill of Rights, under which both the federal government and later the states would find restrictions. The logical meaning of this status is not eventual extinction in a political sense, but independence and recognition on a world scale.

The United States passed legislation shortly after the *Talton v. Mayes* case abolishing the institutions of the Cherokee Nation, particularly its court system. Yet the very act purporting to abolish the tribal government provided that it should remain operative until it had disposed of its property. A shadow government has existed until the present time. The original legislation was amended in the late sixties to provide that the Cherokee people could elect their own chief, a right originally denied them by the requirement that the President of the United States appoint their chief. The tribe's original rights as articulated in the *Talton* case would seem to be unimpaired, if presently inoperative, under the theory of the case.

Talton v. Mayes became very important in defining the rights of tribal governments in the half century following it. A number of cases were taken in the 1950s in which the same basic question arose. In 1954 six members of the Jemez Pueblo of New Mexico filed suit charging that the Pueblos had violated their rights to religious freedom as defined in the U.S. Code. The elders of the Pueblo had refused them the right to bury their dead in the community cemetery, had denied them the right to build a church on Pueblo land, and had refused to allow Protestant missionaries to freely enter the Pueblo to see them.

The federal court was at a loss to decide the case. It was impossible to show that the Pueblos had acted under any color of law whatsoever. The New Mexico statutes did not at any time purport to vest any governmental powers in the Pueblos. And the Pueblos did not derive their powers of self-government from any act of the United States. The Indian Reorganization Act, which defined the right of tribes to establish courts on a formal basis, was understood by the court as having merely recognized the perennial and inherent rights of the Indians to govern themselves, not as having established courts and governments for the tribes.

Since the government of the Pueblos must have originated at some time, the court weakly referred to the *Talton* decision and declared somewhat vaguely that the Indian tribes were subject to the paramount authority of Congress, an enigmatic reference which did not clarify anything. The complaint was dismissed, thus holding intact the somewhat surprising doctrine that tribal governments extended backward into the remote past and had rights which even the United States could not cancel or amend.

A more dramatic case involving the same problem of religious freedom of tribal members was the *Native American Church v. the Navajo Tribe* (1959). Adherents of the Native American Church, which uses peyote in its religious ceremonies, sued the Navajo tribe to enjoin its enforcement of its ordinance forbidding the introduction of peyote on the Navajo reservation in Arizona and New Mexico. The Navajo members of the Native American Church claimed that the tribe was subject to the same limitations as Congress and the states with respect to the constitutional rights of its citizens. The federal court, after reviewing the several cases that have exempted tribes from the constitutional limitations imposed on the federal government, noted:

> The First Amendment applies only to Congress. It limits the powers of Congress to interfere with religious freedom or religious worship. It is made applicable to the States only by the Fourteenth Amendment. Thus construed, the First Amendment places limitations upon the action of Congress and of the States. But as declared in the decisions hereinbefore discussed, Indian tribes are not states. *They have a status higher than that of states. They are subordinate and dependent nations possessed of all powers as such only to the extent that they have expressly been required to surrender them by the supreme law of the land, but it is nonetheless a part of the laws of the United States.* [Emphasis added.]

If the ghost of John Marshall had wandered by while this decision was being written, it certainly would have looked askance at the reasoning of the court. Marshall's problem in the *Cherokee Nation* case was whether the Cherokees were a foreign nation in the sense that they could sue Georgia, a state of the Union, in an original action in the Supreme Court of the United States. Inherent in his decision was the assumption that the Cherokees had not yet reached the lofty civilized plateau of the state of Georgia and were therefore in a state of tutelage. Yet the federal district court in New Mexico described the Navajo tribe as possessing a higher status than a state of the Union as a true dependent nation.

The *Talton* case dominated legal theories in this subject field until 1965, when a case on the Fort Belknap Indian Reservation in Montana paved the way for an eventual enactment of a statute making tribes subject to the Bill of Rights with respect to their own members. The case, *Colliflower v. Garland,* involved imprisonment of a tribal member without due process. The federal court timidly suggested that its decision to allow habeas corpus should be restricted only to that particular reservation, making the holding a precedent but hardly universally applicable.

Opposed to this continuing tradition of regarding the Indian tribes as dependent nations has been the characterization of the administrative rules of the Bureau of Indian Affairs by the federal courts as the proper rules and regulations by which the United States exercises its "guardianship" over its "wards." The tendency of the courts has been to confuse the exercise of trust responsibilities for the property of individual Indians with the arm's-length stance required by the United States when dealing with a dependent nation. The trust responsibility for the property of individual Indians was assumed by the United States with the allotment of tribal lands to tribal members in the period 1854–1934. There is no justification in treaties, statutes, or the Constitution for regarding the corporate political entity of tribal government as a "ward" of the executive branch of government.

In the last century the federal government has developed extensive doctrines outside the constitutional framework justifying its intrusion into the affairs of the tribes. Almost any policy proposed which might change either the nature of federal services or the manner in which they are delivered has been immediately sabotaged by the career bureaucrats of the Bureau of Indian Affairs, on the ground that it would violate the Secretary of the Interior's trust responsibility to Indians. Yet when Indian tribes have asked the Secretary of the Interior to exercise his trust responsibilities toward them, they have been refused.

For nearly a decade during the 1960s, the Pyramid Lake Paiute tribe attempted to get three different Secretaries of the Interior to clarify their rights to water on the Truckee-Carson river system in Nevada. Each time they were refused, on the ground that the Secretary's trust responsibility did not include protection of their water rights if they appeared to be in conflict with the programs of other agencies of the Interior Department. The Quinault Tribe of Washington State has continually petitioned the Interior Department to enforce the federal laws and prevent the timber companies from clear-cutting their timber. They have been told that the Secretary has a "moral" and not a legal duty toward them.

The theory of wardship has proven a tragic farce. It has no constitutional justification for its existence, other than a very broad interpretation of the interstate-commerce clause. On the other hand, the concept of the dependent nation is buttressed by another phrase of the Constitution, which, while it does not directly mention Indians or Indian tribes, is part and parcel of the Indian experience. That phrase is the treaty-making clause.

In Article II, section 2, clause 2, the President is given the power to make treaties "by and with the Advice and Consent of the Senate." Indians are not specifically mentioned in this treaty section, but the practice from the very beginning of the republic until 1871 was to ratify the treaties with Indians under the same powers of advice and consent of the Senate exercised in the field of foreign treaty making. While the War Department and later the Interior Department were given the administrative authority to deal with Indian tribes, the documents pertaining to Indian treaties were maintained by the State Department until 1871, and the special appropriations required by the Indian treaties were appropriated as treaty items.

The question of whether the Indian treaties stand on the same legal basis as treaties with foreign nations consistently has been resolved in favor of the Indian tribes. One of the most frequently cited cases interpreting Indian treaties is *Turner v. American Baptist Missionary Union* (1825). The case involved title to lands in the State of Michigan, and whether the act of the State of Michigan or the Indian treaty ceding the lands to the government determined the true ownership of the land. The federal district court stated:

> It is contended that a treaty with Indian tribes has not the same dignity or effect as a treaty with a foreign and independent nation. This distinction is not authorized by the constitution. Since the commencement of the government, treaties have been made with the Indians, and the treaty-making power has been exercised in making them. They are treaties within the meaning of the constitution and, as such, are the supreme law of the land.

The court described, however, the precise nature of the treaty rights which could be considered "the supreme law of the land."

> A treaty under the federal constitution is declared to be the supreme law of the land. This, unquestionably, applies to all treaties, where the

treaty-making power, without the aid of congress, can carry it into effect.

It is not, however, and cannot be the supreme law of the land, where the concurrence of Congress is necessary to give it effect.

Until this power is exercised, as where the appropriation of money is required, a treaty is not perfect.

In distinguishing the various articles of the treaties which require an act of Congress appropriating money from those which automatically operate without any action of the Congress, the constitutional nature of Indian treaties emerges. The land-cession articles and annuity provisions of the treaties are those which require congressional action. They are being litigated in the Indian Claims Commission, set up by Congress in 1946. Neary half of the 600 or more claims filed in this commission have already been decided. But settling those treaty provisions does not liquidate the constitutional rights of the tribes under treaties.

The most important aspect of the treaties for Indian people is the series of articles limiting the powers of the United States over the lives and rights of Indian people. The third article of the treaty of Medicine Creek, which ceded large portions of the state of Washington, is an example of these limitations. It provided:

The right of taking fish, at all usual and accustomed grounds and stations, is further secured to said Indians in common with all citizens of the Territory, and of erecting temporary houses for the purpose of curing, together with the privilege of hunting, gathering roots and berries, and pasturing horses on open and unclaimed

lands: Provided, however, that they shall not
take shellfish from any beds staked or cultivated
by citizens, and that they shall alter all stallions
not intended for breeding-horses, and shall keep
up and confine the latter.

The above passage is a self-operating article of a
treaty. It requires no positive action on behalf of Congress to be immediately effective. As such, it is the
supreme law of the land under the interpretation
given to treaties by the Constitution. The major difficulty Indians face is getting the United States to
respect these articles which require only the good
faith of the United States.

The relationship of Indian tribes to the United
States in a constitutional sense is twofold. Congress
has the power to regulate commerce with the Indian
tribes. This power must recognize the status of Indian tribes as "higher than states" if it is to be effective. It is presently ineffective because the United
States does not uphold its part of the relationship.
The United States insists on emphasizing the "dependent" aspect of the domestic-nation status, and
interprets this phrase to mean the total incapability
of Indian people to govern themselves. By insisting
on this overly protective stance in its administration
of Indian Affairs, the United States has created for
itself continual financial liabilities. Federal employees
have frequently squandered Indian natural and
financial resources under the guise of "trusteeship,"
and the courts have awarded tribes in excess of $100
million in damages for their losses.

The other aspect of the constitutional relationship
is the vesting of rights in the Indian tribes under the
Constitution through the ratification of Indian treaties and their subsequent elevation to the status of
supreme law of the land. The violations of this

principle have characterized the recent history of federal policy, and have wreaked untold havoc on Indian communities. Various articles of the treaties which are self-operating should be recognized in federal and state law as valid because of their ratification by the Senate. Yet the tendency of the federal and state governments has been to quibble about the interpretation of the articles, or to pretend that the mere passage of time and changing of conditions is sufficient to invalidate them.

The contemporary recognition of Indian tribes as an international protectorate in line with the thinking of the *Cherokee Nation* case and as reconciled by the holding of the *Native American Church* case would clarify the status of Indian tribes and eliminate the inconsistencies that are presently found in the federal relationship with Indians. The history of litigation in the field of Indian law indicates that the United States claims its guardianship primarily when it is beneficial to its interests and acknowledges the protectorate status only when it is convenient to do so. The injustice presently existing in the field of Indian affairs comes from the continual fluctuation of policy and practice between these two conflicting interpretations of the status of the tribes.

A strict construction of the constitutional relationship between Indian tribes and the United States might result in a large reduction in services owed to the Indian tribes and their members. On the other hand, it would undoubtedly free the tribes from the many inconsistent and onerous interpretations of the relationship which presently hinder tribal progress and result in the wasteful use of tribal assets. Considering the many lawsuits that have been filed against the United States for its inept management of Indian assets, the determination of a distinct status of the tribes as advocated by the development of the concept of an international protectorate should be considered.

The major argument of the United States, as articulated in the courts, is that Congress has a plenary power over the property of the Indian tribes. But, as we have already seen, this power is asserted against the nations of Europe under the doctrine of discovery in relation to the land holdings of Indians. It is not a power to be properly asserted against the tribes themselves in a political sense. The Constitution of the United States already has adequate provisions for recognizing the Indian tribes' special international status. The major areas in which the Constitution of the United States has been applied to the special rights of the Indian tribes all have major doctrines which support the recognition of the distinct national character of the tribes rather than the plenary powers of the Congress.

8. The Size and Status of Nations

The proposal to restore the Indian tribes to a status of quasi-international independence with the United States acting as their protector strikes most Americans as either radical or ridiculous. In fact, it is neither. The standard objections raised by non-Indians to a fully sovereign status for tribes are generally based upon a misunderstanding of the concept of sovereignty in modern international law and practice, and on a misconception of Indian eligibility for this status because of their previous relationship with the United States government.

Some say that the land areas presently possessed by Indians are too small to qualify as areas over which sovereignty can be exercised. Still others, accepting the small land area, argue that the United States totally surrounds the respective reservations, in effect locking the tribes into its political and economic system whether they wish it or not. The fact that the tribes have a very small population in comparison with other independent states is often pointed out as a reason why the tribes should not have international status.

The tribes' lack of an independent economic base

presently helps to justify the massive federal expenditures which the government yearly makes available to Indian tribes. It is apparent that for the immediate future the United States will have to continue to appropriate large sums of money to keep the reservation people employed and to provide services for them. Can the tribes, people wonder, maintain any form of economic enterprise without the expenditures of the federal government? Would not independence in a political sense doom those programs now operating on the reservations which show some promise of succeeding? And, finally, the fact remains that many tribes lack sufficient education to succeed in the modern industrial society of the United States.

With all of these factors combining to create a tremendous pocket of poverty on each reservation, many non-Indians feel that the present movement to create an international status for the tribes is foolhardy, that the political and social basis for Indian tribal existence would vanish if the tribes were left to go it alone, and that the whole idea is un-American in some fundamental but ill-defined way.

Indians are not seeking a type of independence which would create a totally isolated community with no ties to the United States whatsoever. On the contrary, the movement of today seeks to establish clear and uncontroverted lines of political authority and responsibility for both the tribal governments and the United States so as to prevent the types of errors and maladministration which presently mark the Indian scene.

The assumption of many non-Indians is that independence of a nation implies that it stands in the same position as does the United States toward the rest of the nations of the world. People visualize a standing army, a massive import-export business, tariffs, gigantic administrative bureaucracies, international intrigue, and the ability to wage wars on distant nations with relative impunity. Such indeed are the characteristics of a superpower, but not of the average nation which has recognition as a self-governing community with inherent rights to its own existence. We shall take these objections in order and show that the status suggested for the Indian tribes today is well within the present nature of national existence as practiced by the other nations of the world.

The first of these objections, that of too small a land area, is perhaps the most common, and clearly the most mistaken. The concept of sovereignty has never attached exclusively to large land areas. Geographically, small nations have existed and been recognized in Europe since the city-states of Greece. Throughout the period following the collapse of the Roman Empire, various small European kingdoms and principalities functioned as sovereign states, entering fully into the political life of that highly volatile continent. To be sure, many of the small nations suffered because of their size and were swallowed up into larger aggregate nation-states. But some small states have survived the vicissitudes of history and continued to function as sovereign, independent nations down to the present day. Belgium, Denmark, The Netherlands, and Luxembourg are all smaller than the Navajo Reservation, yet they have each enjoyed sovereign independence for over a hundred years, and they were each founding members of the United Nations and the North Atlantic Treaty Organization (N.A.T.O.). Five non-European nations (Costa Rica, the Dominican Republic, El Salvador, Haiti, and Lebanon), all smaller than the Navajo Reservation, have enjoyed long-standing international recognition and were also founding members of the U.N. Within Europe, there are five minuscule states (Andorra, Liechtenstein, Monaco, San Marino, and Vatican City) that have survived for centuries as largely autonomous sovereign entities, even though the largest of them is only 179 square miles in size and all are completely surrounded by other countries. Because of both their small size and their interesting political relationships with neighboring countries, we will return to examine these states later for precedents for a sovereign status for American Indian tribes.

The existence of very small independent nations is not, of course, an anachronistic historical development no longer considered acceptable as a basis for emerging countries. On the contrary: Since the end of World War II, the worldwide movement toward decolonization has produced a host of new small nations which have come to enjoy full status in international relations, including that most coveted token of modern sovereignty, membership in the United Nations. Barbados, for example, became independent in 1966 and joined the United Nations, yet it is smaller than fifty American Indian reservations and has a population of only 240,000. Geographically, it is comparable in size to the Chippewa-Cree Reservation at Rocky Boys, Montana, or the Kaibab Paiute Reservation in Arizona, north of the Grand Canyon.

From a more political point of view, even more startling examples can be found. Simply by taking the land area of the four largest Sioux reservations in South Dakota (Standing Rock, Cheyenne River, Rosebud, and Pine Ridge), a geographically larger nation could be created than Israel (which has been a sovereign country since 1948 and a member of the U.N. since 1949). If the United States can participate in the creation of Israel as a national homeland for the Jews in partial compensation for the genocide committed against them by Hitler during the Second

World War, why is the United States incapable of recognizing the Sioux Nation as sovereign over its lands in South Dakota in partial compensation for the genocide committed against it at Wounded Knee and other massacres?

A recent study of the entire question of Indian lands by Kirke Kickingbird and Karen Ducheneaux (*One Hundred Million Acres*, Macmillan Publishing Co., 1973) concludes that Indians have a reasonable and legitimate contemporary claim to that much land. The magnitude of total land potentially available for Indian possession gives the sovereignty question a completely different complexion. With land on this scale, no one can seriously challenge a return to Indian sovereignty on the basis of geographic arguments alone.

What emerges clearly from this review of the relationship of land area to sovereignty is that even tiny political entities have achieved international recognition and function as modern states. Small land area simply is not a valid argument for restricting the Indian tribes from returning to that sovereign status they once enjoyed in relation to the United States. The following table shows forty nations with land areas smaller than the Navajo Reservation, thirty of which are full members of the United Nations. It illustrates plainly how land area per se has become irrelevant as a consideration for the achievement of sovereign status in today's world.

The discussion of the land question so far has focused on total size for sovereign recognition. A related concern of many people is that the granting of sovereignty to the Indians for their tribal reservation lands is impossible because practically all of those reservations are totally landlocked and completely surrounded by the United States. To some degree this is a political-legal misunderstanding of what a

Nation	Square Miles	Indian Tribe	Square Miles
1. Costa Rica	19,575	Navajo	21,838
2. Dominican Republic	18,816		
3. Bhutan	18,147		
4. Denmark	16,619		
5. Switzerland	15,941		
6. Netherlands	14,125		
7. Taiwan	13,886		
8. Belgium	11,781		
9. Lesotho	11,716		
10. Albania	11,100		
11. Equatorial Guinea	10,852		
12. Burundi	10,747		
13. Haiti	10,714		
14. Rwanda	10,166		
15. El Salvador	8,260		
16. Israel	7,993		
17. Fiji	7,055		
18. Swaziland	6,704		
19. Kuwait	6,178		
20. Qatar	6,000		
		Papago	4,460
21. Jamaica	4,411		
22. Lebanon	4,015		
23. Gambia	4,005		
		Hopi	3,862
24. Cyprus	3,572		
		Wind River Tribes	2,947
		White Mountain Apache	2,898
		San Carlos Apache	2,855
		Pine Ridge Sioux	2,600
		Crow Tribe	2,434
		Cheyenne River Sioux	2,210

Nation	Square Miles	Indian Tribe	Square Miles
25. Trinidad and Tobago	1,979		
		Yakima Tribe	1,711
		Uintah and Ouray	1,581
		Colville Tribe	1,569
		Hualapai Tribe	1,551
		Fort Peck Sioux	1,534
		Rosebud Sioux	1,526
		Blackfeet Tribe	1,420
		Standing Rock Sioux	1,320
		Jicarilla Apache Tribe	1,159
26. Western Samoa	1,130		
		Fort Belknap	1,027
27. Luxembourg	999		
		Flathead Tribe	960
		Ute Mountain Ute	917
		Red Lake Chippewa	882
		Warm Springs Tribe	881
		Fort Hall Shoshone	817
		Pyramid Lake Paiute	742
28. Mauritius	720		
		Mescalero Apache	719
		Northern Cheyenne	678
		Laguna Pueblo	652
		Fort Berthold	651
		Zuni Pueblo	636
		Sisseston	629
		Pima	582
		Walker River	500

Nation	Square Miles	Indian Tribe	Square Miles
		Duck Valley	452
		Kiowa, Comanche, Apache	370
		Osage	340
		Spokane	300
29. Tonga	269		
30. Bahrain	231		
31. Singapore	226		
		Quinault	200
		Kaibab Piute	188
32. Andorra	179		
33. Barbados	166		
		Rocky Boys Chippewa-Cree	162
		Nez Perce	137
		Hoopa Valley	134
34. Malta	122		
35. Maldives	112		
		Coeur d'Alene	108
36. Liechtenstein	62		
37. San Marino	23.5		
38. Nauru	8		
39. Monaco	.6		
40. Vatican City	.17		

sovereign status would imply for the Indian tribes, but let us leave that for later and focus only on the geographic problem for now.

Technically speaking, in terms of international law, sovereign Indian tribes within the United States would be enclaves. Such independent entities have a long history of acceptance in international diplomatic practice, even though at times the states in question have had difficulty maintaining their independence. Enclaves are to be distinguished from countries which are simply landlocked. At the present time, more than twenty countries with no outlet to the open seas function as independent states in the world. Some, like Austria, Switzerland, Hungary, Bolivia, and Paraguay, have had a long history of independent existence, while others, like Zambia, Mali, and Chad, have achieved independence only recently. They exist on every continent except North America, but differ from true enclaves in that they have borders with several neighboring countries. Currently functioning sovereign states which are total enclaves include Lesotho, which is surrounded by South Africa; San Marino and Vatican City, which are islands in the Italian state; Singapore, which is enclosed by Malaysia; Monaco, which is embedded in the French Riviera; and Gambia, which is surrounded by Senegal. All are surrounded, but each retains sovereign control of its affairs and its destiny. The fact that Indian lands are dotted across the map of America can thus be no excuse for not considering the restoration of sovereign status, if international practice is the determining factor.

A perhaps more substantial objection to the granting of sovereignty is that the Indian tribes are too small in terms of population to be able to function in an independent status. Indeed, many people reject the argument that small territory is irrelevant to sovereign status by pointing out that countries like Belgium and The Netherlands, while geographically small, have populations of 10 and 14 million respectively. It is true, of course, that in a comparative sense, American Indian tribes are much smaller than many geographically small countries around the world. But not all. The 1970 U.S. census (which probably undercounted Indians by as much as 10 to 15 per cent) showed a total population of 791,839, of whom 588,000 live on or near federal reservations. The larger tribal populations are: Navajo (131,000), Lumbee (45,000), Sioux (32,000), Pueblo

(26,000), Cherokee (21,000), Creek (15,000), Choctaw (10,000).

An examination of the population statistics for the world's small countries as shown in the following table reveals some startling facts. Seven sovereign

Countries with Fewer than 1,000,000 Population

1.	Vatican City	1,000
2.	Nauru	7,000
3.	San Marino	20,000
4.	Andorra	20,550
5.	Liechtenstein	21,550
6.	Monaco	23,000
7.	Tonga	90,000
8.	Maldives	110,000
9.	Qatar	115,000
10.	Western Samoa	146,000
11.	United Arab Emirates	200,000
12.	Sikkim	200,000
13.	Iceland	210,000
14.	Bahrain	220,000
15.	Barbados	240,000
16.	Equatorial Guinea	290,000
17.	Malta	330,000
18.	Luxembourg	340,000
19.	Gambia	380,000
20.	Swaziland	420,000
21.	Gabon	500,000
22.	Fiji	533,000
23.	Cyprus	640,000
24.	Botswana	670,000
25.	Oman	680,000
26.	Guyana	740,000
27.	Kuwait	830,000
28.	Mauritius	840,000
29.	Lesotho	930,000
30.	Congo (Brazzaville)	960,000

states have fewer than 100,000 population, 20 have fewer than 500,000 and 30 have less than 1,000,000.

The table reveals that some of the American tribes can quite easily compete in terms of population as a claim to sovereign status. The Navajo tribe is larger than the first nine countries listed in the table, with a population approximately the size of Western Samoa. It is 145 times larger than Vatican City, to which the United States Government accredits an ambassador.

As interesting as straightforward comparisons of this kind may be, they ignore the fundamental differences in condition between the American Indian tribes and most of the world's small countries. The 1970 census revealed that the Indian population of the U.S. had finally begun to make a statistical recovery from the decimation of the previous century. In the decade of 1960 the Indian population grew by over 50 per cent. But in the previous hundred years the Indian tribal population had failed to grow at anything like a normal rate, owing to the cumulative ravages of war, disease, poverty, and emigration. Indeed, in the period from 1890, when the first official U.S. census of Indians was taken, to 1920, the recognized Indian population in America actually was decreasing and reached an all-time low of 244,000.

But what is the significance of population size to a claim for sovereignty? The preceding table shows that even very small populations have achieved independence as nations in the world. The notion that a country needs a given minimum of population to assure its security and economic self-sufficiency is clearly outmoded. The survival of nations and world peace no longer depends on the ability of each country to mount an army or navy large enough to secure it against all potential aggressors. In today's world that is plainly impossible for all but a few nations. In an absolute sense, the United States or the Soviet Union can, with their nuclear weapons, threaten the security of any other country in the world. So security in the modern world is no longer a simple function of a national defense capability. It is more and more a function of alliances, diplomacy, arms control, international understanding, and good will. Small, weak nations, which exist in abundance in the world today, have no choice but to rely on their ability to stay out of the affairs of the major powers and seek peaceful solutions to those issues which affect them directly.

The world's attitude toward large populations has also undergone profound changes in the last two decades. We have come to understand that not only are large populations not an absolute guarantee of security, but they can also pose enormous obstacles to economic development and national well-being, as India and China have learned. Thus, the accepted attitudes toward population growth and large families have been completely reversed. Now, throughout the developing world, and in many of the small countries, there is a strong emphasis on population limitation and birth control. Thus, the argument against Indian sovereignty on the ground of small population lacks real credibility in the world today. It may be an excuse for an unwilling government, but it is not a valid reason.

The argument that the tribes are not economically self-sufficient units and therefore cannot function as sovereign entities like other nations also lacks credibility. This becomes vividly apparent when we examine both the current economic condition of various countries and the record of U.S. economic support to struggling nations in every part of the globe over the past twenty-five years. The idea (known as *autarky*) that a nation must be totally economically self-sufficient has been completely discredited in international economic theory and practice. No nation has all the resources, production capability, know-how, and capital to be entirely economically self-reliant, and even if it did, there is a strong economic advantage to specializing in the production of certain items at lower cost and trading with other countries that also specialize in products which they can make at lower cost. This concept underlies the whole international economic system today. Total self-sufficiency is neither feasible nor desirable. Countries like Japan and the United Kingdom rely on trade for 10 per cent or more of their gross national product.

If economic strength is the criterion for sovereignty, then most of the countries of the developing world would never have qualified in the first place. Indonesia requires over $800 million in foreign assistance every year just to maintain the stability of her economy. For India, the figure is over one billion dollars. With the exception of the oil-rich Middle East, most of the Third World nations require either direct grant assistance from the industrial nations to support their economies and continue their development or long-term credits to finance the continued flow of import commodities necessary to maintain their international financial solvency.

The United States government has, of course, been the largest single contributor since World War II in these international assistance efforts. Senator J. William Fulbright, in a recent speech on the floor of the U.S. Senate, pointed out that, since the end of the Second World War, the U.S. has provided *$180 billion* in assistance to foreign countries, $80 billion of it in various forms of military assistance! U.S. Marshall Plan aid to European recovery in the three-

year period of 1947–1950 alone amounted to over
$12 billion. In fiscal year 1973, the U.S. spent over
$2.5 billion in military and developmental foreign
aid. It has been, in fact, the long-term willingness of
the United States, and more recently of some of the
other countries, to make these major continuing
financial contributions that has made sovereign independence economically feasible for the majority
of the smaller developing nations.

It is entirely reasonable, therefore, to consider a
form of sovereignty for American Indian tribes in
which the United States government would continue
to provide necessary economic assistance. The $582
million which the federal government spent on Indians through the B.I.A. in 1973 does not, of course,
compare with the sums we continue to appropriate
for foreign aid. But the time has clearly come when
we must consider whether it is just to neglect a significant population residing within the borders of
the United States while we continue to pour such
huge sums into assistance to peoples of far less interest to us in the four corners of the world.

Compounding the problem is the B.I.A. system,
through which Indian funds are administered. It
amounts to nothing more than a system of domestic
colonialism which demeans the Indian recipients and
perpetuates the abusive psychological frame of reference within which the federal government has dealt
with Indians for nearly two hundred years. Apart
from the question of land control, the most urgent
arguments for restoring Indian sovereignty as the
basis for future Indian-U.S. relations are in the
economic area. In no other way can dignity, mutual
respect, equity, justice, and, perhaps, one day, trust
be returned to the relationship between Indians and
non-Indians on this continent.

The last refuge of those who would continue to

keep the tribes in a condition of dependence vis-à-vis the U.S. is the argument that the Indians have neither the education nor the sophistication to manage their own affairs and shape their destiny. One finds this mentality for the most part throughout the Bureau of Indian Affairs administrative apparatus, which controls the lives of Indians in such excruciating detail. These people, of course, have a heavy vested interest in the preservation of the tutelary parent-child concept of the B.I.A.-Indian relationship. But on any kind of comparative educational basis, the Indians of America are far better qualified for sovereignty than many, if not most, of the nations of the Third World that have achieved independence in the past twenty years.

While literacy among Indians is far from universal, it is still high by international standards—about 15 per cent. Literacy in India is only 28 per cent; in Egypt, 25 per cent, and in Pakistan, 19 per cent; in Indonesia and Nigeria, 15 per cent; in Saudi Arabia, Afghanistan, and Ethiopia, 5 per cent. All of these are large independent nations, fully self-governing, and recognized in the international system. Many of the small nations with low literacy rates have also achieved independence. In Haiti literacy is only about 11 per cent; in Burundi, 10 per cent; in El Salvador (independent for over 100 years), 42 per cent; in the Dominican Republic, 43 per cent. Literacy rates have thus been ignored in international practice as a criterion for sovereignty.

More important perhaps than current literacy is school enrollment as an indicator of the future educational-achievement level and basis for intelligent self-government. B.I.A. reported that in fiscal year 1972, 92.5 per cent of all Indian children between the ages of 5 and 18 were enrolled in school, a level comparable with that of most West European nations and far higher than the standard of the developing countries of the Third World. The argument against Indian sovereignty on educational grounds, therefore, falls on its own weight. Like the other arguments, it is simply an excuse for those who wish to see no change in the Indian's dependent status in American society.

We have now dealt with the major arguments against restoring a status of sovereignty to the Indian tribes and reestablishing a U.S. Federal Government-Indian relationship on that basis, and shown that in each case the argument against sovereignty is without solid foundation in contemporary international practice. But how do small states exist and survive in today's world? What form does their sovereignty take? What kinds of relationships do they develop with their contiguous, or proximate larger nation neighbors? In the remainder of this chapter, we will examine these questions and try to draw conclusions for the kinds of Indian-U.S. relationships that might be most feasible.

The oldest independent states we have dealt with in this chapter are the mini-states of Europe: Monaco, Andorra, Liechtenstein, San Marino, and Vatican City. Each exists in substantial sovereign independence, yet each has also negotiated certain agreements, understandings, and treaties with its larger neighbors. These larger countries have been willing to fully recognize the small states as sovereign entities and contract with them on specific issues, an example the United States might well examine when deciding how to deal with the Indian demand for sovereignty. Once a dependency of Austria, Liechtenstein declared its full independence in 1918 and in 1920 negotiated a treaty with Switzerland under which the latter assumed responsibility for posts and telegraphs, customs, and foreign affairs for the small principality.

Andorra has enjoyed nearly seven centuries of sovereign independence by jointly recognizing the French chief of state and the Catholic bishop of Urgel as co-princes. Monaco, which enjoys substantial independence, has at times feuded with France but today enjoys a comfortable relationship covered by a variety of formally negotiated agreements. San Marino and Vatican City, both with ancient claims to independent sovereignty, have each negotiated formal treaties with the modern Italian state guaranteeing their independence and mutual friendship and covering various aspects of their relationship. Because of the importance of Catholicism in Italy, the Lateran Treaty on the status of Vatican City (originally negotiated in 1929) was actually incorporated into the new constitution of Italy in 1947.

As can be seen in the cases of these small old European states, a sovereign country is perfectly free to contract with a neighbor for the transfer of certain governmental functions without prejudice to its status. If we can judge from this European experience, the fairness and equity of those relationships is far greater than anything ever enjoyed by Europe's colonies around the world—and probably the best current analogy for the U.S. relationship to the Indian tribes.

Examples of this kind of "contractual sovereignty" are, of course, not confined to Europe. The Himalayan kingdoms of Sikkim and Bhutan also have developed more or less close contractual governmental relationships with India. Bhutan, the larger of the two, enjoys reasonably full sovereignty, including membership in the U.N., but under the terms of a 1949 treaty India guides its foreign policy in exchange for guaranteed access to the sea and an Indian subsidy. Here, plainly, is a precedent of serious interest to the question of American Indian sovereignty, because it includes a contractual agreement with another government for economic assistance in exchange for control of foreign policy. Sikkim, the smaller of the two areas, has a far more intimate relationship with India. Throughout the nineteenth century, Sikkim existed as a protectorate, a form of dependent status of which the British made extensive use during their colonial period. In 1950, following India's independence, Sikkim ended its connection with the U.K. and negotiated a new protectorate arrangement with India. Under the terms of this agreement, India not only handles defense and foreign affairs but also has a right to intervene in Sikkim's internal government.

Great Britain adopted the protectorate concept in a great many of its possessions around the globe in the nineteenth century because, unlike a colony, a protectorate was a negotiated arrangement with traditional local or tribal leaders which gave the British suzerainty, particularly in external affairs, but did not supplant the traditional leaders. The British tended to negotiate such arrangements in areas with small populations or territory which they did not want to have to garrison heavily but over which they did want control for strategic reasons. Examples of British protectorates, most of which are now independent, include Aden, Bahrain, Qatar, the Trucial States, Brunei, Somaliland, Swaziland, Tonga, and the Solomon Islands.

Following World War I, when the League of Nations was established, a problem arose as to the disposition of the former German and Turkish colonies in Africa, the Middle East and Asia. The League decided to establish a system of mandates. Control of the former German colonies and other areas was given to various countries under mandates from the League, to which they were responsible for the administration of the territory and the social and political development of its population. In Africa, the former German colonies of Tanganyika and Togoland were mandated to the U.K., Ruanda-Urundi went to Belgium, the Cameroons to France, and Southwest Africa to South Africa. In the Middle East, the U.K. was placed in charge of Palestine, from which a separate sub-unit of Trans-Jordan was created in 1922. France took over the former Turkish possessions of Lebanon and Syria, and the U.K. was granted the mandate for Iraq in order to shore up her position in the Persian Gulf. In the Pacific, New Guinea and Nauru were mandated to Australia, Western Samoa and the Cook Islands to New Zealand, and all of the German possessions in Micronesia to Japan.

While the mandate concept that countries were internationally accountable for how they administered overseas territorial possessions was a distinct step forward in international law and benefited the mandated people, none of the mandate powers made serious efforts to develop local self-government or move these territories toward independence before World War II. As a practical matter, the administering powers looked on their mandates in much the way they did other overseas possessions, as territory granted to them in recognition of their war efforts and their big-power status, and which they were largely free to use to their own best interest.

When the United Nations was set up after the Second World War, the League of Nations' mandate system was transferred to the U.N. under the Trusteeship Council. The mandate countries of the Middle East all achieved independence before, during, or just after the war (Iraq, 1932; Syria, 1944; Israel and Jordan, 1948) and so did not fall under the new system. In almost all other instances, mandate powers simply became Trust powers under the U.N.

for the territories they had held previously under the League. The two major exceptions were Japan, whose Pacific islands of Micronesia were confiscated and given to the United States as a Trust Territory, and South Africa, which refused to recognize the U.N.'s authority and incorporated Southwest Africa into the South African Republic, against the will of its black-majority population.

An important innovation of the U.N. Trust system was the explicit adoption of the goal of eventual self-government and/or independence for all Trust Territories. In fulfilling that goal, the system has been remarkably effective, and another indication that granting sovereignty is now feasible in a very flexible range of circumstances. Indeed, the only remaining U.N. Trust Territories are the Micronesian Islands, administered by the U.S. but currently negotiating for a permanent self-governing, quasi-independent status. Trust-administering countries granted independence to Togoland and the Cameroons in 1960, Tanganyika (now Tanzania) in 1961, Western Samoa in 1962, and Ruanda-Urundi (which became the two countries of Burundi and Rwanda) in 1962. All are now members of the United Nations. In 1968, the Island of Nauru became independent; it retains a close political relationship with Australia. The Cook Islands, a former New Zealand Trust, became self-governing in 1965, with New Zealand retaining responsibility for defense and foreign affairs and providing economic assistance. Papua–New Guinea, formerly administered by Australia, achieved independence in 1975.

Apart from the case of Southwest Africa, which has been the subject of intensive U.N. debate over the years and several cases at the International Court of Justice, the largest remaining Trust issue is the future of the Pacific island territories administered by the United States. The U.S. has taken the position that because it has an incorporated state in the mid-Pacific (Hawaii), the Trust islands farther to the west are of strategic importance to its defense. For that reason, it has been reluctant to enter into negotiations with the islanders for independence or even total self-government. One of the major concerns of the American government has been that a totally self-governing or independent Trust Territory of the Pacific Islands (T.T.P.I.) would require the sacrifice of the U.S. right of eminent domain; it regards as essential the ability to confiscate land for military purposes in the future (much as it does where Indian lands are concerned). However, under pressure from the United Nations and the Micronesian legislature, the U.S. finally agreed to start negotiations on the future status of the islands in 1970. These negotiations have proceeded through several formal rounds with long adjournments between them, and no final resolution is currently in sight.

Several concepts of serious interest to the question of future Indian status under the United States have been discussed by the Micronesians. However, the apparent divisions among the islanders themselves, not unlike some of the internal disputes of the American Indian community, have prevented them from uniting on a single approach. One group, apparently a minority, favors complete independence. A larger element appears to favor a concept of "free association" with the U.S., which would put future relations on a time-limited but renewable contractual basis. In general terms, this approach would give the islanders total internal self-government and would confer responsibility for defense and foreign affairs on the U.S., with the U.S. providing a fixed annual financial subsidy in exchange for access to a limited amount of Micronesian land for military purposes.

The whole agreement would have a fixed time limit, and the Micronesians could in the future opt for total independence if they chose. Further complicating the negotiations is the fact that the northern islands, the Marianas, are interested in a much more intimate relationship with the U.S., perhaps something like the commonwealth status Puerto Rico enjoys.

The U.S. government has apparently found the concept of "free association," which might serve as a useful model for future Indian sovereignty, sufficiently uncomfortable that it has sought to divide the islanders by negotiating separately with the Mariana Islands for some type of more integrated status, while putting off negotiations with the remainder of the T.T.P.I. until the status of the northern islands is settled. Whether these divide-and-conquer techniques will succeed remains to be seen, but Indian proponents of a sovereign status would do well to study carefully the ideas of the Micronesian negotiators. In this connection, it is interesting to note that in preparing for their negotiations with the federal government, the advisers to the Micronesian delegation apparently reviewed the entire history of the U.S.-Indian relations and negotiations so as to avoid falling prey to the U.S. government in the same way.

Before leaving this discussion of U.S. territorial possessions, it is worth noting that besides the Micronesians and the Indians, there are other peoples and territories under various types of U.S. administration well short of statehood. Puerto Rico is, of course, the largest, and enjoys clearly the optimum relationship. As a commonwealth, Puerto Rico is totally self-governing; its population has U.S. citizenship and is free to migrate to the U.S. without quota. Puerto Rico has non-voting representation in Congress, but Puerto Ricans do not vote for President unless they reside in the continental U.S.

Other territories with significant populations which, like the Indians, also come under the wardship of the Interior Department are the Virgin Islands, Guam, and American Samoa. Each is ruled by an American governor appointed by the President but does have a local legislature. Residents of these islands are American citizens but cannot vote for President. It is important to note that none of these areas has formal Territorial status. That status was created originally by the U.S. government as a preparatory phase for newly acquired land which, it was expected, would one day achieve statehood. Obviously, statehood is no longer available for the remaining dependent peoples. What should be observed, however, is that the U.S. federal government has enormous flexibility where questions of status for people and territory are concerned, and those who argue against Indian sovereignty on the grounds that there is no precedent for it in U.S. policy are simply ignoring the flexibility available to the federal government in this area.

One further case must be considered before completing this review of the law and practice of sovereignty in international relations and its relevance to the Indian status question: Israel. Israel's achievement of independence, the international recognition of her sovereignty, and her membership in the United Nations are a dramatic vindication of the validity of traditional, historic claims to specific territory as the sovereign heritage of a particular people. Israel's victory is a great tribute to the strength of a culture and the tenacity of a people in pursuit of a homeland. Expelled from Palestine in the second century A.D., the Jewish Diaspora lasted nearly two millennia before dedicated men began the systematic attempt to recover their ancestral home. The Zionist movement, begun in the nineteenth century, saw its first real success in the British Balfour Declaration of 1917, which acknowledged the right of Jews to settle in Palestine.

The influx of Jews from Europe was slow but steady in the 1920s and 1930s, and a solid political foundation was laid in a functioning Jewish community with the old British mandate of Palestine. Hitler's reign of terror against Jews in Europe during World War II shocked a formerly comfortable and complacent people into the recognition that creating a strong Jewish nation was the only secure future for the Jewish people. The destitute survivors of the horrors of Hitler's concentration camps streamed to Israel in the late 1940s. No longer content to leave their fate in the hands of other people, the Jews in Israel began an insurrection against the British administration to achieve political control of their own lives.

Under strong Jewish pressure within Palestine, and with strong U.S. and international support, Great Britain persuaded the U.N. in 1947 to create separate, independent states for Jews and Arabs. On May 15, 1948, the British withdrew their troops from Palestine and the state of Israel came into formal existence on the land their ancestors had first settled over 3,000 years before. The Arab governments immediately launched attacks on the fledgling nation, but the Israelis rose to their own defense and protected the territorial birthright it had taken them centuries to recover. With the defeat of the Arab armies, the new nation had a stronger claim to life, and in May 1949 was admitted to the United Nations. Since then, of course, Israel has had to fight two more wars to secure its claim to sovereignty, but today is a strong and fiercely independent member of the international community.

The role of the United States in the birth of Israel must not be ignored, because if the U.S. can recognize the historic claim of a specific people to land in the Middle East, there is no reason in fact or logic for it to continue to ignore the claim of the native Americans to territorial sovereignty over a small portion of their historic land. In the years following the end of World War II, President Truman took a particular interest in the plight of the Jews in Europe and put international pressure on Britain to permit greater immigration of Jews to Palestine. In close touch with Jewish leaders in the U.S., he strongly backed the creation of a Jewish state, and the U.S. was among the first to recognize the new state of Israel, in spite of Arab legal claims that the Jews had no current right to the land of Palestine. Since then, of course, the U.S. has become Israel's strongest ally and her major source of military aid. The U.S. has backed her position in the Middle East against the Soviet support for the Arabs. If the U.S. is capable of recognizing Jewish rights to sovereign land in Israel, it must be capable of acknowledging a similar right for American Indians in the U.S.

Having reviewed international law and practice where the concept of sovereignty is concerned, what conclusions can be drawn about the Indian demand for a sovereign status as a basis for their future relations with the United States? First, there is no reason for rejecting such a demand on the grounds of inadequate Indian land, since many geographically minuscule nations function with full sovereignty and international recognition in the contemporary world. Second, the fact that most Indian lands are almost totally landlocked by the United States is not a valid argument against Indian sovereignty, because the same precedent has been set through international practice. Third, the population size of many Indian tribes equals or exceeds those of some small nations of the world and is adequate for a sovereign status. Fourth, economic deficiencies should not discredit the Indian claim to sovereignty, given the low standard in the independent Third World and the fact that continuing U.S. assistance can be a formally negotiated part of any sovereignty agreement. Fifth, insufficient educational levels used as an argument to prove that Indians should not totally govern themselves will not withstand the test of international practice; indeed, American Indians have a higher literacy rate than many of the Third World countries. Finally, in the world today sovereignty permits an abundance of different forms of relative dependence or independence, any of which could be available as a model for a future U.S. Government–Indian relationship. Therefore, the proposal advanced in this book and by other Indian spokesmen for a return to the sovereign relationship of the early nineteenth century has every justification from an international point of view.

9. The Indian Reorganization Act

The Wounded Knee protest brought sharply into focus a century-long controversy over the nature of tribal governments. Wounded Knee basically pitted the assimilationist and mixed-blood Indians of the Pine Ridge village against the traditional fullbloods who lived in the back country of the reservation. The 1868 treaty appeared to many traditionalists as symbolic of the status which the tribe had lost through bureaucratic betrayal. They saw as symptomatic of their loss of sovereignty the adoption of the Indian Reorganization Act of 1934, under which the present tribal government is organized. Many regarded the establishment of the present government as the ultimate violation of the treaty.

The Indian Reorganization Act (or Wheeler-Howard Act) of 1934 was perhaps the most fundamental and far-reaching piece of legislation passed by Congress in this century. It has, at the same time, proven to be the piece of legislation most frequently misunderstood, more often subverted by the bureaucracy, and most subject to criticism by the succession of Congresses. Some traditional Indians have charged that by adopting the I.R.A. many tribes voluntarily limited their sovereignty, thereby surrendering their aboriginal status as nations in favor of a quasi-corporate status which the United States refused to recognize anyway. In order to get a perspective on the I.R.A., one must understand the nature of life during the early reservation days.

By the beginning of the 1880s, intense pressure was growing in Congress for a further division of tribal lands in order to release more lands for white settlement. The Indian wars left the more powerful tribes with large reserves, which non-Indians considered a permanent block to further growth of the western states. The Sioux, for example, owned western South Dakota. The Kiowa-Comanche-Apache coalition, along with the Cheyennes and Arapahos, owned western Oklahoma. The Blackfeet and Flatheads controlled most of western Montana, and the Crows owned a substantial portion of southern Montana. Railroads needed rights-of-way to cross the continent. They sought not only land for their tracks but additional lands to encourage settlement along their lines and insure an adequate supply of farmers and ranchers to use their railroads to ship agricultural produce to the two coasts.

Immigrants were recruited by the railroads in the West in order to insure settlement of farmlands along the major roads. It was partially through the sale of land to these settlers that some railroad magnates planned to keep their lines financially solvent. James Hill of the Great Northern, for example, badly needed to develop settlements in the very sparsely populated northern states. In the Oklahoma Territory the Indian lands were surrounded by whites who wished to get the last piece of unsettled frontier under cultivation. The various groups of "Boomers" and "Sooners" in the territory agitated continually for the division of the large tribal estates and the opening of more land for homesteads.

Coupled with the desire for new lands was the equally adamant demand of the Christian churches for the breakup of the "tribal mass" through allotment. Missionaries had visited nearly every tribe, and in many of the remote tribes they discovered a relative immunity to their overtures in the religious field. The custom in most tribes of living in small groups or bands within the large reserved areas meant that the religious traditions of the tribes were being preserved through community religious ceremonies. Siphoning off a few converts for the little missions became a difficult task for the missionaries. They demanded that the reservations be divided into allotments according to the number of individuals in the tribe. In that way, the community groups would be destroyed and each family would be isolated from the rest of the tribe, and so, theoretically, vulnerable to conversion efforts.

The result of this pressure was the passage of the General Allotment Act of 1887, which gave the President the authority to make agreements with the tribes for the allotment of their lands and the purchase of the "surplus" by the United States. The sponsors of the bill visualized a period of relative calm as the tribes deliberated on the inevitability and necessity of changing from hunting to farming and agreed to allotment. But the executive branch, which always seems to pay its political debts with Indian resources, pushed the policy on the tribes as rapidly as possible. Tribes were forced to agree to land cessions almost continually from the 1890s to the 1920s, and soon nearly all the tribes had been approached on the allotment question, with only a handful successfully rejecting it outright.

In 1891, after four years of operation, the General Allotment Act was amended to provide authority for Indians to lease their lands. In 1906 the Burke Act amended the period of trust from its original twenty-five-year term to provide that the Secretary of the Interior could issue certificates of competency whenever he found an Indian capable of handling his own affairs. Because of these two amendments, Indians had lost a substantial portion of their lands by the 1920s, and the Bureau of Indian Affairs was leasing a major portion of their remaining lands through the device of exercising a "trust" over the property of the individual "incompetent" Indians. Most of the lands which had been sold were allotments of mixed-blood Indians, who had often been declared "competent" because of their infusion of white blood.

Conditions reached an all-time low when Albert Fall was appointed Secretary of the Interior by President Harding. Fall had been a Senator from New Mexico for eight years prior to his appointment as Secretary of the Interior, and in that time had done everything possible to stall the settlement of the Pueblo Lands question.

His proposals concerning the reform of Indian affairs were shockingly corrupt. One idea was to appraise the holdings of every tribe (except the Five Civilized Tribes and the Osage of Oklahoma) and distribute the proceeds on a per capita basis, in effect severing all responsibilities of the United States for Indians. At that time some of the tribes were still receiving treaty annuities, and many of the reservations were defined by treaties. The policy would have broken many of the treaties protected by the courts and the Constitution, and probably would have caused an Indian war in several states. Wounded Knee might have become a battleground sooner had Fall been successful.

Another of his proposals involved mineral rights on the executive-order reservations. These lands were set aside by an order of the President for those tribes that did not have treaties or that lived in extremely remote areas not served by the federal government. There had always been a question, because of the lack of a definite treaty commitment by the United States, whether the Indians owned the lands or were temporary settlers on the land at the government's pleasure. Fall wanted to divide the royalty income of those lands among the states, the Bureau of Reclamation, and the tribes concerned. The legal status of the lands fell under unextinguished aboriginal title, and thus presented a unique legal question.

Fall's fondness for oil finally got him into trouble when he was implicated with Harry Sinclair and Attorney General Daugherty in the Teapot Dome scandal. Fall spent two years as Secretary of the Interior, and several more in a federal prison for his "accomplishments" as Secretary of the Interior. He was succeeded by Hubert Work, who had a difficult time restoring the confidence of the Indians in the federal Indian policy.

The Committee of One Hundred, prominent people who pressured Work for reforms, advocated a better understanding of the nature of Indian tribal traditions and customs shortly after Work took office. So the new Secretary asked the Brookings Institute to prepare a major study of the federal Indian policy and its administration. The Brookings Institute hired the famous Lewis Meriam to head their survey. Meriam was an acknowledged expert on the federal government's administrative structure and procedures. In a two-year-long survey of the conditions of Indians, Meriam developed a powerful and shocking report. The allotment policy was discredited, as well as the government policy of educating Indian children in boarding schools far from the reservations. Among the recommendations of the Meriam Report was that the Bureau of Indian Affairs consider itself primarily an educational agency, with its function to prepare Indians to live in the larger society in terms which they could understand.

The political impact of the recommendations of the Meriam Report was less than expected, even though its publicity made it appear the major statement on Indians in American history. Most of the recommendations were disregarded when President Hoover timidly appointed Charles Rhoads to supervise the suggested reforms. Rhoads did little to implement the policy suggestions which Meriam and his associates had made, and the Great American Depression precluded any substantial changes in federal policy which required financial commitments. By 1932 the pressures for a change in Indian policy were tremendous.

Major credit for the change of political climate in Indian affairs should be given to the man who became President Franklin Roosevelt's Commissioner of Indian Affairs, John Collier. Collier was a former social worker in New York City who had come west after a disquieting working experience with industrial America. Depressed with the many social problems of urban America, Collier found a whole new concept of society among the Pueblos and Navajos of the Southwest. He saw in their blending of individualism and communal interest a sense of integrity which he had found lacking in the Western European tradition. Collier remained a student and enthusiastic supporter of the Pueblo way of life all of his life.

It was singularly fortunate that Collier was so entranced with Indians, for the Pueblos surely needed his help. In 1913 the *Sandoval* case had clarified the federal responsibility for the Pueblos and thrown into question the land titles of the whites who had moved onto the Pueblo lands over a sixty-year period. The whites of New Mexico, trying to solve this complex problem, proposed a solution encompassed in the infamous Bursum bill of the early twenties. The effect of the Bursum bill, if passed, would have been to make the Pueblos prove which lands they still owned, rather than to force the white squatters to prove their rights to the lands.

Collier was enlisted to lead the fight against the bill by the General Federation of Women's Clubs and the New Mexico Association on Indian Affairs. He rounded up the Pueblo leaders and reconstituted the Pueblo Council, which had not been formally in existence since the revolt against the Spanish in 1680. The Bursum bill was defeated, and in its place the Pueblo Lands Act was passed. This statute reversed the procedure for proving title to lands; white men had to prove how they had obtained their titles, not the Indians.

Collier then jumped into the fight to preserve the religious freedom of the Pueblos. Some missionaries had spread malicious stories about the atrocities perpetrated during the secret ceremonials held in the Pueblo kivas, and the Interior Department was pressuring the Pueblos in an effort to restrict their religious activities. Collier got the Interior Department to reverse its position. Throughout the 1920s Collier was either leading or highly involved in nearly every fight between the Indians and the federal government. When he felt that the Hoover administration was not serious about undertaking the reforms suggested in the Meriam Report, Collier pressed the Senate Indian Committee to undertake its own investigation of the conditions of Indians in the United States.

From 1928 to 1932 the Senate Indian Committee toured Indian country, visiting tribes and getting a firsthand view of what was happening on the reservations. Their general impressions were eye-opening. On many reservations the Indians' stories shocked even the most hardened Senator. The abstractly phrased suggestions of the Meriam Report began to take on flesh as the committee saw instance after instance of deprivation in their investigation of allotments, competency commissions, and arbitrary actions of the government. The printed hearings ran some thirty volumes and brought the need for reform to the fore in Congress.

As the New Deal assumed command of the nation's destiny, it was apparent that there could be only one choice for Commissioner of Indian Affairs: John Collier. By this time Collier had developed a full theory of Indian society, and he was determined to institute reforms which would enable the tribes to exploit their natural communal strengths in an America that was growing more complex and industrially sophisticated. Collier worked hard to incorporate some features of his understanding of Indian culture into a major piece of reform legislation.

In mid-February of 1934, the Roosevelt administration was ready to present its Indian program to Congress. Under the sponsorship of Representative Edgar Howard of Nebraska in the House of Representatives and Senator Burton K. Wheeler of Montana in the Senate, the Indian Reorganization Act was introduced. The forces of reform had been working for this moment for over a decade, but not even the most farsighted of Indian advocates was able to anticipate Collier's vision.

The bill itself was over fifty pages long, and included four titles in its original form. Title One was called "Indian Self-government." It declared as a federal policy the right of tribal societies to control their lives by establishing their own governments. Tribes could receive federally approved constitutions and by-laws for reservation government. Their lands would be exempt from state and federal taxation until Congress removed the exemption, and they could operate businesses as tribal enterprises. The intent of this title was to translate the old tribal forms of government into a modern legal vehicle for community government, thereby allowing the informal processes of Indian decision-making to formalize themselves in a recognized institutional structure which the federal government would be bound to respect.

The second title of the bill was called "Special Education for Indians." It must have warmed Lewis Meriam's heart to read it, since the title went far beyond his recommendations, which had been made at a time when it was not popular to acknowledge the validity of Indian culture or traditions. The policy of the government in education under this title would be to emphasize the value of Indian culture. Government schools would be required to develop materials for their curricula from the tribal traditions and folklore, thereby bringing to the Indian communities a sense of their own immediate past and the values inherent in their way of life. The title even made provisions for a scholarship fund for formal education of Indians of academic ability.

The third title of the original legislation prohibited future land allotments and restored to tribal ownership those lands which had been declared surplus under the respective allotment acts but never settled. The title authorized an annual appropriation of $2 million for land purchases for existing reservations and the creation of reservations for landless Indians. One unfortunate feature of the original legislation, and a feature that did more to subvert Collier's plans than any other, was the provision that there would be no more inheritance of lands by individual Indians. The existing pieces of land held by multiple owners would revert to the tribal holdings, and the Indian owners would receive a certificate showing that they owned a proportionate interest in tribal lands.

This feature of banning the inheritance of property interests in lands severely hurt the Collier program. It was particularly objectionable to the tribes of Oklahoma, which were not included in the bill anyway. The other tribes picked up the refrain that it deprived them of their rights to property from the Oklahoma Indians and opposed this provision even though they stood to gain by the cessation of land losses under this policy.

The last title of the bill was a half century ahead of its time. It provided for a Court of Indian Affairs. The court was to consist of seven justices appointed by the President with the consent of the Senate. It would have authority over all legal controversies affecting Indian tribes. The justices of this special court would have ten-year terms, thus avoiding any one administration's packing the court either against or in favor of the Indians (although it was doubtful if any President would consider packing the court in favor of the Indians). The court would have eliminated the perennial problems of the tribes' having to litigate their treaty rights in state courts with appeal to the federal court system.

As a reform measure, Collier's original draft of the Indian Reorganization Act was so thoughtful, philosophical, and ahead of its time that it had a hard time gaining credibility. The reformers of the day, Indian and white, had only wanted to amend certain laws to correct the blatant practices of the Interior Department, and perhaps write in a few safeguards for individuals. They had not contemplated a total revolution in thinking which conceived of tribal governments as modern organizations with rights of substantial political sovereignty. Dissension over the concepts of the bill began to escalate, and soon Collier found that he had more enemies than friends.

Missionaries, for example, were content to support some of his educational reforms, but chafed at the thought that, with full powers of self-government, the tribes would be able to reinstitute their old religious ceremonies or, at a minimum, guarantee religious freedom to non-Christian religions. Rumors rumbled through the country that Collier was trying to revive paganism and destroy the work of a century of missionary effort. Some church leaders saw self-government on a tribal basis as undoing a century of their work in making the people adhere to white culture.

Most Indian tribes were delighted at the prospect of renewing their land base. Some tribes had ceded immense areas of land only twenty or thirty years before, and these areas had not then been completely settled. Now Collier was proposing to have the lands restored to them. The bill's provision for a $2-million fund for land purchase would have allowed the tribes to pick up individual allotments which had gone into multiple ownership. But the provisions of the bill which forbade further inheritance and reversion of individual allotments to tribal title irritated many influential tribal leaders who anticipated inheriting choice lands within their reservations. Some Indian leaders were against the proposed land-reform legislation for personal reasons and not because the proposal was bad for the tribe.

Some career federal employees greeted the movement toward self-government with enthusiasm. They had grown tired of the constant harping of the reform elements outside the federal establishment, and they saw the legislation as a means of placing the responsibility for conditions of the Indians on the tribal governments. Others welcomed Indian participation in solving long-standing problems, some of which had been insoluble because of the lack of Indian cooperation. Yet, among the provisions which Collier supported was one giving Indians preference in hiring and advancement in the Bureau of Indian Affairs. This idea was not greeted warmly by people who had their career advancement at stake.

As the controversy swelled and reached epidemic proportions, Collier took an unprecedented and decisive step to gain Indian support for his proposals: He decided to consult the Indian people on the legislation, and called a series of Indian congresses around the nation. The move took everyone by surprise. The only time previously that Indians had seen a Commissioner of Indian Affairs was during a perfunctory good-will tour prior to changing a policy or during a traditional final tour of the reservations at government expense prior to leaving office. The idea of a Commissioner of Indian Affairs consulting them on legislation boggled most Indian minds.

The first Indian congress was held in Rapid City, South Dakota, on March 2, 1934, and was attended by most of the tribes of the Northern Plains. The meeting was stormy indeed. Many of the Sioux were fearful of losing their treaty rights, and protested against the legislation. Other tribes sent progressive representatives who had been coached by their local missionaries and who opposed the legislation on the ground that it was a step backward. One of the biggest disputes, and one that would eventually surface at Wounded Knee in 1973, was the objection by the Sioux fullbloods that any governments organized under the act could be dominated by mixed bloods who had already sold their lands and simply hung around the agencies looking for a handout.

Collier withstood the objections and convinced the assembled delegates that he would seek amendments on those points about which they felt strongly. The congress of Indians finally gave support to the proposal, albeit reluctantly. Collier had pretty much the same response to his proposals at the other congresses, but he failed miserably with the Navajos, whom he admired so much. The Navajos had been going through the traumatic experience of a sheep-reduction program in line with their current soil-conservation ideas. They wanted no part of any more government schemes to help them. On the whole, Collier was able to communicate some of his ideas to the Indians around the nation, but it was apparent that too many tribes had lost confidence in the ability of their own culture to survive. Collier had more faith in Indians than they had in themselves.

On his return to Congress, Collier saw his program virtually gutted. Various Senators and Congressmen added or subtracted their favorite sections of the legislation, and many of the good reforms of the proposal were lost. The Court of Indian Affairs was dropped completely. The ban on inheritances was dropped. Collier was accused of trying to institute soviet collectivism in his efforts to restore the tribes to a position of political stability. Oklahoma and Alaska Indians were made ineligible for the legislation.

Perhaps the most devastating aspect of the amendments to the Collier proposal was the option clause that was added, making the acceptance of the act dependent upon a referendum vote of the people on the reservations. True, it was the first effort to put self-government to work, but it overlooked several important factors and had the effect of complicating matters in Indian affairs for all time.

First, the tribes were given a period of one year to vote whether to accept the legislation and organize a tribal government under it. Most of the people could not possibly understand what it was that the government was asking them to do, and the one-year time limit made it appear as if a hidden agenda was present in the proposal. Many tribes that refused to accept the provisions of the act might have done so if they had had more time to consider the act.

The second important factor, which also involved the operation of the option clause, was the fact that there was no way to determine tribal membership. Some Indians had retained their allotments and were therefore, without doubt, entitled to federal services. Others had long since sold their lands but remained in the vicinity of the reservation, living on the income from seasonal jobs and participating in tribal affairs. A strict interpretation of the federal statutes would have meant that they were no longer considered eligible for federal services. Yet they were allowed to vote in the referendum to determine if the tribe should approve the act. No tribe had an accurate roll of its membership, and because the elections were being held under the one-year time limit, they involved generally whichever Indians happened to vote at the time.

The third factor affecting the referendum vote was that the Bureau of Indian Affairs counted as affirmative votes those Indians who had refused to vote. The traditional method of indicating displeasure or disapproval in many tribes was to boycott the proceedings. When many traditional Indians refused to vote in the referendum, they believed that by not voting they were indicating their refusal to accept the act. When they discovered that the government had counted them as affirmative votes, they were livid—and helpless to reverse the decision.

The final version of the act, after all of the compromises forced by the Indians and the several Senators and Congressmen, did not remotely approach Collier's original version of the proposal. The titles were all destroyed, and in their place were nineteen sections that could be called, if one were in a kindly mood, miscellaneous provisions. There was no rhyme nor reason to the sequence of the law as written, and it reflected scattered points of view that were nearly irreconcilable philosophically, if not legally.

Even the gutted version of the reforms which Collier pushed through to enactment proved very important in reviving the tribal governments. Two years later, in 1936, the natives of Alaska and the tribes of Oklahoma were given the right to organize under similar laws negating the original objections of the Oklahoma Indians. Congress made a gesture toward providing rules and regulations for tribal elections under the act by passing a law which required at least 30 per cent of the reservation residents to vote in order to have a valid election. But since few tribes had any record of tribal membership, the amendment did little to clarify the situation.

The Indian Reorganization Act has had a tenuous existence in the years since it became law. The bureaucrats of the Bureau of Indian Affairs have acted as though the mere passage of time has been sufficient to void the provisions of the act. Consequently, many of the reforms which did survive the amendment process of Congress have become useless because of the refusal of the Bureau of Indian Affairs to abide by them. The Secretary of the Interior was authorized, for example, to proclaim new reservations under this act. Very quickly, this authority was subverted by bureaucrats who decided that they did not want any more reservations than already existed.

One of the worst abuses of the bureaucracy was the subversion of section sixteen of the act. That section dealt with the powers of the new tribal governments, and one clause in this section made it mandatory for the Secretary of the Interior to consult with the tribal governments concerning the annual federal expenditures on their reservations:

> The Secretary of the Interior shall advise such tribe or its tribal council of all appropriation estimates or Federal projects for the benefit of the tribe prior to the submission of such estimates to the Bureau of the Budget and the Congress.

The section was inserted to insure that the tribes would know what the federal government was doing on their reservations, and to insure that the tribes would have some voice in the development of federal programs and federal priorities. Over the years Indians found government appropriations escalating, with no way of tracing where the moneys were going. Today, estimates of federal expenditures for Indians run as high as a billion dollars a year, and Indians are still unable to discover where and how the funds are being spent.

Congress rejected the Indian Reorganization Act almost as soon as it had passed it. Even Senator Wheeler had rejected it by 1937 and sought its repeal. The House members cut appropriations to a minimum level and refused to allow the concept of tribal self-government to have any chance for sustained growth. In doing so, they not only subverted their own legislation but turned their backs on the Meriam Report, which had made many of the same recommendations concerning the investment of federal funds in reservations projects. As late as the 1950s, people in Congress sought to repeal the I.R.A. They found dealing with tribal governments onerous when they were trying to slip bad legislation past the Indians, and sought a way to abolish tribal governments by getting rid of the I.R.A., which had given them the legal structure to develop political savvy.

In retrospect, the Indian Reorganization Act was not all that it could have been. It was a reversal of unmeasured proportions in both philosophy and practice from what the United States had been doing to Indians for nearly a century and a half. As such, the violence of the opposition which the new program aroused was understandable. Had Collier's original program been enacted by Congress, there is little doubt that it would have achieved outstanding success. Collier's plan incorporated a comprehensive philosophy of social existence based upon ancient Indian values and beliefs. The parallels between Collier's fully developed legislative proposals and the Twenty Points of the Trail of Broken Treaties are startling.

Some of the parallels are certainly the paths along which the future changes in federal policy must lie if it is to be effective. The Collier proposal to establish a Court of Indian Affairs, for example, is very similar to the suggestion by the Trail of Broken Treaties of encompassing all Indians within a federal treaty relationship and setting up a treaty commission to determine violations of the treaties. When a particular solution is advanced by diverse and unrelated groups a number of times over the period of a century, it would appear that the problem area is one that must be taken seriously.

At least part of the problem faced by the Indian Reorganization Act was the refusal of Congress to support the program. Hardly any members of Congress thought in either sociological or philosophical terms. They were used to passing Indian legislation the chief characteristics of which were coercion and restraint of the tribes. Lacking these familiar factors, Congressmen and Senators suspected a subversive presence lurking in Collier's comprehensive ideas, since the proposal was quite bland in the manner in which it imposed restrictions on the tribes.

The persistent argument over the I.R.A. between Indians and the Bureau of Indian Affairs concerns whether acceptance of the act limited the sovereignty of the tribes. In general, the bureaucrats have interpreted the act as having been in the nature of a trade—aboriginal sovereignty for limited but formally recognized powers as a federal corporation. It is questionable whether the act itself can be interpreted as having irreversibly limited the powers of the tribe. Section 16 declares:

> . . . in addition to all powers vested in any Indian tribe or tribal council by existing law, the Constitution [tribal constitution adopted by the tribe under the act] shall also vest . . . the following rights and powers.

Far from limiting the political powers of the tribe, the Indian Reorganization Act seems to have either added powers or defined existing powers more specifically. The present contention of Indian activists and others that the Indian Reorganization Act was a step away from the traditional right of Indians to govern themselves is inaccurate if they mean that the scope of legal powers was reduced by the adoption of the act. The manner in which governmental powers were expressed may be changed, but that was a result of the General Allotment Act and not the I.R.A.

What, then, do we understand to be the effect of the I.R.A. on tribal existence as a political entity? The answer is probably contained in the decision of the *Toledo* case. In that case, as we have seen, the Pueblo of Jemez forbade Protestant missionaries to enter the Pueblo, and six Indians sued in an effort to enforce their rights to religious freedom. The court found that the Pueblo had preserved its rights to self-government, and stated that:

> Their right to govern themselves has been recognized in such statutes as the Indian Reorganization Act.

Had the Pueblo been limited in the exercise of its aboriginal sovereignty, the court would have surely found that by the adoption of the Indian Reorganization Act by Congress, the federal government intended to bring to an end the mysterious subject known as aboriginal sovereignty in favor of a limited but constitutional exercise of powers of local self-government.

The Indian Reorganization Act was intended to be and was a major change of federal policy. With the exception of the period from 1954 to 1961, when Congress tried to terminate the federal relationship of the tribes, the policy of the government has been supportive of tribal sovereignty and self-government. Presidents Johnson and Nixon endorsed this principle without reservation (if that is an apt term for it). The I.R.A. has often been considered a law directed primarily toward a domestic problem of the United States. It was more than that, however, since it confirmed the inherent and aboriginal right of self-government of Indian tribes.

The fundamental principles which John Collier presented in the Indian Reorganization Act were based upon the assumption that Indians had not lost their rights to political existence but had been partially submerged by the events of history. Instead of seeking to subvert the power and influence of the traditional tribal Indians in favor of the assimilation-oriented progressives, Collier strongly supported the revival of Indian customs. That the fullblood Indians would be unable to take advantage of the provisions of the act was probably a foregone conclusion. Too many of them sought to return to the days of Fort Laramie, forgetting that in the intervening decades the world had changed. If they believed, with Collier, that customs could be preserved, they should also have realized that new customs had to be devised so that the tribes could survive their encounter with the modern world.

One of the interim steps which the federal government could take in its effort to create a new Indian policy would be to recognize the genius of John Collier's original suggestions and reconsider the titles contained in his original proposal as separate pieces of legislation today. Collier spent his remaining years working to get Indian affairs placed on the political agenda of the American nations of the Western Hemisphere. His intent in creating the Indian Reorganization Act was to use this newly clarified legal status as the prototype for legal reform in the conditions of Indians in both Americas. That is precisely the proposal of this book, at least with respect to the Indians of the United States.

10. Litigating Indian Claims

When the protesters of the Trail of Broken Treaties presented their Twenty Points to the White House Task Force, they asked the administration for a response within sixty days. The hope was that the White House Task Force would consider some of the points and introduce a new package of legislative proposals based on the ideas they had presented.

The response of the White House Task Force was hardly encouraging. For the most part, it avoided the questions which plagued Indian communities by insisting that individual Indians had become citizens and therefore could look forward only to the rights that other citizens enjoyed. Point Four of the Twenty Points concerned the creation of a commission to review treaty commitments and violations. The White House Task Force, which was apparently unfamiliar with Indian affairs to an appalling degree, responded to this point as follows:

> We already have a Commission: the Indian Claims Commission, a quasi-judicial agency created by Congress in 1946. Its mandate is to settle financially any and all legal, equitable and

moral obligations the United States might owe to the Indians, including the loss of aboriginal lands or inadequate payment for them through treaties or otherwise. The Commission has decided on some 190 awards, and has certified $424 million for appropriation as award payments. There are about 250 dockets still pending before the Commission, and in the last Congress the Commission's life was extended another five years.

In its response the White House Task Force made the same error which non-Indians have been making ever since the Indian Claims Commission was established. That assumption is that the commission was designed to hear and make decisions on the accumulated claims of the tribes against the United States. Such is not the case. The commission has restricted its activity to a very narrow scope of claims and has failed to consider alternative interpretations of its powers or authority.

With numerous tribal claims falling outside the province of the Indian Claims Commission through procedural rulings and the narrowing of rules of evidence, many Indians have felt that they will get justice only by protests. The major point of contention of many activists, the settling of treaty issues, has been avoided by the Indian Claims Commission, and as tribal lawyers are unable to deal with this issue, the activists have taken it up. If there is a moral in the Wounded Knee incident, it is that treaty issues must be resolved either peaceably or violently, but they must be resolved.

The story of Indian claims against the United States goes back almost to the beginning of the republic. The ink was hardly dry on the treaties before white settlers began their trek overland into Indian country, breaching the solemn promises of the

United States. When the executive branch of government refused to use the army to enforce the provisions of the Indian treaties, the tribes had but two recourses: war or relief through the United States court system. When they were pushed to the limit of their patience by the advancing tide of settlement, many tribes fought for their lands. But several times before a crisis occurred, tribes had attempted to use the federal courts for redress. The sad story of *Cherokee Nation v. Georgia* indicates the dead end which the tribes found in the legal processes of the United States. A year following the *Cherokee Nation* case Samuel Worcester, a missionary to the Cherokees, appealed what was basically the same case as *Cherokee Nation* to the Supreme Court in *Worcester v. Georgia*. The Supreme Court upheld the validity of the Cherokee treaties and held against enforcing the laws of the state of Georgia which had been passed to harass the Cherokees. When President Andrew Jackson learned of the Supreme Court decision he is said to have remarked, "John Marshall has made his decision, now let him enforce it."

Following the two Cherokee cases, the tribes knew better than ask a federal court to enforce their treaty rights through injunctions. The executive branch was determined to disqualify Indian treaties as the law of the land, and the refusal of the respective Presidents to give credence to the treaty provisions was something over which the Indians had no control. While a President might promise the tribes that no whites would be allowed in their land, as was done by President Grant in the Treaty of Fort Laramie in 1868, whenever the settlers illegally moved into Indian country, the first response of the executive branch was to make another treaty with the tribe concerned in order to somehow give legality to acts that were already illegal.

There was one weapon that the tribes discovered

in the mid-1850s which partially helped to soothe their tempers. That was the lawsuit to compel the United States to pay either damages for lands taken in breach of treaty rights or damages for annuities and payments promised but not paid by the United States. In 1854 Congress created a Court of Claims as a tribunal in which the United States would voluntarily submit itself to suit on its contractual obligations. The Indian treaties and treaties with foreign nations were, of course, the foremost contracts outstanding against the United States, and tribes began to file suits in the Court of Claims to get some redress. The situation looked optimistic, but when the tribal cases got near judgment, Congress recognized the danger of allowing the court to handle the many breaches of treaty obligations and decided to restrict the jurisdiction of the court to exclude any claims deriving from treaties. In March of 1863 a law was passed withdrawing from the Court of Claims jurisdiction over all claims arising out of treaties that were not pending on December 30, 1862. The legislation also provided that no interest be allowed on any claim up to the time of judgment where the payment of interest had not already been stipulated expressly prior to suit.

After the 1863 legislation, the tribes had no legal recourse when the United States violated their treaties. They could not sue in federal courts seeking injunctions and writs to prevent violation of their treaty rights. And they could not sue in the Court of Claims and get compensation for damages once the treaties had been violated. For all practical purposes, the tribes had been denied any type of formal legal relationship through which they could plead their case with the United States, which was allegedly their guardian acting in good faith toward them. The tribes stood on the same basis as foreign nations.

They could go to war or they could lobby the respective Congresses to get legislation opening the Court of Claims to them on a single-claim basis.

For the next thirty years tribes with claims against the United States had to seek jurisdictional legislation to sue the United States. Sometimes they would be told that they were wards of the government and could not sue their guardian. Other times they would get their case into the Court of Claims only to find the court interpreting their jurisdictional statute so narrowly that their claim was dismissed through the manipulation of words and phrases which they did not understand.

In the meantime the West was being settled in rather bloody fashion. Tribes left with no appeals to law took up the tomahawk, and while the United States claimed the lands of the interior under the doctrine of discovery, it was a hardy pioneer who ventured into Apache, Shoshone, or Sioux country. The Indians felt that they still owned their lands, and rightly so. The Apaches, for example, controlled their desert lands until the late 1880s. Most of the tribes had, at one time or another, signed peace treaties with the United States, and over the course of years these treaties were violated by the United States or its citizens. Some of the treaty provisions required that if an Indian tribe committed depredations against a citizen of the United States, the tribe could be held liable for damages. As the wars for control of the West spread across the land, these potential claims against the tribes mounted.

As the depredation claims by the whites mounted, political pressure to settle them grew more intense. In 1891, bowing to the pressure of western whites who saw a bonanza in the Indian-depredation claims, Congress passed the Indian Depredations Act. The act provided that in addition to any jurisdiction which the Court of Claims might have to settle claims by whites for injuries suffered in the Indian wars, the court would have jurisdiction to adjudicate claims of the following classes:

> First. All claims for property of citizens of the United States taken or destroyed by Indians belonging to any band, tribe, or nation, in amity with the United States, without just cause or provocation on the part of the owner or agent in charge, and not returned or paid for.
> Second. Such jurisdiction shall also extend to all cases which have been examined and allowed by the Interior Department.

In effect, Congress was making the Indian tribes vulnerable for almost unlimited liability for acts committed in the Indian wars if they had signed treaties and were supposed to be in amity with the United States. The courts, however, remained closed to the tribes for injuries they had suffered in the same engagements.

The law provided that any questions concerning a time limitation for bringing the suits or the method of presenting the claim would be waived for all claims accruing after July 1, 1865. The injured party could simply file a petition with the Court of Claims outlining the circumstances under which he believed he had suffered his injury. The court could make its own rules and regulations for taking testimony in the cases, and no party was barred from giving testimony or from filing a claim simply because he was an injured or interested party. In effect, the rules of evidence were waived and the claims filed by the whites were to be given credence, with few provisions for cross-examination or other legal defense techniques.

The claims were to be settled with priorities determined according to the amount of funds available to the tribes. The first priority was a deduction from the annuities due to the tribe from the United States. If no annuities were available or owing the tribe, then any other funds which the tribe might have on deposit in the federal treasury could be taken to satisfy the judgment. Those tribes which did not have funds in the federal treasury from sales of their lands would have the amount of the judgment deducted from any funds which the government might have appropriated for their benefit. Thus, a current appropriation for education or health might be curtailed to fulfill a judgment for an incident occurring a generation before. Finally, the judgment could be paid from the federal treasury by the United States and would remain as a charge against the tribe until such time as it did have money available.

The tribes had the right of appeal on any judgments rendered against them. But the tribes that were most vulnerable to suit under the law were those which had most recently been restricted to the reservations: the Sioux, Cheyennes, and Apaches. On the whole they had little knowledge of the law, few lawyers available to defend them, and little understanding of the appeals process. The United States was holding the tribes at bay while its citizens were busy picking their pockets.

Abuses under this legislation were incredible. Claims were filed for every conceivable incident that anyone could remember. Not all were upheld by the Court of Claims, but in general it was a field day for the Westerners, who saw themselves as the injured parties even though a good many of them had violated the treaties in the first place. One claim involved the destruction of a steamboat which had run aground three miles from a Yuma village. The claimant maintained that the careless burning of his boat by one of his employees constituted an act of war by the Yuma Indians. That the Yumas had not signed a peace treaty with the United States and were not in a state of amity with its citizens did not seem to bother the plaintiff. In any event, the Indians won.

Many claims were filed against the Sioux for depredations allegedly committed by their warriors in the Black Hills during the gold rush, even though the Black Hills specifically belonged to them and whites were forbidden by federal law to enter the area. The Cheyennes were sued for depredations allegedly suffered during their famous "Cheyenne Autumn" flight from Oklahoma through Kansas and northern Nebraska. Contemporary newspaper reports made note of their avoidance of depredations as they made their way north. It is said that they skirted white settlements so successfully that they had come and gone before anyone knew they were around. Yet the depredations claims filed against them for the loss of cattle and horses, when figured cumulatively, totaled more livestock than had existed in Nebraska and Kansas at that time.

The most important part of the Indian Depredations Act was the theory under which it was justified. A very strict interpretation of the responsibilities of nations signing treaties was used as a justification for passage of the law. The tribes had signed treaties with the United States in which they had promised not to injure the citizens of the United States. Tribal members had broken the treaty provisions, and therefore the tribes were legally liable for damages. No mention was made of the depredations committed by the citizens of the United States or the United States itself. The facts which were used to substantiate the claims often failed to mention how the Indian wars began—only that the Indians had committed such and such an act.

The claims lasted from 1891 to about 1919. It was during this period that the Supreme Court handed down its famous *Lone Wolf v. Hitchcock* decision, which denied that the tribes had ever had an independent status but concluded that they had always been subject to the plenary power of Congress. Thus, while one court of the United States was denying the status of Indian tribes as dependent nations, another court was holding them to the highest concept of reparations shared by independent nations under the laws of treaties. This inconsistency in purpose has never been satisfactorily explained.

Following the Indian Depredations era, the courts were closed to claims by white citizens, but they were not opened to the tribes. The old pattern of seeking jurisdictional statutes allowing the tribes to sue was maintained. As the years passed, the claims became more complicated and encompassing. They began to cover more than the violation of treaties and included other causes of action, such as violation of rights accruing under statutes. The United States was now governing the tribes almost exclusively by legislation, and it had set certain minimum standards which it alleged to uphold. Yet in the Bureau of Indian Affairs even these minimum standards were being violated, and the tribes were being deprived of their lands and funds by a bewildering variety of policies and decisions.

The government policy was clearly to prepare the Indians for eventual assimilation into white society, and to that end schools were operated, buildings for administration of tribal affairs were constructed, and roads and irrigation projects were authorized. The purpose of these projects and expenditures was to further the federal policies regarding Indians, not specifically to benefit the Indians. Most tribes had no choice in what programs they were offered. The educational programs consisted primarily of "kidnapping" Indian children and taking them off to government boarding schools, where they were to be brainwashed of any memory of their Indian heritage. Often the parents were denied treaty annuities unless they allowed their children to be taken away. It was a choice of selling one's children in order to eat or keeping the children, only to see the whole family starve.

The United States had the gall to claim many of these expenditures as funds gratuitously expended for the benefit of the tribes and therefore deductible from any judgments which the tribes might win in the Court of Claims. Treaty provisions were interpreted very narrowly, and the government would not allow any expenditures which it had made without specific treaty authorization to go unaccounted for in the claims litigation. The case of the Fort Berthold Indians was a classic example of the government attitude. A federal law had been passed denying rations to any family on the reservation that would not work or allow its children to be taken to government schools. Yet the United States introduced as an offset claim the expenses of keeping the children prisoners in the school during the period of time when the tribes were suing the government.

The Bureau of Indian Affairs continually mismanaged the assets of the tribes, and with each violation of federal law another claim was added to the growing list of claims against the government. Each Congress saw frantic delegations of Indians making the rounds of their Senators and Congressmen asking for the introduction of legislation to allow them to sue the United States. As claims went to judgment in the Court of Claims, the tribes rushed back to Congress seeking redress from adverse decisions, since the tendency of the Court of Claims was to deny the tribes satisfaction because of alleged defects in the legislation which enabled them to sue the United States. If ever a party was required to pass rigorous standards to get a claim satisfied, it was the Indian tribe during the 1920s and 1930s.

In the comprehensive investigation of the conditions of Indians conducted by the Senate Indian Committee between 1928 and 1932, one of the most frequent complaints lodged against the United States by Indians was about the handling of tribal claims. The chief complaint was that tribes had to go to Washington many times before they could even get their claims legislation introduced. Then they had to make several more trips to insure passage of their bill, and, finally, they might get a bill which did not serve the purpose of supporting their claims, thus making the whole process fruitless and extremely costly.

Cases seemed to drag on for years and years, even when the tribe did get them into the Court of Claims. When decisions did come down, those claims that appeared to establish certain liability for the United States were often denied by procedural devices, and strange interpretations given to provisions of treaties and agreements. Then there were a number of claims which had accrued because of an admitted liability of the United States which had never been liquidated. These claims generally involved an admission of guilt by the United States at some remote time in the past, coupled with the promise to pay the tribe for damages resulting from the incident. The question raised by the tribe involved when, if ever, the United States would keep its promises.

The liability for the Sand Creek massacre of the friendly Cheyenne and Arapaho tribes was a classic example of this type of claim. In December of 1864 a contingent of Colorado militia under Methodist preacher John Chivington was on the prowl, looking for a fight with the Plains Tribes before the enlistment time of the militia ran out. Knowing that Chief Black Kettle of the Cheyennes had pitched his camp at Sand Creek and was flying an American flag under instructions from the Army, Chivington approached the sleeping Indian camp at dawn with full intentions of attacking. Various officers protested the proposed action, but to no avail.

Chivington's men virtually destroyed the Cheyennes and Arapahos in an attack in the early morning. Numerous atrocities were committed on the friendly Indians, including the taking of scalps of infants and the mutilation of the sexual organs of the Indian women. The happy militia returned to Denver with their trophies and paraded them at the Opera House, to the delight of Colorado citizens. In later years white historians would claim that Chivington had raised the "siege" of Denver by attacking a peaceful Indian camp some two hundred miles from the city.

The Indians were furious, and the Sioux, under Crazy Horse, promptly burned Julesburg, Colorado. For several years the frontier blazed with incidents as the tribes of the Northern Plains sought revenge for the slain Cheyennes. One of the provisions of the treaty of 1867 at Medicine Lodge between the United States and the Cheyennes and Arapahos was the admission of guilt by the United States and the promise to pay a substantial sum of money to those tribal members who had lost relatives or property in the massacre. While the United States had signed the treaty, it never fulfilled the payment provision, since political pressures in Washington by the Army high command called into question whether the massacre was a battle, as the Army maintained, or a bloody massacre, as a House of Representatives investigating committee classified it. The Cheyenne and Arapaho tribes sought compensation, but the courts refused to consider the claim.

Another classic case uncovered by the Senate field hearings was that of the Fort Sill Apaches. The majority of the Apaches had been scouts employed by the United States Army to catch Geronimo. Following Geronimo's capture, the Army had taken the whole Chiricahua Apache tribe, scouts and all, to Florida as prisoners of war. The loyal scouts were told they would receive their usual pay of $2 a day as scouts if they went to Florida quietly and allowed the Army to straighten out the bureaucratic foul-up through its regular channels. The scouts, trusting the Army, agreed and left for Fort Marion with Geronimo's band of followers. In 1928 they were still waiting for their pay, having been classified as prisoners of war from 1886 to 1906, and having been moved several times by the Army, finally ending up in Fort Sill, Oklahoma. With unusual patience, they explained that they felt that the United States owed them something for their troubles.

Sometimes the tribal claims would involve the refusal of a government agency to bow to the facts and/or to submit its interpretation of history to the court. A typical example of this type of claim involved the reparations due the people at Pine Ridge who had been victims of the Wounded Knee massacre. The Army, even against the legally admitted judgment of General Nelson Miles, who supported the Indians, claimed that the massacre had in fact been a battle and that the survivors were not entitled to compensation. Legislation was introduced during several Congresses to get the claim satisfied. Some of the survivors gave testimony before the Congressional committees, but the tribe was not paid for the depredation.

Pressure to settle the outstanding Indian claims

did not come only from the tribes visited by the Senate Indian Committee. The Meriam Report of 1928 mentioned claims as an important subject matter which should be handled as quickly as possible.

> The unsettled legal claims against the government should be settled at the earliest possible date. A special commission should be created to study those claims which have not yet been approved by Congress for submission to the Court of Claims. This commission should submit recommendations to the Secretary of the Interior so that those claims which are meritorious may be submitted to Congress with a draft of a suitable bill authorizing their settlement before the Court of Claims.

Perhaps it was this recommendation from the prestigious Brookings Institute that triggered a number of bills introduced in Congress during the 1930s to settle Indian claims by a special commission. Almost immediately following the Meriam Report, Senators and Representatives began to introduce bills designed to provide a forum for Indian claims.

In January 1930, a bill was introduced in the House of Representatives which sought to create a United States Court of Indian Claims. The proposed court was designed to handle any claim brought by an Indian tribe. Unfortunately, the climate for reform had not yet reached the point where the United States wanted to have its past sins recited in a legal forum, and the bill failed to become law. In 1934 and 1935, Senate bills were introduced to create an Indian Claims Court but these bills also failed, in spite of the fact that the Democrats who introduced them controlled Congress and could have easily passed the legislation.

At that point a strange thing happened. A bill was introduced to create an Indian Claims Commission. The idea of the adversary nature of a formal court apparently became distasteful to Congress. This feeling was shared by then Secretary of the Interior Ickes who commented to Senator Elmer Thomas of Oklahoma, chairman of the Senate Indian Committee, that the cause for delay in the existing claims cases was the endless bickering of government agencies charged with preparing materials for the defense of the United States. Congress began to think that a commission could cut through this kind of red tape in a nonadversary proceeding. The investigatory commission appeared to be the only feasible vehicle for handling claims which involved history and anthropology as much as they involved legal theories.

Senator Thomas introduced a Senate bill to set up a commission, and the attention of Congress shifted from a desire to set up a formal court to the goal of setting up a commission to hear Indian claims. Even then Congress did not understand either the nature of the claims or the complicated types of evidence which might be required in order to make decisions on the claims. Thomas' bill failed, and similar bills were introduced in 1937, 1940, 1941, 1944, and 1945. The Indian Claims Commission was definitely a future possibility, except that no one knew how to define its role and the scope of its powers. Finally, in 1946 then Representative Henry Jackson (the late Senator from Washington State and former chairman of the Senate Interior Committee) introduced a bill which became law in August of that year.

The law turned out to be a hybrid which created an entity, called a commission, halfway between a court and a true commission, thus causing untold confusion. The commission was given very broad powers to hear and determine all claims against the United States which arose before 1946. Tribes had five years from the signing of the bill to file their claims. The major problem with the law was that few Indians knew what kinds of claims would be accepted. Would claims which had previously been turned aside because of defects in the jurisdictional statutes be eligible for consideration? Would the claims then being litigated in the Court of Claims be transferred to the Indian Claims Commission for final settlement? Congressmen and lawyers might have claimed to understand the scope of the new commission, but it was clear that the Indians didn't.

The Indian Claims Commission covered claims in several areas. Any tribe, band, or identifiable group of American Indians could file a claim. These words were interpreted liberally in some cases, narrowly in others, and ignored in still others. Some claims involving lands covered cessions during which the United States had insisted that the tribes be considered as one legal entity for the purpose of the treaty. The tribes of the Pacific Northwest, for example, were all gathered together as the "Medicine Creek Nation" for the purposes of the Medicine Creek treaty. Yet, when they sought entrance into the claims commission, it was decided that they would be considered as individual groups. The Chippewas, Ottawas, and Potawatomi were merged to form the "United Nations of Chippewa, Ottawa and Potawatomi" for several treaties, yet they were forced to file separate claims. But the California tribes who had signed a number of treaties as individual nations were gathered into one new group, aptly called the "California Indians," and forced to sue for the whole state, thus merging what had been distinct tribal claims.

The commission had jurisdiction over all claims in

law or equity arising under the Constitution, laws, or treaties of the United States, executive orders of the President, and all claims for which the claimant tribe would have been entitled to sue the United States had the United States previously been subject to suit. In contrast to former cases decided in the Court of Claims, the commission was empowered to go behind the treaties and include all claims which would arise if any treaties, contracts, or agreements with the United States had been revised on the grounds of fraud, duress, unconscionable consideration, mutual or unilateral mistake, or any other equitable concepts which have traditionally been cited to correct injustices of the law.

The final section of eligibility of claims was to admit those claims based upon "fair and honorable dealings which are not recognized by any existing rule of law or equity." This phraseology would have appeared to cover all treaty violations, settling as of that date all failures in the exercise of trusteeship or violations of the concept of fair dealings between the United States and the Indian tribes. But the Indian Claims Commission, when it finally began to hear tribal claims, studiously avoided this section of its jurisdiction and refused to consider any claims except those which dealt with land cessions or an accounting of tribal funds held by the United States in the federal treasury.

One of the purposes of the bill was to settle the question of depredations committed by the United States at Sand Creek, Wounded Knee, and other infamous incidents. The Indians regarded these claims as tribal claims. But the court termed them "individual claims," on the ground that they were incidents which injured individuals. And individual claims were disallowed. The claims of the Apache scouts, which had been an important factor in spurring Congress to consider the Indian Claims Commission bill, failed to qualify for consideration. Thus, even in a court established for that purpose, the United States failed to deal honorably with the Indians—a dealing which, incidentally, should have also been considered by the commission under the rubric of fair and honorable dealings.

Three hundred and seventy claims were originally filed in the Indian Claims Commission. Most tribes had some semblance of notice from the Bureau of Indian Affairs about the five-year time limit during which they could file claims. Nevertheless, some claims were haphazardly filed within minutes of the deadline. Some tribes, primarily those living in federally unrecognized communities east of the Mississippi River, were never notified of either the Commission or their eligibility to file claims. With the exception of the Creeks and Miamis, who had previously sued the United States in the Court of Claims, the Indian tribes without federal recognition east of the Mississippi were excluded from the operation of the act because of a failure of notification.

The complicated nature of the issues became apparent when the 370 claims were broken down into subcategories according to the specific land-cession areas and dates of cession. The result of this reclassification was the creation of a total of 605 docketed cases to be heard. The original intent of Congress was that the commission would finish its work within ten years. This expectation was based partially upon the authorization of an investigative division within the commission, which was designed to screen claims and make reports to the commission concerning their relevancy. With this additional arm for the commission, it was thought that the old delays which claims had been subjected to in the Court of Claims might be avoided. Such was not the case.

In 1969 then Chief Commissioner of the Indian
Claims Commission John Vance, writing in the *North
Dakota Law Review*, found that the failure of the
Indian Claims Commission to make use of the investigative division was one of the major causes in
delay of the dockets. By December 1968, some
twenty-two years after the Indian Claims Commission had been authorized, less than half of the dockets
had been settled, and the end was nowhere in
sight. The old difficulty with the Court of Claims
cases emerged again in the Indian Claims Commission. The government spent so much time preparing
its list of offsets and counterclaims that the cases
dragged on indefinitely. Bureaucrats were making
lifetime careers in simply working on the claims of
certain tribes.

Not only were the government agencies infinitely
slow, the Indian Claims Commission had an appeals
process which allowed either a tribe or the government to appeal to the Court of Claims and then to
the Supreme Court on any part of a decision of the
Indian Claims Commission. As the Indian Claims
Commission began to break the cases down into a
procedural sequence—determining the tribe's title
to the lands, the value of the lands, the value of the
government's offsets against the tribe, the date of
taking, and the attorney's fees, in addition to any
other motions raised by either the tribe's lawyer or
the government—the possibilities for either party to
appeal an adverse ruling were fantastic. Much of the
delay in settling the cases has come from this constant appeal of points and remanding the cases back
to the Indian Claims Commission by the higher
courts.

The point which John Vance raised was that the
Congress had authorized a *commission*, not a court.
The first commissioners, the tribal lawyers, and the

government attorneys had promptly transferred all the procedures and theories developed in the old Court of Claims Indian cases to the new Indian Claims Commission, thus transforming it into a court and not allowing it to become a commission.

What John Vance either did not know, or had been too modest to mention, was that the attorneys who lobbied for the passage of the Indian Claims Commission had carefully structured the new law to give themselves the best of all possible worlds. Many of the best cases had already been filed in the Court of Claims prior to the passage of the Indian Claims Commission act. The attorneys were worried that these claims might be transferred to the new commission, so they had section eleven inserted in the act, forbidding the transfer of existing cases to the Indian Claims Commission. The reason was evident to the careful observer. The Indian Claims Commission act barred lawyers' fees from exceeding 10 per cent of the amount of recovery. The fees for a case in the Court of Claims often ran to 25 per cent.

Consideration of lawyers' fees might also have been responsible for the 1951 cutoff date for filing claims. All claims arising since 1946 which would now be ineligible for consideration by the Indian Claims Commission would have to be filed in the Court of Claims—with the higher legal fees available. The high moral purpose of settling the Indian claims boiled down in the end to a lucrative bonanza for a select group of attorneys possessing the special skills to practice Indian law and the career employees of the United States who saw the complicated Indian cases as a lifetime career in a specialized field.

The effects of the Indian Claims Commission act have been varied. Some tribes have been torn apart internally in political fights between progressives wanting to settle the tribes' claim on the land issue and traditionals wanting a full accounting by the United States of its illegal acts against the tribe. Some traditional leaders have counseled their people that no claims for land should be settled, since the original taking by the United States was a violation of their treaty. They have demanded that the treaty be honored and the stolen lands returned. It was this attitude toward the 1868 Fort Laramie treaty that brought the old Oglala men to Wounded Knee in droves. Their argument—that in an illegal taking by the government the land title of the tribe remains intact and the land should be returned today—remains a difficult one to answer.

Many government officials who have come into government service since 1946 have misunderstood the nature of the legal effect of the Indian claims decisions. They do not liquidate the rights Indians have under treaties, since these rights are not examined by the commission. The Indian Claims Commission's refusal to honor the "fair and honorable dealings" clause of eligibility has precluded a settlement of these claims. Its sole function and the effect of its decisions is to update the legal parity of the land purchases as of the date the United States took the tribal lands. In the accounting-claims cases, the decision is simply to reimburse the tribe for unwarranted or foolish expenditures of tribal funds by government employees.

The present payments from claims cases received by tribes does not settle treaty obligations, but is more in the nature of compensating tribes for the real-estate-contract aspect of their treaties. The issue of political status and sovereign rights of the tribes remains the important and unresolved issue. There has been no liquidation of the political claims against the United States, and the national status of the Indian tribe remains intact. Rather than finally settling the Indian claims against the United States, the Indian Claims Commission works merely to clear out the underbrush and allow the claims created by the forced political and economic dependency during the last century to emerge.

The present movement among American Indians to force the United States to honor its treaties and agreements and to institute a new treaty relationship with the tribes is the significant movement of our time, and perhaps of this century. The Indian activists are trying to force the United States to live up to its own laws as they have been developed by the federal courts, the Congress, and the executive branch. The movement thus concentrates on the moral and political issues of Indian existence in this century and not on the events of the last century, except insofar as they have crippled the Indian communities in their effort to survive.

The pressing need today is that the United States not only recognize the international status of the Indian tribes, which survives the determinations of the Indian Claims Commission, but that it also authorize the creation of a special court to settle treaty violations. Until a Court of Indian Affairs, developed along the lines originally suggested by John Collier, is created, the perennial feeling of betrayal and resentment among Indians will continue. The claim of American Indians against the United States is not simply a demand for compensation for lands lost, but also a demand that a way of life that was nearly lost be protected from further depredations. The movement to reclaim that life and the independence which characterized it lies at the heart of the current Indian unrest and demonstrations.

11. The International Arena

Many Indians had predicted a widespread revolt against the conditions of the reservations long before Wounded Knee. Hank Adams, the fishing-rights activist, forecast nearly two years ago that before 1976 the activist movement would demand the dismantling of the Bureau of Indian Affairs and a reinstitution of the treaty-making procedures. And many a conference has witnessed a demand by some Indian or group of Indians that the whole subject of the status of American Indians be taken to the World Court for action.

To have found in either the takeover of the Bureau of Indian Affairs or the siege at Wounded Knee a conspiracy by activists funded by foreign money, as the federal government tried to do at one point, was to admit to a profound ignorance of the attitudes and beliefs of Indians. The pressure for international recognition has been building up for at least a generation among the traditional Indians, and more recently has become intense among the activists. The federal government may continue to pretend that it cannot deal with the tribes as sovereign nations, but two things for which it has responsibility are beginning to loom as important stumbling blocks in the campaign to sweep Indian affairs under the rug.

In this century the nations of the Western Hemisphere have been holding frequent meetings to determine what relationships must exist among the nations of the two continents. Inevitably, of course, the subject of the Indians has arisen. Every nation looks into its historical closet and discovers there the dispossessed native peoples. Most of the nations of the two continents have justified their treatment of Indians by depending upon the doctrine developed by the United States—that they had fallen heir to the claims exerted by their colonial predecessors to the right to extinguish the land titles of the native peoples. But many of the nations have not even had the sense of morality of the United States and have refused to purchase the lands, merely taking them as they were needed.

During the course of the present century, the International Conference of the American Nations began to meet, and at the eighth meeting the assembled nations resolved: "That the Continental Conference on Indian Life study the advisability of establishing an Inter-American Indian Institute and, if the occasion arises, set forth the basis for its organization and take the necessary steps for its immediate installation and organization." The resolution received serious attention because many of the nations were on the verge of final exploitation of their Indian populations, and there was considerable discussion among the other nations as to the advisability of this final step of disenfranchisement. As one might suspect, John Collier, the United States Commissioner of Indian Affairs, played an important role in admonishing the other American nations concerning their treatment of Indians.

The resolution was made effective by the First Inter-American Indian Conference in Patzcuaro in April 1940, which was attended by many of the nations of the hemisphere. The assembled nations passed a resolution creating the Inter-American Indian Institute and recommended to themselves an international convention which would finalize the creation of the institute. In December 1940, the convention was approved by a sufficient number of governments and the Inter-American Indian Institute was formally established.

The terms of the convention reflected both a desire of the nations to assume some responsibility for the conditions of Indians on a hemispheric basis and a frantic effort to shore up their images before the rest of the nations of the world. While the nations agreed to hold periodic meetings and cooperate with one another in the preamble of the convention, they also pledged "on a basis of mutual respect for the inherent rights of each to exercise absolute liberty in solving the 'Indian Problem' in America." There might be discussions in the future, but if Brazil, for example, decided to embark on a policy of genocide, it was free to do so with the blessings of the other American nations.

Under the provisions of Article L, each state promised to establish a number of organizations. There was to be an international institute called the Inter-American Indian Institute, to which each nation would contribute and which would be administered by a governing board. There was also to be an Inter-American Indian Conference, meeting every four years. And each nation promised to establish a National Indian Institute in its own country for research and policy formation.

Attendance at the quadrennial meetings of the conference was strictly limited. Delegates were to be appointed by the respective governments. Persons of recognized interest could attend the meetings provided they were invited by the organizing government and authorized by their own governments. They could attend the sessions but express themselves only through their own nation's delegates. Effective criticism was thus eliminated from the very beginning.

The institute itself was to solicit, collect, arrange and distribute reports on subjects pertaining to Indians. The major emphasis was research of a rather deadening kind, but it was also authorized to act in an advisory capacity to any Bureau of Indian Affairs of the American nations. The focus of the Institute was away from the difficult legal and philosophical problems involving Indian populations toward the collection of data that could interest only a tourist who had expressed a sudden fascination with the Indians.

The National Indian Institutes were supposed to be organized whenever the subscribing nations deemed it advisable. It was theoretically possible for nations to join the Inter-American Indian Institute and pledge to create their own National Indian Institute but legally postpone any action toward this goal. As one might suspect, the United States has yet to fulfill its responsibilities under this convention, and has not yet created its National Indian Institute. The institutes of each nation were to be affiliated with the hemispheric institute and file annual reports with it.

A complicated formula was worked out to create an annual budget of $30,600 for the operation of the Inter-American Indian Institute. The formula was revised in 1963 to raise a budget of $93,771.04, a goodly sum to solve the problems of the nations of the hemisphere. The United States was assessed some $61,000 under the new formula, and the other nations contributed much smaller sums, Brazil's $7,400 being the next largest contribution.

The creation of the Inter-American Indian Institute did not do much for the native peoples. It was, however, a clear indication by the nations of the Western Hemisphere that Indians were not simply a domestic problem which they shared but a subject of concern that spanned all nations. For nearly thirty years the nations met in conference, shared anecdotes, and adjourned to mourn the passing of the noble red race. In recent years the consciousness of Indians around the hemisphere has increased, and with this rising consciousness has come a change of attitude among the nations of the world.

Perhaps again the Iroquois should be given credit for embarking on a new course of action. The famous Wallace "Mad Bear" Anderson of the Tuscaroras made contacts all over the two continents, particularly with some of the Indians in Mexico and Central America. Anderson earns his living as a merchant seaman, and in his travels has visited nearly every port in the Western Hemisphere. As Mad Bear traveled, be began to build up a demand by Indians for closer contact. As early as the beginning years of the sixties, Indians were visiting back and forth between Mexico and the United States, and American Indians were becoming more aware of what was taking place in South America.

Then came the revelations by European journalists that Brazil had been conducting a genocidal war against its Indians for some time. Cries of outrage began to be heard, and the National Congress of American Indians demanded that something be done by the United States to show its concern over the destruction of whole tribes of Indians in the Amazon.

The fact that Indians of the United States were becoming more vocal themselves began to worry the bureaucrats in the nation's capital, and the specter of American Indians demanding that the United States go on record against the genocide of Indians by other nations in the hemisphere, particularly with the repeated failures in hemispheric policy that had marked the ventures of the United States during the twentieth century, resulted in a change of emphasis by the federal government.

Prior to the 1960s, the constitution of the American delegation to the quadrennial conferences had been largely farcical. The conference was viewed as a pleasant political junket which could be used to reward the party faithful by whichever party controlled the White House. No serious confrontation of the issues was expected, the delegates all received spending money and purchased souvenirs for their relatives, and the conference was quickly forgotten. But with the rising tide of Indian discontent in the United States, delegations had to be chosen to reflect the policy of the government rather than the designs of the party in power. Indians began to be chosen to attend the conference as delegates—but only those Indians who would bring credit to the United States. That is to say, those who would not ask embarrassing questions of Brazil or the other nations busily engaged in genocide against Indians.

The conference before Wounded Knee was in 1972, and a well-trained delegation of Indians was sent to Brazil as representatives of the United States. It is particularly enlightening to read the position papers prepared by the United States prior to the conference. As explained by Anthony Perkins, a State Department employee:

> The Inter-American Indian Institute is a specialized organization of the OAS that assists member governments in their efforts to develop national policies on Indian affairs through the

exchange of publications and information, and by the organization of training programs designed to improve the well-being of the Indian population in the Western Hemisphere. As part of its regular activities, it holds seminars, studies the migration patterns of Indians, encourages Indian handicrafts, and promotes community development projects among isolated and marginal tribes. In the field of publications, it has reprinted numerous studies on Indian populations, including one on the Pueblo Indians in the Southwest United States. In view of the large Indian populations in Latin America, the United States supports the Institute as a significant contributor to the economic, social, and cultural development of human resources in that area of the world. *The Institute also serves as a useful international forum for the United States to explain our government's policy towards Indians in this country.* [Emphasis added.] [Report of the Delegation.]

The participation of the United States, it would seem, is based upon the opening of opportunities for propaganda rather than any real concern for the problems of Indians.

This suspicion is verified by another short paper prepared for the last conference, listing four reasons why the United States continues to participate in the Inter-American Indian Conference and the benefits which it receives from its participation:

1) Our participation *demonstrates to Latin America U.S. concern* about the condition of its Indian minority.

2) It allows *U.S. specialists in the field to exchange information* on a face-to-face basis with specialists from other countries.

3) The Institute serves as a *clearing house* for information *about Indian Programs* in the United States and Latin America.

4) Nonparticipation in the Institute might *provoke the accusation by organized Indian groups in this country,* i.e. like the National Congress of American Indians, that the United States is neglecting its international obligations towards the Indian. [Emphasis added.]

And there you have it. The demonstration of concern by the United States is ephemeral at best. U.S. specialists in the field of Indian affairs go to conferences of anthropologists and sociologists which are far more profound than the Inter-American Indian Conference, and the clearinghouse function of the conferences is ridiculous at best. The fourth reason is primary—that the federal government is afraid that the Indian organizations might accuse it of failing to fulfill its *international obligations* to Indians.

There is, then, an international dimension to Indian problems and Indian existence, recognized by the nations of the Western Hemisphere and carefully obscured by the United States government through rhetoric, that continues to emerge with the rising consciousness of peoples around the world becoming aware of the conditions of Indians on the American continents. The fear of the United States is that Indians may become a world issue and that the carefully constructed theories concerning the demise of the American Indian may be revealed to a startled world as slightly premature.

Fortunately for the United States, the delegation of Indians chosen to represent it during the 1972 meetings in Brazil behaved like well-oiled puppets. They not only failed to raise the question of Brazilian genocide but actually offered a resolution applauding Brazil's handling of its Indian problem. Who could ask for a better group of Indians?

We are seeing in the Wounded Knee confrontation the beginning of a period when the Indian problems of the Western Hemisphere can no longer be hidden behind the Monroe Doctrine or the Inter-American Indian Convention of 1940. The question of the status of Indian tribes and peoples is arriving on the world agenda as surely as it did upon the discovery of the New World. Debates and arguments will once again rage, as they did in the Spanish court of the 1500s. Thus, while the United States might like to protect the status quo of its present Indian policy, to do so would be the highest folly. The other American nations are anxiously watching to see how the United States arrives at a satisfactory status for its Indian population. Continued protest and discontent among American Indians may well trigger movements in other countries. The situation remains tense in spite of the American Indians, hand-picked by the administration, who applauded Brazil in 1972.

It would not be bad if the movement in the modern world were confined to the Inter-American Indian Institute, for, were that the case, the United States could surely find the means to drop a buckskin curtain on the events in the Indian world and choke off any semblance of discontent from the outside world.

Another movement of nearly thirty years' duration is also beginning to present difficulties for the United States, and the combination of these two forces may well propel the subject of Indian status out into the world arena beyond the point where it can be easily contained by the United States. This other force, moving quietly but firmly today, is the movement to get the United States to ratify the Convention against

Genocide. The story of this convention is strange, considering the actions of the United States during the Second World War and its recent actions in Viet Nam and Cambodia. One of the first major acts in foreign policy by President Nixon during his first term, however, was to send a message to the Senate Foreign Relations Committee asking that they consider sending the Genocide Convention to the Senate floor for ratification. It had remained in committee for twenty-three years, so Nixon's action was hardly premature.

The Genocide Convention was one of the major reforms in international law to come out of the Second World War. Previous wars had been waged over territories, imagined and real insults between nations, and as wars of trade and economic rivalry. The Second World War was the only extensive war of modern times that featured as a grisly sideshow the advocation of the extermination of a racial group. The world watched with almost evil fascination as Adolf Hitler assumed power in Germany and began an extensive campaign to deny German Jews their legal and civil rights. As Hitler's campaign of lies and oppression escalated, it became apparent that something demonic was happening in Nazi Germany, but few people in the outside world wanted to consider exactly what that something was.

As the end of the war saw the invasion of the German homeland, the horrible truth of Nazi depravity became known. Concentration camps with massive gas ovens were found inside Germany, and estimates were that over six million people had been systematically exterminated in these camps. The world recoiled in horror at the Nazi excesses and resolved to make genocide an international crime.

On November 2, 1946, the delegations of Cuba, India, and Panama requested the Secretary-General of the United Nations to include on the agenda of the General Assembly the topic of the prevention and punishment of the crime of genocide. The subject was referred to the Sixth (Legal) Committee for study. The committee reported a draft resolution a month later, at the fifty-fifth plenary meeting on December 11, 1946, and the Assembly adopted, unanimously and without debate, the report of the Legal Committee.

The genocide resolution states that

> Genocide is a denial of the right of existence of entire groups of human beings, as homicide is the denial of the right to live of individual human beings.

The resolution further stated that the extermination of entire groups of human beings impairs the self-preservation of civilization itself, and that civilized society is justified in branding genocide an international crime.

A draft convention on genocide was prepared under an ad hoc committee in the spring of 1948 under the chairmanship of the United States representative to the committee. On September 23, 1948, Secretary of State Marshall reflected the attitude of the United States toward genocide when he remarked that

> Governments which systematically disregard the rights of their own people are not likely to respect the rights of other nations and other people and are likely to seek their objectives by coercion and force in the international field.

The fear of fostering further international conflict by allowing nations to persecute racial or ethnic minorities within their own borders was persuasive, and on December 9, 1948, the General Assembly unanimously adopted the convention to outlaw genocide.

The United States signed the convention two days following United Nations approval of the document. When signing on behalf of the United States its representative noted:

> I am privileged to sign this convention on behalf of my Government, which has been proud to take an active part in the effort of the United Nations to bring this convention into being.
>
> The Government of the United States considers this an event of great importance in the development of international law and of cooperation among states for the purpose of eliminating practices offensive to all civilized mankind.

President Truman forwarded the convention to the Senate Foreign Relations Committee in mid-1949, and the committee considered it for nearly a year. The following year, 1950, the committee failed to get the convention to the floor before Congress adjourned, and with the onset of the Korean War the attention of Congress was tragically diverted from the convention. Eisenhower, Kennedy, and Johnson all studiously avoided the question of seeking ratification of the Genocide Convention. Finally, in 1970, President Nixon, as part of his forward thrust in foreign policy, sent a message to the Senate requesting action on the convention. "I urge the Senate," President Nixon wrote, "to consider anew this important Convention and to grant its advice and consent to ratification."

Between the time that the United Nations unanimously endorsed the Genocide Convention and President Nixon sent his message asking Congress to reconsider it, seventy-four nations had approved the convention. Soviet Russia and its satellite nations had approved the convention during the mid-fifties, but both the United States and the United Kingdom, supposedly the moral leaders of the West, refused to ratify it, the United Kingdom finally approving it in 1970, an event which probably triggered the action by the Nixon administration. In the interim period, the United States and Great Britain were hard put to complain about the treatment of minorities by the Soviet Union. How could they accuse Russia of violating a convention which they had refused to sign? The moral issues of the Cold War were not, apparently, on as lofty a plane as we have been led to believe.

The first article of the convention declared that genocide would be considered a crime before the nations of the world. It was in the second article, the definition of genocide, that problems began to arise for the United States. The second article specified that any of the following acts, if accompanied by the intent to destroy, in whole or in part, a national, ethnical, racial, or religious group, constituted the crime of genocide:

  1) Killing members of the group;

  2) Causing serious bodily or mental harm to members of the group;

  3) Deliberately inflicting on the group conditions of life calculated to bring about its physical destruction in whole or in part;

  4) Imposing measures intended to prevent births within the group;

  5) Forcibly transferring children of the group to another group.

The third article of the convention specified that five acts would be defined involving genocide that would be considered criminal:

1) genocide itself
2) conspiracy to commit genocide
3) direct and public incitement to commit genocide
4) attempt to commit genocide
5) complicity in genocide.

The remainder of the convention deals with procedures for the ratifying nations to change their domestic legislation to conform with the provisions of the convention, agreements to punish guilty parties, provisions for trials of the accused, and a recognition of the aggrieved parties by the United Nations when such parties petition for redress.

Article IX provided that disputes between parties relating to the interpretation of the convention should be submitted to the International Court of Justice. It was the key provision in the convention, since if parties did not agree to the interpretation of the acts alleged to be genocidal, the remainder of the convention would be useless. It was at this point that the United States led the fight to gut the convention. Although voting in favor of the convention, the representative of the United States made the following exception on behalf of the United States:

> Article IX provides that disputes between the contracting parties relating to the interpretation, application, or fulfillment of the present convention, "including those relating to the responsibility of a state for genocide or any of the other acts enumerated in article III," shall be submitted to the International Court of Justice.
>
> If "responsibility of a state" is used in the traditional sense of responsibility to another state for injuries sustained by nationals of the complaining state in violation of principles of inter-

national law and similarly, if "fulfillment" refers to disputes where interests of nationals of the complaining state are involved, these words would not appear to be objectionable.

If, however, "responsibility of a state" is not used in the traditional sense and if these words are intended to mean that a state can be held liable in damages for injury inflicted by it on its own nationals, this provision is objectionable and my Government makes a reservation with respect to such an interpretation.

The idea of the Genocide Convention, if you will recall, was to prevent such horrors as the Nazi extermination of the Jews. Yet the reservation which the United States demanded would have allowed Nazi Germany to escape any responsibility or liability for its treatment of the Jews. Most were citizens of Germany, and hence the convention would have exempted them from its operation under the United States version of the convention.

What the American representative was considering was that, for the most part, American citizens are from a varied background of European countries, with a scattering of Asians. If a European nation could force the issue of mistreatment of its racial or ethnic descendants who had become citizens of the United States, quite obviously there would have been the possibility of endless intervention by other countries into the domestic affairs of the United States.

The question of American Indians did not arise in conjunction with the discussions on genocide. Yet, quite obviously, the American Indian situation is the area where genocide has occurred in the past, where present policy flirts with genocide, and where no foreign nation finds any racial or ethnic relationships. Realistically, it is the only area in which the United States could be accused of genocide. Are American Indians nationals of the United States within the interpretation of this convention? That question has never been answered. It has not even been asked.

Theoretically, under the convention one nation could file a protest or accusation against another nation on the subject of genocide. With the creation of Israel, the international problem of the Jews was solved. Israel could complain if the other nations embarked on pogroms once again. But who would protest if the Basques, Flemish, Celts, or American Indians were subjects of genocide? Their only nations were the remnants of their old tribal or political forms which had survived or been allowed to continue by the nations that engulfed them. Yet they were so distinct a group as to be the beneficiaries of the convention.

The question of the Genocide Convention has not yet been settled by the Senate Foreign Relations Committee. Perhaps the disgusting behavior of the United States in Southeast Asia has made some Senators hesitant about endorsing a convention that the United States has systematically been violating for nearly a generation.

Even if we allow the courts of the United States the luxury of developing their own, very favorable interpretation of the Genocide Convention's words and phrases, questions regarding the treatment of American Indians will eventually arise. Federal policy for the major portion of this century has been oriented toward the systematic destruction of Indian communities. "Break up the tribal mass" was the cry of the supporters of allotments, and this ideology was revived during the termination era, when the Congress decided to remove all federal services from the tribes and disperse the tribal members to the cities of the Midwest.

What will become of the educational system of the Bureau of Indian Affairs, which seeks to deprive Indian children of their heritage through a concentrated program of federal schools at which speaking the tribal language is covertly forbidden? What will become of the children of Indians who are taken from their homes by state agencies, well-intentioned do-gooders, and church programs with the intent of transforming those children into cultural white men? How will the United States answer charges concerning its off-reservation boarding schools, which transport children thousands of miles from their homes?

The states also will have a problem with American Indians if the Genocide Convention is approved. How can the states avoid Indian treaty rights any longer when they have themselves blurred the definition of rights under those treaties? Will they be able to deny that they are persecuting Indian fishermen because they are fishing under a treaty and still deny genocidal policies? What will happen to the National Guard in the State of Washington when they use the Nisqually tribe as hypothetical enemies on their summer maneuvers? Mental harm deliberately inflicted is a crime under the convention.

The present time is one of extreme complexity. Indians are demanding that their sovereign rights be recognized by the United States. While part of the Indian protest movement is political, its major thrust is religious and historical and sees the revocation of Western ideas of the inevitability of history, derived primarily from the Christian religious teachings, as a major step in reform. The United States has neglected to enforce the provisions of Indian treaties either against itself or against its citizens when they have violated them.

Indians have somehow managed to survive the past century with some aspects of sovereignty still intact. Now the movements of the world are beginning to form a relationship with the American Indian struggle for survival, and by doing so are lifting the Indian struggle out of its context as a domestic problem of the United States. The Inter-American Indian Conference and Convention, for example, are both indications that Indians are more than an internal problem of any particular nation of the Western Hemisphere. And the Genocide Convention, if ratified, will bring with it certain procedural problems as well as the major problems of interpretation. Ratification of the convention will almost certainly provoke Indian protests under its provisions, while failure to ratify will result in accusations by minority groups within the United States and an increasingly bad image for the United States overseas.

Had all of these things happened in an earlier time, the subject of Indian political and cultural existence might not have proven so explosive. A generation ago, Indians were still well within that period of their experience where they regarded the techniques and material goods of the white man as an indication that the white man knew what he was doing. Many Indians felt humbled in their reservation existence and deferred to whatever the white man wanted.

Today the situation is reversed. Indians have traveled in almost every nation in the world. They have fought in the major wars of this generation. They have watched as industrial pollution, pesticides, and urban sprawl have reduced the country to a pitiful state of affairs. As the cartoon produced at Wounded Knee remarked, "If the white man cannot take care of his own land, why do you think he can tell you what to do with yours?" Thus, to postpone consideration of a new legal status for Indian tribes is merely to court continued protest and discontent. Within a foreseeable time, Indians will want to know why the United States has failed to set up its National Indian Institute under the Inter-American Indian Convention and why it refuses to ratify the Genocide Convention, and protests may well revolve around those issues.

The time has come when it is clearly in the best interests of the United States to clarify the legal status of Indians.

12. Reinstituting the Treaty Process

After four centuries of conflict between red and white and nearly two centuries of intimate struggle with the United States, American Indians stand today on the verge of their greatest crisis. The old years of freedom have long since vanished. Tribal customs, religions, and beliefs formed in the days of independence have been badly eroded, and the temptation to surrender the remaining customs and beliefs and merge with the white man's society remains a fascinating alternative for many Indians.

It has been only within the last decade that Indians have taken a critical look at their history, their conditions, and the answers that American society have given them to explain their fall from prosperity. The drama is still unfolding. More and more Indians are questioning both their knowledge of the tribe and their understanding of how the tribe has been split into a quarreling, scattered conglomerate of people. For the first time in history, American Indians are exploring the old legal doctrines, the cultural attitudes of themselves and white society, and the history of the peoples of the world to find an answer to the present confusion.

As this search has proceeded, the rejection of the old ideology of the innate inferiority of the tribal culture and the superiority of the Western European way of life has been profound and extensive, especially among the younger and more educated Indians. The more that Indians discovered about themselves and about American history and the history and fate of the other peoples of the world, the more they have sought refuge in the tribal customs, beliefs, and traditions that have remained.

Instead of vanishing, therefore, the American Indian has redoubled his efforts to bring the tribe back together. With this movement has come a realization that the tribe must stand before history and reclaim its political and cultural identity and independence. Not all tribes lost their sense of independence. The Iroquois always maintained that they had never surrendered any part of their independence. From the very beginning, they saw themselves as allies of Great Britain, free and sovereign, even when Great Britain was no longer a viable political force on the North American continent.

The Sioux submerged their feelings and suffered in silence but never forgot the defeats they had inflicted upon the white man in numerous battles. Beneath the façade of defeat was the urgency to have one more battle, losing perhaps to overwhelming odds, but in losing finding that eternal affirmation that it is a "good day to die" and thus confirming to future historians that it did mean something to be a Lakota. Other tribes felt the same way, and for nearly a century kept their feelings well hidden from the white man but simmering just beneath the surface so that if the time should arise when a chance existed to reclaim freedom, there would never be a question whether the price was too high.

Through some mysterious intuition, the Indian

activists divined the presence of this perennial resistance and began to exploit it nearly a decade ago. The movement began to get its bearings, first in political ideology, then in religious doctrine, then back again to practical politics, and finally in the explosions of Alcatraz, Fort Lawton, and other invasions of federal lands.

From the initial protests, one can draw a straight line in ideology and type of confrontation from the first invasion of Alcatraz in 1964 to the snowy hills of Wounded Knee, South Dakota, in 1973. Politically, the issues revolved around the treaty of 1868 as symbolic of the hundreds of treaties and agreements that had proven less valuable than the paper they were printed on. Religiously, the movement set its roots in the desire to reclaim a sacred place for the tribal community which existed partially in time and space and partially in the determination of unknown Indians who preserved a dignity that was timeless.

No matter how Indians approached their problems, the answer appeared to be the same. If one was primarily a political activist, one could not remain in that field for long before the question of religious morality and history asserted itself. Did it make sense to fight for change and take risks when the next generation of whites might well destroy the hard-won agreements, eroding their meaning, as the treaties of the previous century had been reduced to rhetoric? Political gains could be solidified only if the enemy were taught a higher sense of morality and one's own people learned the lessons of sacrifice and devotion to the cause.

Conversely, the religious men among the tribes could not remain true to themselves unless they found a way to express the value of their religion in the events of the day, in some tangible manifestation of the tribal religion through a change of the conditions under which the people lived. In the former days of glory the religious men predicted, prophesied, lamented, warned, rejoiced, and reflected, but they were always involved in the fate of the community. For Indian religious leaders, the past decade has been a time of gradual reintegration of their beliefs and ceremonies into the life of the people once more.

The culmination of these emerging forces and attitudes, as we have seen, was the eager participation by reservation people in the Trail of Broken Treaties caravan. The wide spectrum of Indian people represented in that march proposed a new method of dealing with Indian tribes based upon the treaty-making process. Their explanations of the process which would emerge if this course of action were adopted was sketchy at best, and involved an assumption that the federal government understood their legal status far better than they did. As we have seen, the federal conception of the Indian tribe as a political entity has ranged over a number of concepts which appear mutually conflicting without the definition of political status encompassed by the protectorate concept.

Affirmative action by the Congress of the United States to define Indian tribes as smaller nations under the protection of the United States would be the first step in defining the nature of the new relationship. Such an action would eliminate the errors of the past regarding the nature of Indian tribes and bring to a close the nebulous period of history which has plagued us since the days of discovery of the New World. In effect, this action would mean a surrender by the United States of its right to extinguish Indian aboriginal title to land, and would freeze the present Indian lands within the context of national boundaries rather than reservation boundaries.

Eliminating the claim of the United States to first-purchase rights of tribal lands would mean that no further sales of Indian lands would be possible. The lands of individual Indians would have to be sold to the tribal government under the same legal terms by which the United States government now purchases tribal lands: the right of first refusal and, following that first refusal, sale to other tribal enterprises or individual tribal members. It would also mean that the trust relationship presently imposed by the United States government on tribal and individual lands would become a passive trust instead of an active trust. Bureaucrats would enter the land picture only as an appellate commission to determine the validity of the transfer, not as energetic real-estate salesmen attempting to reduce the tribal land holdings.

Reduction of the trust relationship from an active to a passive trust would have a profound impact on the federal budget. The great numbers of bureaucrats who now find a restful home in the offices of the Interior Department would not be needed. Great reductions in unnecessary staff would be possible, resulting in great financial savings. Perhaps even better would be the release from liability of the United States for those acts which its employees committed not wisely but too well. This factor alone would be significant, since nearly a hundred claims presently filed against the United States by Indian tribes involve a misuse of federal funds. The liability of the United States continues so long as it insists that it must supervise or actually perform all business functions of Indian tribes. The international status of tribes would mean an automatic shifting of liability from the United States to the tribal government.

Of more immediate importance to people on the

reservations would be the clarification of the status of their lands and rights with respect to state governments. At the present time, tribes all over the country are under continual attack by departments of state governments on the vague and untenable theory that the reservations are somehow part of the states. The fact that Indians draw some services from the states seems, in the eyes of those states, to justify intrusion into tribal affairs and erosion of outstanding treaty rights.

With the tribes having international status, the states would have no more power to interfere with tribal governments or reservation affairs than they would to interfere with the operations of the Canadian or Mexican government. The lines of civil and criminal jurisdiction would be clearly set, with no doubts remaining in the minds of state officials or Indians concerning the limits of political power each entity would exercise. In those instances where Indians have rights outstanding on lands now under the jurisdiction of the state, new arrangements could be worked out regarding the extent and nature of those rights. Tribes could issue membership cards to all tribal members, and under the agreements concluded with the states a definite time and place to exercise tribal rights would be made available to tribal members.

At the present time, the two Indian committees of Congress that deal with Indian legislation spend the majority of their time working on minor and petty pieces of legislation. A typical legislative calendar of either the Senate or House Indian Subcommittees would show that Congress is called upon to exercise its wisdom on whether reservations should have five- or ten-year leasing periods authorized, whether the United States should return eight acres of surplus school lands to the tribe, and whether a tribe shall divide its claims award a certain way. The work that these members of Congress are asked to do under the present method of operation is demeaning at best, insulting at worst.

Under the theory of international protectorate, the necessity of Congress' performing tribal housekeeping chores would be swept away. In its place the treaty or agreement relationship would exist. Congress would authorize a delegation of people to go to the respective reservations and there make arrangements for a treaty or agreement with the tribe. A full discussion of the problems of the tribe would ensue, and the various proposals for a total development of human and natural resources of the tribe would be conducted. Both the tribe and the treaty-making commission would be empowered to authorize studies, reports, surveys, or whatever hard research work was needed to enable the tribe and the commission to reach an intelligent solution to the problems they were confronting.

When the commission and the tribe reached an agreement, the rights and responsibilities of both parties, the tribe and the United States, would be clearly defined. If the tribe wished to operate its own school system, the nature of the relationship would be carefully defined. If the tribe wished the United States to provide roads, health services, or development funds, the amount and extent of such services and funds would be carefully defined. All aspects of the relationship would be covered, and a final responsibility would be assigned to each area that came under discussion.

Following the negotiations of the tribe and the commission, a formal agreement would be drawn up and signed. This agreement would cover a period of years agreeable to both the federal government and the tribe. At the end of the term of years for which the treaty or agreement had been made, another treaty or agreement would be needed. Again, only those areas which indicated a need for cooperative efforts would be the subjects of discussion, and the agreements reached would define precisely which entity, the United States or the tribe, would accept responsibility for handling the problem.

Following the formal signing of the agreement, the document would go to both the tribal council and the Congress of the United States for consideration and ratification. Congress would have open hearings on the ratification of the treaty or agreement and allow any witnesses that wished to appear to be heard. All agencies of government that would have commitments under the new agreement would be asked to file a report with the committee, and it would prepare a final report on the agreement to be submitted to both houses of Congress for approval.

The tribal government would publicize the agreement on the reservation and among its tribal members who lived off the reservation. Open hearings would also be held at various places on the reservation and in those urban areas where a substantial number of tribal members lived. Every tribal member would have an opportunity to comment on the agreement, and the tribal government would be responsible for informing its members concerning their rights and responsibilities under the document when approved.

If any differences resulted either from the meetings of the tribal members or the open congressional hearings, a special subcommittee composed of Senators and Congressmen and tribal officials would be appointed to work out a compromise text. The final version of the agreement or treaty would be submitted to a vote of the tribal members, with a specific percentage of tribal members required to approve before it would take effect. Some tribes already have the requirement that two-thirds or three-fourths of their adult male members approve any further agreements with the United States.

Assuming that the tribal members approved the agreement, the only remaining step would be the formal endorsement by Congress of the treaty or agreement. Following endorsement or ratification, the tribe and the United States would be expected to perform their respective functions on a contractual basis, with legal remedies available to each party at any step in the process. Both the United States and the tribe would waive sovereign immunity for the purposes of the treaty or agreement, and the remedies for each infraction of the agreement would be specifically given.

The problem with this proposal is its very simplicity. At the present time, each session of Congress may find a number of pieces of legislation introduced affecting a certain tribe. A leasing bill, a bill to return submarginal lands, a bill to return school lands, a bill funding roads, a bill adding a member to the tribal roll, a bill authorizing a dam, a bill distributing a claims award, and a bill authorizing trading of lands may all be introduced on behalf of a tribe. The agreement process would cover all of these problems plus any others that might arise. Congress would be relieved of its onerous burden of pondering over minutiae and simply have responsibility for determining the legal relationship that will be considered to exist between the United States and a tribe.

One of the objections that has been raised against this process is that there are a multitude of federal laws that apply to all phases of Indian affairs, and unless the federal government followed those laws or was aware of them, it might be creating unusual or unwanted precedents. The effect of the treaty-making process would be to negate the large body of existing laws that presently affect tribal and individual rights and place the whole responsibility for the legal relationship on the treaty or agreement that was worked out between the tribe and the government. Using the treaty-making process, the whole concept of precedent would soon be eliminated, since the rights and responsibilities of each party would depend upon the most recent treaty or agreement and not upon a precedent made, perhaps with another tribe, some years ago.

Another objection that has been raised is that the majority of the tribes in the country are very small. Only about thirty tribes have either the population, land area, or income to attempt any significant venture in self-government. The people of the Trail of Broken Treaties anticipated that question and advocated that regional treaties be signed with those tribes that are too small to negotiate on their own.

There is a lot of merit and substantial legal precedent for considering such a move. During the treaty-making days of the last century, the United States frequently signed treaties with smaller bands of larger nations, and occasionally made a number of tribes share treaties. An examination of the existing treaties and agreements will reveal that a *majority* of them were treaties signed with more than one tribe and provided for a type of government or land cession affecting the lives of people on a regional basis. With several regional treaties, the federal government could easily provide a definite program for the majority of tribes around the nation.

Finally, in the area of the relationship between Indian tribes and the various states of the union, the treaty-making process would prove fruitful. At the present time, hardly a soul, Indian or white, knows the extent to which the tribe and the state have or should have formal legal relationships. During the 1950s Congress attempted to solve the problem when it passed P.L. 280, which unilaterally gave the states permission to extend civil and criminal jurisdiction over Indian reservations. The result was disastrous. In many places the states claimed to have assumed criminal jurisdiction, but failed to provide any services to the reservation people. Some reservations were legal no-man's-lands because the federal government could not provide police protection and the state would not provide it.

With that special irony that history records, many states made no effort to tax income or property of Indians on the reservation until after Congress had amended P.L. 280 to provide that the states had to get the tribe's consent before they could extend their jurisdiction over the reservations. Following the amendment of P.L. 280, a number of states attempted to tax Indians, on the theory that they were given that right by implication by Congress in 1954. The argument of the states was that this receipt of implied powers had survived a clear statement of Congress that limited state action to instances where the state had received the tribe's consent.

The agreement process (or regional treaty-making, in the case of most tribes) would carefully define the relationships that would exist between a state and a tribe as understood on the part of the federal government. But within the agreement made on the federal level tribes could provide for agreement-making with states on certain topics of mutual interest. In that way, no area of contact between a state and a tribe need go to litigation, since all areas could be covered by mutual agreement. The question of eligibility for state programs could be handled in a far better setting than having the states dictate to the tribe or the federal government dictate to the states on behalf of Indians.

One of the most pressing problems of today concerns the right of the tribe to police its own reservation. Many of the reservations have boundaries set in the 1880s, over which the tribe is expected to exercise some control. Yet some of the lands within these ancient boundaries have long since left Indian hands and are therefore theoretically under the jurisdiction of the state. The question of both boundaries and jurisdiction over lands could be handled on a contemporary basis reflecting the true state of conditions at the local level and not the magic lines drawn on a territorial map nearly a century ago.

To insure proper functioning of the agreements, Congress could provide a special federal court to handle all questions arising under the treaties, agreements, and laws pertaining to Indians. The court could be composed of judges and a research staff, including scholars who had an intimate familiarity with the history behind the respective treaties and agreements of the past which affect the relationship between Indians and the federal government today.

In addition, the special court would send observers to the respective treaty- or agreement-making sessions then being held with tribes. A transcript of the sessions could be filed in the special court for reference in interpreting the document when the occasion should arise. The whole area of legal rights of Indians would be compressed into a concise and compact package. All questions arising concerning past or present treaties and agreements could be settled quickly, instead of the decades that settlement of such questions presently takes.

The idealism in this idea is obvious. It assumes good will on the part of both the United States and the Indian tribes. History has shown that such good will is a rare thing. Yet the alternative which presents itself is hardly comforting. Today, the federal government is spending nearly a billion dollars a year on Indian problems, the majority of the money going to support a large and inefficient bureaucracy, and the problems continue to get worse. Instead of preparing Indians to confront the modern world, the Bureau of Indian Affairs spends its money to train yet another generation of bureaucrats to handle the affairs of Indians.

Indian country today simmers with discontent. That discontent has manifested itself at Wounded Knee and other incidents where the people have cried out for more self-government. The response of the federal government has been to subcontract some functions of the Bureau of Indian Affairs to the tribal governments, but in no case to clarify the legal status or legal rights of the tribe so that it could begin to function as a political entity. Rather, the trend has been to view the tribal government as a childlike extension of the Bureau of Indian Affairs—a junior chamber of commerce, as it were.

Without a clear understanding of their rights, neither Indians nor their tribal governments can function effectively in the modern world. There has been no effort by the federal government to clarify those rights. Long-standing legal doctrines that favor the tribes are shucked off as relics of the past when the federal government opposes a tribal plan of action, and hailed as inherent powers of the tribe when the federal government favors an action of the tribal government. Indians are thus left without a clear legal status, yet bound helplessly in legalities.

We would strongly recommend that the United States government face the Indian problem squarely. That it acknowledge to the nations of the world the international status of Indian nations as perhaps among the smallest and weakest nations of the world but yet as nations with an inherent right to political and cultural existence comparable to any other nation.

We would strongly recommend that the United States reinstitute treaty-making with Indian tribes on a tribal or regional basis, and that that mechanism be used to clarify and define the rights which an Indian tribe has. In conjunction with the treaty-making process, we recommend that those programs which the United States and the tribe reach an agreement on be the programs of the reservations, and that the Department of the Interior be forbidden to develop programs of its own design which are then forced upon the reservations under the guise of federal policy.

We believe that the program outlined in this book is the most rational alternative to the present federal policies and programs, which have spawned the take-over of the Bureau of Indian Affairs, Wounded Knee, numerous incidents in every state, and widespread discontent among American Indians. They have not been able to solve one single problem of American Indians, because they have taken dignity away from Indians. Until that dignity is restored, no lasting progress can be made by the United States or the respective tribes. The best way to restore dignity to the tribes is to fulfill the original promises made to the tribes in the treaties and agreements of former years.

Attorney General William Wirt, writing an opinion for then President Andrew Jackson concerning the Cherokees and the state of Georgia, commented regarding the validity of the Cherokee Treaty:

> If it be mean to say that, although capable of treating, their treaties are not to be construed

like the treaties of nations absolutely independent, no reason is discerned for this distinction. . . . The point, then, once conceded, that the Indians are independent to the purpose of treating, their independence is, to that purpose, as absolute as that of any other nation.

We think that's still pretty good law.

Afterword

The occupation of Wounded Knee is now a matter of history for most people. Some Indians remember it as the most important experience of their lives; others see it as a terrible disruption in the steady march of progress during the postwar years. Many non-Indians are still not clear what it was all about, but a clear majority seems to have generated great sympathy for the Sioux as a result of Wounded Knee II. The turmoil on the reservation did not stop with the end of the occupation. Violence between the two factions on the reservation continued during the remainder of Dick Wilson's term of office. The F.B.I. became severely oppressive toward the traditional people, constantly harassing them, until finally two F.B.I. men were killed in June 1975. Several Indians were brought to trial for these killings but only one person, Leonard Peltier, was convicted—and that conviction may have been based on manufactured evidence. F.B.I. incursions on the reservation stopped with the killings of the two agents. The agency realized that the Indians would fight back when they felt they were being unjustly used.

The reservation is now relatively calm and people have started putting their lives back together. Credit for this recovery should be given to a remarkable tribal member, Albert Trimble. First as superintendent of the reservation for the Bureau of Indian Affairs and then as tribal chairman, a post to which he was elected after resigning from his federal job, Trimble worked hard to bring the warring factions together. By demonstrating that the tribal government could be administered in an impartial manner once again, Trimble finally achieved a measure of stability on the reservation and laid the groundwork for the peaceful transfer of the reins of tribal government after the biennial elections. Although Trimble died shortly after his term as tribal chairman ended, the work he had done was enough to restore the functioning of the reservation institutions.

In June 1973 representatives of the White House journeyed to Kyle, South Dakota, a small village on the Pine Ridge Reservation, and met with the traditional leaders. The 1868 treaty was discussed and it was decided to hold periodic meetings to deal with some of the problems on the reservation. But the Nixon administration was then in the fatal coils of the Watergate scandal and, as the year passed, less and less time and energy could be devoted to the Indians and no other meeting was ever scheduled. The Indians lost faith in the government after Wounded Knee and in 1974 decided to hold their own conference to discuss what could be done to restore their treaties to some kind of enforceable political status.

The Standing Rock Sioux Tribe of North Dakota agreed to act as host for a meeting of Indians to discuss this subject and in 1974 the first International Indian Treaty Council was convened on that reservation. Indians from all over the United States came to the meeting and conducted workshops for several days.

After discussing all the different remedies that tribes might have in getting their treaties enforced, the conference participants decided that they should take their case to the United Nations. Later that year the International Indian Treaty Council was established with offices in New York City across from the United Nations. With a small staff headed by Jimmy Durham this office began the difficult task of creating a constituency for American Indians among the countries sending delegations to the United Nations.

Durham did a remarkable job for the Treaty Council. He obtained sympathetic hearings for the Indian cause from several nations belonging to the United Nations and made friends with numerous staff people on the committees and subcommittees that were part of the vast United Nations administrative apparatus. It was the ideal time for American Indians to have started this kind of work. In 1969 the U.N. General Assembly had adopted the International Covenant on Economic, Social, and Cultural Rights and this document had boldly stated that "all peoples have the right of self-determination" and further stated that "in no case may a people be deprived of its own means of subsistence." It was not at all clear that American Indians were included within the scope of these principles but, having articulated this policy as a matter of international human rights, the United Nations would have to backtrack publicly if it were not to take the Indian matter under consideration.

Two years later, in 1971, under the auspices of the U.N. Human Rights Commission, the Subcommission for the Prevention of Discrimination and Protection of Minorities initiated the "Study of the Problem of Discrimination against Indigenous Populations." This study originally meant to examine the condition of indigenous peoples in different parts of the world and, because the United States was so highly industrialized, had not intended to include American Indians within its purview. But the incident at Wounded Knee had received worldwide publicity and the case of the American Indians could hardly be ignored. The International Indian Treaty Council had moved onto the world stage at precisely the right time, for the United Nations could hardly shunt aside an aggressive organization which sought to represent the indigenous people of the most powerful nation on earth.

By 1977 the Treaty Council had received consultative NGO (nongovernmental organization) status as an observer at the United Nations and it used this status as a means of getting American Indians included in an NGO Conference on Discrimination held at the Palais des Nations in Geneva, Switzerland, on September 20–23 of that year. Of the six hundred NGOs recognized by the United Nations, sixty organizations attended the Geneva hearings, with more than four hundred people present in the sessions, one hundred of whom were Indians from the Americas making presentations.

The sixty indigenous nations attending the meeting at Geneva drafted a special "Declaration of Principles for the Defense of Indigenous Nations and Peoples of the Western Hemisphere." Two principles mentioned in this document are particularly worthy of mention. The first principle concerned the recognition of indigenous nations and articulated four characteristics that these smaller nations possessed. Recognition should be granted, the delegates felt, if the smaller nations had (*a*) a permanent population, (*b*) a defined territory, (*c*) a form of government, and (*d*) the ability to enter into relations with other states.

This last characteristic was deliberately vague. Did it mean that these groups had once possessed the political power to choose the kind of relationship they wanted with the larger nations of the world? Or did it mean that the smaller indigenous nations had the ability to enter into various kinds of agreement with larger nations, including the governments which presently exercise control over them, and possessed the self-discipline and internal domestic structure to carry out their part of the bargain? The description was sufficiently broad to allow many future interpretations of the basis for formal political recognition.

The other principle that played an important role in defining the "defense" of indigenous nations of the Western Hemisphere involved the guarantee of rights. The delegates insisted that "no indigenous nation or group shall be deemed to have fewer rights, or lesser status for the sole reason that the nation or group has not entered into recorded treaties or agreements with any state." This provision was included in order to preempt any efforts by the larger nations to discard the status of indigenous groups on the basis that they had always been regarded as internal citizens of the countries in which they lived. This phrasing was meant to provide a basis for establishing recognition of political rights for groups in Central and South America which, because of the Spanish method of colonization, had not had their inherent political rights as peoples respected in the past. Large areas of some countries south of the American border were populated wholly or predominantly by one particular tribe or people— and always had been the lands of these people. The artificial divisions and subdivisions imposed on these lands when the Central and South American nations threw off the Spanish yoke could not thereby be cited as reasons for refusing to recognize the rights of indigenous populations.

Although much of the discussion at Geneva concerned political recognition and protection of indigenous populations, the moral basis for proposing such fundamental changes was considerably broader.

"There is only one color of mankind that is not allowed to participate in the international community," Russell Means told the conference, "and that color is red." Political status, therefore, was inferior to the recognition of common humanity in the minds of the delegates. The reasoning was sound but perhaps not welcomed in the deliberations of the larger nations. But if these larger nations had the power to disrupt local communities all over the globe and literally decide the fate of the earth with their arsenals of atomic weapons, then, the indigenous peoples believed, they should have some voice in deciding the fate of the human species.

Indigenous peoples were finally a part of the world agenda, albeit only as a moral force, after the Geneva conference. Although they had been the objects of international concern before Geneva, they had not been allowed to make their own presentations about those things that concerned them. Other people spoke for them. Now they would play an active role in defining the issues to be discussed and the policies to be considered. A significant number of Indians attended the Fourth Russell Tribunal, held in November 1980 at The Hague. This conference, as might well be suspected, was concerned primarily with discovering instances of abuse of indigenous peoples and leveling accusations against the larger nations which had committed them. Although many real instances of injustice were brought to the attention of the Tribunal, its obvious political orientation and bias made it seem as if the injustices were artificial and had been devised primarily for propaganda purposes.

In 1981 the Subcommittee on Racism, Racial Discrimination, Apartheid, and Decolonization of the Special NGO Committee on Human Rights sponsored a conference at the U.N. offices in Geneva, "Indigenous Peoples and the Land." Again American Indians were well represented at this meeting. The subject of land was subdivided into four categories: (*a*) the land rights of indigenous peoples, (*b*) the indigenous philosophy and the land, (*c*) transnational corporations and their effect on the land of indigenous peoples, and (*d*) the impact of the nuclear arms build-up on the land and life of indigenous peoples. These topics seemed to be of overwhelming importance and nicely complemented the previous meeting on political status. But, like the question of political status, there was not much the subcommittee could do except record the evidence of abuse of indigenous peoples by the nations within which they resided. The subject of land title, like the subject of status, had been regarded as settled several centuries before under the doctrine of discovery by the nations who possessed the Indian lands.

In May 1982 the U.N. Economic and Social Council established a Working Group on Indigenous Populations to continue to gather data on the conditions under which these peoples lived and to evolve new standards for the protection of indigenous rights. And in August 1983 the United Nations convened the Second World Conference to Combat Racism and Racial Discrimination for two weeks in Geneva. Recognizing that racism was becoming a more serious international problem, the conference declared a "Second Decade to Combat Racism." Since many of the problems suffered by indigenous peoples in the Americas involved racism, there was no question that American Indians would be able to continue to work to focus world attention on their problems.

Although the traditional people from American Indian tribes believed they had accomplished a good deal in the years since Wounded Knee, they realized that any true reform in their status would require an immense shift in moral sensibilities by the larger nations, particularly the United States. The United States would have to voluntarily forswear the exercise of some of the administrative controls it had imposed upon the tribes during the previous century. With Indian tribes owning and partially controlling large tracts of mineral wealth in the American West it was not likely that this shift in morality would occur within the American political system without significant pressure from the rest of the world.

There was also a larger problem within the United Nations that seemed incapable of resolution. The United Nations was founded at the height of power of the nation-state and it had been sustained by the unparalleled development of industrial activity experienced by the Western nations. In Article 2, paragraph 7, of the U.N. Charter the founding nations carefully protected themselves against independence movements by indigenous minorities. The paragraph reads: "Nothing in the present Charter shall authorize the United Nations to intervene in matters which are essentially within the domestic jurisdiction of any State or require the Members to submit such matters to settlement under the present Charter." Hence all a nation had to do to prevent inquiry into the conditions of its indigenous peoples was to declare them a matter of internal jurisdiction. This escape clause served the Russians as well as it did the countries of the Western Hemisphere and the chances of having it amended, revoked, or overridden were nonexistent.

The decolonization process which followed the Second World War did not deal with indigenous groups that were geographically contained or contiguous to larger nations. In every instance where a people received political independence their lands were not geographically part of the larger nation from which they received their independence. Therefore, if the native peoples of the Americas wished to achieve complete independence from the countries in which they were located, they were seeking the kind of political miracle which history has not yet experienced. It seemed likely, however, that the indigenous peoples wished simply to create quasi-independent enclaves in which they would have a maximum of social and domestic freedom without surrendering the military protection against invasion which the larger nations offered. The problem, as they saw it, was to stop the military invasions by the nations which alleged to be protecting them.

The international arena was very fruitful in many ways for American Indian tribes. Visits to Geneva to make presentations about the actions of the United States toward them were of inestimable value in bolstering their morale. The United States' response was puzzling. Although there have been many abuses of American Indian tribes by the federal government in the past and abuses are presently occurring, the condition of American Indians in the United States is dramatically better than is the condition of every other indigenous minority. Thus the United States did not have a bad record to hold out to other countries. Yet efforts were made to discourage the Indian delegations from attending the meetings in Geneva and at The Hague and the federal government made numerous efforts to cover up its minor misdeeds, often by simply misrepresenting the truth as it knew it. No one could determine whether this attitude represented guilt for past deeds or a guilty conscience for what federal officials knew was being planned for the future.

The movement to seek international help originated in the minds of the Sioux and Iroquois traditional people and was at first an effort to establish a political status that would be recognized by the nations of the world and respected by the United States. This movement has since expanded to become a more powerful quest for representation of the indigenous peoples of the Western Hemisphere in world councils. Traditional people, relying firmly on the religious prophecies and beliefs, have now sought to move the international conscience away from political sovereignties toward a more comprehensive view of peoples and races. The movement thus goes beyond the question of political theory to include, at its very roots, the idea of the origin of humans. These ideas are powerful and capable of gaining an allegiance and commitment which neither parochial patriotism nor cold war rhetoric can command. We can but hope that the indigenous people will get a fair hearing as they pursue this worthy goal.

THE DOMESTIC ARENA

The confrontation at Wounded Knee severely shook the foundations of federal Indian policy and administration. For nearly a decade prior to Wounded Knee the federal government had greatly expanded its services to American Indian tribes. The War on Poverty had seen a significant number of programs developed on the reservations. The 1968 Indian Civil Rights Act tried to introduce a measure for the consistent application of law within the tribal court system and had guaranteed the tribes that states could not seek to extend their civil and criminal jurisdiction over the reservations without the consent of the tribal government involved. The Indian Education Act of 1972 created a National Advisory Committee on Indian Education and recommended Indian control of education.

The federal government did not have a bad record in its recent dealings with Indians—at least not superficially. But there were many unresolved questions lying beneath this seemingly benign exterior. The federal government was far too zealous in its support of the Indian establishment—the tribal chairmen and national organizations and federal Indian employees. Corruption was fairly common in many of the federally funded programs and little was done to ensure that federal funds would be used for the benefit of the people of the reservations. Sporadic outbreaks of racial discrimination against Indians in the western states, which should have been investigated by the Justice Department, were shunted aside or quickly closed with only a perfunctory investigation. The Bureau of Indian Affairs was pressuring some tribes to sign leases for the exploitation of their mineral wealth which returned few benefits to the people. The frustrations of Indians were unlike those of any other American racial minority. Other groups might complain of a lack of federal funding; Indians complained of a misappropriation of funds. They knew monies were available to them; they just could not seem to get the funds allocated where they would do some good for the mass of Indians.

While the traditional Indians were planning to seek recognition on the international scene, other Indians and some members of Congress sought to create a commission to look into the administration of Indian programs within the United States. Senator James Abourezk of South Dakota introduced a resolution in the Senate in 1974 to create an "American Indian Policy Review Commission." His original idea was to have an intensive study of the conditions existing on the reservations and produce a set of policy recommendations which could set the proper course for the future. Unfortunately, his resolution was substantially amended in the course of its travels through Congress and, while he did get his commission established in 1975 for a two-year period, it was not a commission that could do much significant work in the policy area. Amendments had created ten "task forces" organized along topical lines (an eleventh task force was later created by the commission) and these groups were authorized to conduct field hearings and investigations on behalf of the commission. No commissioner would actually visit the reservations during the course of the study unless accidentally—or for some personal political purpose known only to himself.

The Policy Review Commission, which was quickly nicknamed the "Abourezk Commission" after the popular senator who was appointed co-chairman with Representative Lloyd Meeds of Washington, was composed of three senators, three representatives, and five Indians. Unfortunately, the Indian membership on the commission became the subject of much political infighting by Indian politicians and the final appointments were an undistinguished lot who represented a number of bad political compromises. The positions on the task forces were filled by a similar political struggle and some Indians who served on these committees had only their political base as a strength, some persons knowing little if anything about the topical area they were responsible for investigating. The Abourezk Commission failed to learn the lesson of Wounded Knee— that much discontent was centered on Indian leadership as well as federal authority—and it filled its positions almost exclusively from the professional Indian class. Few traditional Indians were asked to serve in any capacity on the task forces and no Indian clearly identified with the traditional movement did work with the commission.

The Abourezk Commission filed its final report in May 1977. During the last months of its existence the commission staff had to rely on people from the Bureau of Indian Affairs to write up its report and numerous mistakes occurred. The first draft of the report on economic development concentrated exclusively on the mineral wealth of the tribe (perhaps verifying the suspicions of the traditional people that the federal government was planning to use or otherwise confiscate Indian mineral resources) and failed to mention some 40 million acres of farming and grazing land, which composed the bulk of Indian real estate. The final draft of the report fortunately corrected glaring errors of this kind. On the whole the final report did not reflect many of the findings of the task-force investigations because most of these proceedings were not transcribed and made available to the staff.

The final report contained over two hundred recommendations, many of which were simple housekeeping procedures which might better have been handled in consultation with a few knowledgeable staff people. The report was stridently militant in advocating the elevation of tribal governments to a more exalted status and reflected a belated effort to speak to some of the issues the traditional people had been supporting. Representative Lloyd Meeds, fearing that the report was too blatantly nationalistic to win congressional support as a policy for the future, reversed his previous sympathetic stand and wrote a markedly anti-Indian dissent, thereby counterbalancing some of the ideological progress the majority believed it had made. Little was done to implement the recommendations of the report and within a few years most people who had served on the commission, including several of the members of Congress, were denying they had played any significant role in its deliberations.

The Abourezk Commission was a frantic but unimportant sideshow in the 1970s, however, and the major direction in federal policy moved toward strengthening tribal governments. In both legislation and litigation the status of the recognized tribal governments improved considerably. The success in litigation can be partially attributed to the rising interest in Indians and the widespread feeling that they had been wronged in the past and needed the support of federal institutions in the present. The positive movement in legislation was the culmination of various strands of thought which had been advocated by the tribes and national organizations for over a decade and which were finally coming to fruition.

In 1973, the Supreme Court decided the *Morton v. Ruiz* case in which the question revolved about the Bureau of Indian Affairs' requirement that Indian recipients of federal services live "on or near" the reservation. This rule had effectively eliminated many Indians from receiving federal services and was used by the Bureau to keep the Indians fighting among themselves. The Court ruled that the Bureau had to allocate the limited benefits which Indians received among those Indians who were statutorily eligible for Johnson-O'Malley educational funds and could not create artificial standards and requirements for participation in programs funded from this source. The case was widely regarded as a major step forward in affirming the status of the tribe as a major recipient of federal funds, and tribal membership, not reservation residency, became the criterion for receiving federal assistance. A closely related case, *Morton v. Mancari*, arrived at the high court the following year (1974) and involved a determination of the meaning of the Indian preference in employment policies of the federal government. Again the Court adopted a pro-Indian stance and ruled that Indian tribes and the federal government could hire on this basis of Indian ancestry since the relationship between Indians and the United States was political and not racial.

A critical case for understanding the concept of tribal membership, *United States v. Mazurie*, was decided in 1975. The Indians of the Wind River Reservation in Wyoming passed an ordinance regulating the sale of liquor on the reservation, and the Mazuries, owners of the Blue Bull bar located on a piece of fee simple land (not owned by Indians) within the reservation, challenged it. The Appeals Court described the tribe as comparable to a voluntary membership association and ruled that allowing the tribe to pass ordinances which affected nontribal members was not constitutional. But the Supreme Court reversed the appellate ruling by noting that the tribes were not voluntary membership groups and possessed sufficient political sovereignty to receive certain municipal powers from Congress and carry out various political functions. This decision, more than any other of recent times, supported the Indian argument that tribes possessed a residual sovereignty, which they had not surrendered.

In 1978 three important cases were decided by the Supreme Court involving some determination of Indian political status. In *Oliphant v. Suquamish Indian Tribe* the question was raised whether or not a tribe had jurisdiction over non-Indians coming onto the reservation when a clear notice was displayed informing them that they were submitting to tribal jurisdiction if they entered the reservation. Unfortunately, the Supreme Court turned aside this effort to clarify the scope of tribal civil and criminal jurisdiction, ruling against the extension of tribal powers over non-Indians in this instance. Many Indian leaders were despondent over this ruling but most experts agreed that it had been a bad case, on the facts of the situation, to take to the Supreme Court.

The two other cases decided by the Court during that session were more encouraging. In *United States v. Wheeler* tribal sovereignty was enhanced a bit when the Court decided that an Indian convicted of an offense under a tribal code could not claim double jeopardy if indicted under a federal law which covered the same kind of behavior but described a different offense. *Santa Clara Pueblo v. Martinez,* the third case, involved the question of tribal membership. Although the Martinez children were clearly descended from an enrolled member of the tribe, they were not allowed to become members of the tribe themselves due to the tribe's membership requirements. The Court decided that a fundamental right of an Indian tribe was that of deciding its own membership and ruled against the Martinez claim. Although civil libertarians thought the decision unusually harsh, many tribal leaders supported the decision because it meant that courts could not intervene in a tribe's affairs and determine its membership.

Finally in 1982 a unique case came before the Supreme Court. The Jicarilla Apache tribe had leased some mineral lands for exploitation and received an income which was not commensurate with its value. This lease was made in the tribe's role as a landowner. Thereafter the tribe in its political capacity passed an ordinance levying a tax on minerals extracted from reservation lands. In *Merrion v. Jicarilla Apache Tribe* the Supreme Court was asked to rule on the constitutionality of this unique situation. The Court saw clearly the two roles the tribe was forced to play because of the manner in which federal Indian policy had evolved, and it ruled in favor of the tribe in exercising its various powers and performing functions for itself and for its membership. Following the decision the Bureau of Indian Affairs began to write "rules and regulations" for the promulgation of such taxing ordinances, hoping to nullify the Court's ruling. A clear victory enhancing the scope of tribal political powers thus became an administrative struggle in which the tribal guardian sought to handicap the powers of tribal government.

Legislative progress in expanding the status and powers of tribal government had actually begun prior to the occupation of Wounded Knee. Tribal governments were made eligible to receive federal revenue-sharing funds in the State and Local Fiscal Assistance

Act of 1972, an election year benefit, but the population requirements meant that most tribes did not receive enough funds to make eligibility worthwhile. The funds had to be spent for restricted activities, mostly for municipal improvements. The importance of Indian inclusion in this legislation was that it recognized the government-to-government relationship between the tribes and the federal government. This phrase, "government-to-government," soon became the rallying cry of the tribal leaders in seeking expanded opportunities for the tribes. All subsequent legislation dealing with tribal governments was seen in the context of this fundamental advance brought about by inclusion in the revenue-sharing act.

An almost immediate response to Wounded Knee was the passage of the Indian Financing Act of 1974. Ever since the New Deal the Congress had been creating various kinds of development funds and revolving loan funds but, as is the habit of Congress, had not provided more than minimal funding for these programs. The Indian Financing Act merged these various loan and development accounts and authorized an additional $50 million to be appropriated for use by tribes on reservations. Unfortunately, Indian credit needs far exceeded this amount and, since the intent of the act was to industrialize the reservations as much as possible, traditional people who wished to prevent uncontrolled development of the reservations cringed at the idea that more money would be made available for development schemes.

While Senator Abourezk was working to get his resolution passed establishing a policy review commission, Senator Henry Jackson, chairman of the Senate Interior Committee, which had responsibility for Indian legislation, proposed his own bill to expand the powers of tribal governments. Enacted in 1975, the Indian Self-Determination and Education Assistance Act amended longstanding statutes which hinted at Indian participation in directing federal programs but had been sidetracked administratively by the Bureau of Indian Affairs in the years since their passage. The most important provision of this act was to allow tribal governments to subcontract certain program functions from the Bureau of Indian Affairs and operate them according to tribal guidelines. Here, as might be expected, the Bureau of Indian Affairs balked, and implementation of the provisions of this act was made almost impossible by bureaucratic foot dragging. Nevertheless, some tribes did work their way through the tangled mess of regulations which the Bureau had created and assumed control of some vital programs on their reservations.

With major authorizations now made for greatly expanded activity by tribal governments in programs affecting Indians, Congress took up topical legislation seeking to reform areas where the federal government was deficient. In 1976 the Indian Health Care Improvement Act was passed upgrading Indian health services; in 1978 the Tribally Controlled Community College Act was passed authorizing a fund for the operation of these institutions on reservations. And 1978 also saw the passage of the Indian Child Welfare Act, which changed some forms of procedure in child adoption and placement and provided for the participation of tribal governments in the disposition of Indian children who were tribal members. Whether or not these laws were meant to expand and enhance the status of tribal governments, many Indians saw them as advances and believed they were meeting some of the objections raised by traditional people. There was no question that providing badly needed health and educational services was also on the agenda of the traditional people in their presentations before the U.N. committees.

The problem of credit for development of Indian projects continued to plague tribal governments, however, and the tribes rallied around a new concept—amending the tax statutes to provide that tribal development corporations, sponsored by the tribe, could issue tax-exempt bonds to fund their enterprises. This concept was highly controversial because it meant a basic recognition of the permanency of tribal governments, and a number of people in Congress still saw tribal governments as a temporary and expedient way of handling Indians until they assimilated into American society. Nevertheless, there was sufficient Indian support for the movement into tax-exempt bonds and one version of the proposal was passed in 1984 as the Tribal Tax Status Act. But almost immediately bills were introduced to amend this legislation and it seemed likely that getting this kind of adjustment in tribal tax status would take several sessions of Congress.

The movement toward clarifying and enhancing the political status of Indian tribes was seen from two different perspectives by American Indians following the occupation of Wounded Knee. While the Twenty Points were not adopted by the federal government as its Indian policy, significant steps were taken in the direction which the participants of the Trail of Broken Treaties suggested to indicate that some of their ideas had been accepted by the government. Perhaps the traditional Indians wanted to hear a dramatic pronouncement by the federal government and a solemn, public pledge to reassure them for the future. Such a clear indication of national will is rare, perhaps it occurs only in wartime. It would be completely out of character in Indian affairs where nothing has been clear since the constitution was adopted.

There has been decreasing animosity between traditional people and tribal governments in the last decade. Primarily we have seen the strong resurgence of Indian values as articulated by traditional people having strong impact on the way that tribal officials look at themselves and their programs. So Indian tribes are healing the breeches which the tensions of the postwar years created. This process of reconciliation is badly needed if Indians are to be in a position to exploit any significant opportunity that may come to them on the international scene. The recommendations made in the Twenty Points and the justification for such a change as articulated in this book may well come to pass in our lifetime.

Index